Fichte's *System of Ethics*

The *System of Ethics* was published at the height of Fichte's academic career and marks the culmination of his philosophical development in Jena. Much more than a treatise on ethics narrowly construed, the *System of Ethics* presents a unified synthesis of Fichte's core philosophical ideas, including the principle I-hood, self-activity and self-consciousness, and also contains his most detailed treatment of action and agency. This volume brings together an international group of leading scholars on Fichte, and is the first of its kind in English to offer critical and interpretive perspectives on this work, covering topics such as normativity, belief, justification, desire, duty, and the ethical life. It will be an essential guide for scholars wanting to deepen their understanding of Fichte's ethical thought, as well as for those interested in the history of ethics more broadly.

STEFANO BACIN is Associate Professor in Philosophy at the University of Milan. He is the author of *Il senso dell'etica: Kant e la costruzione di una teoria morale* (2006), *Fichte in Schulpforta (1774–1780)* (2007). He is also the coeditor (with Marcus Willaschek, Georg Mohr, and Jürgen Stolzenberg) of *Kant-Lexikon* (2015) and (with Oliver Sensen) of *The Emergence of Autonomy in Kant's Moral Philosophy* (2019).

OWEN WARE is Associate Professor in Philosophy at the University of Toronto. He is the author of *Kant's Justification of Ethics* (2021) and *Fichte's Moral Philosophy* (2020).

CAMBRIDGE CRITICAL GUIDES

Titles published in this series:

Hume's *An Enquiry Concerning the Principles of Morals*
EDITED BY ESTHER ENGELS KROEKER AND WILLEM LEMMENS
Hobbes's *On the Citizen*
EDITED BY ROBIN DOUGLASS AND OHAN OLSTHOORN
Hegel's *Philosophy of Spirit*
EDITED BY MARINA F. BYKOVA
Kant's *Lectures on Metaphysics*
EDITED BY COURTNEY D. FUGATE
Spinoza's *Political Treatise*
EDITED BY YITZHAK Y. MELAMED AND HASANA SHARP
Aquinas's *Summa Theologiae*
EDITED BY JEFFREY HAUSE
Aristotle's *Generation of Animals*
EDITED BY ANDREA FALCON AND DAVID LEFEBVRE
Hegel's *Elements of the Philosophy of Right*
EDITED BY DAVID JAMES
Kant's *Critique of Pure Reason*
EDITED BY JAMES R. O'SHEA
Spinoza's *Ethics*
EDITED BY YITZHAK Y. MELAMED
Plato's *Symposium*
EDITED BY PIERRE DESTRÉE AND ZINA GIANNOPOULOU
Fichte's *Foundations of Natural Right*
EDITED BY GABRIEL GOTTLIEB
Aquinas's *Disputed Questions on Evil*
EDITED BY M. V. DOUGHERTY
Aristotle's *Politics*
EDITED BY THORNTON LOCKWOOD AND THANASSIS SAMARAS
Aristotle's *Physics*
EDITED BY MARISKA LEUNISSEN
Kant's *Lectures on Ethics*
EDITED BY LARA DENIS AND OLIVER SENSEN
Kierkegaard's *Fear and Trembling*
EDITED BY DANIEL CONWAY
Kant's *Lectures on Anthropology*
EDITED BY ALIX COHEN
Kant's *Religion within the Boundaries of Mere Reason*
EDITED BY GORDON MICHALSON
Descartes' *Meditations*
EDITED BY KAREN DETLEFSEN
Augustine's *City of God*
EDITED BY JAMES WETZEL
Kant's *Observations and Remarks*
EDITED BY RICHARD VELKLEY AND SUSAN SHELL
Nietzsche's *On the Genealogy of Morality*
EDITED BY SIMON MAY
Aristotle's *Nicomachean Ethics*
EDITED BY JON MILLER

(Continued after the Index)

FICHTE'S
System of Ethics
A Critical Guide

EDITED BY

STEFANO BACIN
University of Milan

OWEN WARE
University of Toronto

CAMBRIDGE
UNIVERSITY PRESS

University Printing House, Cambridge CB2 8BS, United Kingdom

One Liberty Plaza, 20th Floor, New York, NY 10006, USA

477 Williamstown Road, Port Melbourne, VIC 3207, Australia

314–321, 3rd Floor, Plot 3, Splendor Forum, Jasola District Centre,
New Delhi – 110025, India

79 Anson Road, #06–04/06, Singapore 079906

Cambridge University Press is part of the University of Cambridge.

It furthers the University's mission by disseminating knowledge in the pursuit of
education, learning, and research at the highest international levels of excellence.

www.cambridge.org
Information on this title: www.cambridge.org/9781108480628
DOI: 10.1017/9781108635820

© Cambridge University Press 2021

This publication is in copyright. Subject to statutory exception
and to the provisions of relevant collective licensing agreements,
no reproduction of any part may take place without the written
permission of Cambridge University Press.

First published 2021

A catalogue record for this publication is available from the British Library.

ISBN 978-1-108-48062-8 Hardback

Cambridge University Press has no responsibility for the persistence or accuracy of
URLs for external or third-party internet websites referred to in this publication
and does not guarantee that any content on such websites is, or will remain,
accurate or appropriate.

Contents

List of Contributors		*page* vii
Acknowledgments		ix
List of Abbreviations and Translations		x
	Introduction *Stefano Bacin and Owen Ware*	1
1	Fichte's Ethics as Kantian Ethics *Allen Wood*	10
2	Fichte on Normativity in the Late Jena Period (1796–1799) *Benjamin Crowe*	28
3	Fichte on Autonomy *Ulrich Schlösser*	47
4	Feeling, Drive, and the Lower Capacity of Desire *Owen Ware*	66
5	Fichte and the Path from "Formal" to "Material" Freedom *Daniel Breazeale*	85
6	Fichte on the Content of Conscience *Dean Moyar*	109
7	Fichte's Theory of Moral Evil *David James*	131
8	Embodiment and Freedom: Fichte "On the Material of the Ethical Law" *Angelica Nuzzo*	150

Contents

9 Ethics as Theory of Society: Morality and Ethical Life
   in Fichte's *System of Ethics*   178
   Luca Fonnesu

10 My Duties and the Morality of Others: Lying, Truth,
   and the Good Example in Fichte's Normative Perfectionism   201
   Stefano Bacin

   Bibliography   221
   Index   229

Contributors

STEFANO BACIN is Associate Professor in Philosophy at the University of Milan. He is the author of *Il senso dell'etica: Kant e la costruzione di una teoria morale* (2006), *Fichte in Schulpforta (1774–1780)* (2007). He is also the coeditor (with Marcus Willaschek, Georg Mohr, and Jürgen Stolzenberg) of *Kant-Lexikon* (2015) and (with Oliver Sensen) of *The Emergence of Autonomy in Kant's Moral Philosophy* (2019).

DANIEL BREAZEALE is Professor Emeritus in Philosophy at the University of Kentucky. In addition to numerous articles, he is the author of *Thinking through the Wissenschaftslehre: Themes from Fichte's Early Philosophy* (2013). He is also the editor and translator of J. G. Fichte, *Foundation of the Entire Wissenschaftslehre and Related Writings* (forthcoming) and the coeditor (with Tom Rockmore) of *Fichte and Transcendental Philosophy* (2014) and *Fichte's Addresses to the German Nation Reconsidered* (2016).

BENJAMIN CROWE is Lecturer in Philosophy at Boston University. He is the author of *Heidegger's Religions Origins* (2006) and *Heidegger's Phenomenology of Religion* (2007). He is also the editor and translator of J. G. Fichte, *Lectures on the Theory of Ethics (1812)* (2016).

LUCA FONNESU is Professor of Philosophy at the University of Pavia. He is the author of *Antropologia e idealismo: La destinazione dell'uomo nell'etica di Fichte* (1993), *Storia dell'etica contemporanea: Da Kant alla filosofia analitica* (2006), and *Per una moralità concreta: Studi sulla filosofia classica tedesca* (2010).

DAVID JAMES is Professor of Philosophy at the University of Warwick. He is the author of *Fichte's Social and Political Philosophy: Property and Virtue* (2011), *Rousseau and German Idealism: Freedom, Dependence and Necessity* (2013), and *Fichte's Republic: Idealism, History and Nationalism* (2015). He is also the coeditor (with Günter Zöller) of *The Cambridge Companion to Fichte* (2016).

viii *List of Contributors*

DEAN MOYAR is Associate Professor of Philosophy at Johns Hopkins University. He is the author of *Hegel's Conscience* (2011). He is also the editor of *The Routledge Companion to Nineteenth Century Philosophy* (2010) and of *The Oxford Handbook of Hegel* (2017), and the coeditor (with Michael Quante) of *Hegel's Phenomenology of Spirit: A Critical Guide* (2008).

ANGELICA NUZZO is Professor of Philosophy at City University of New York. She is the author of *Kant and the Unity of Reason* (2005), *Ideal Embodiment: Kant's Theory of Sensibility* (2008), *Memory, History, Justice in Hegel* (2012), and *Approaching Hegel's Logic, Obliquely: Melville, Molière, Beckett* (2018).

ULRICH SCHLÖSSER is Professor of Philosophy at the University of Tübingen. He is the author of *Das Erfassen des Einleuchtens: Fichtes Wissenschaftslehre 1804* (2001).

OWEN WARE is Associate Professor in Philosophy at the University of Toronto. He is the author of *Kant's Justification of Ethics* (2021) and *Fichte's Moral Philosophy* (2020).

ALLEN WOOD is Professor Emeritus in Philosophy at Indiana University. He is the author of *Kant's Moral Religion* (1970), *Kant's Rational Theology* (1978), *Karl Marx* (1981), *Hegel's Ethical Thought* (1990), *Kant's Ethical Thought* (1999), and *Fichte's Ethical Thought* (2016). He is also the editor of J. G. Fichte, *Attempt at a Critique of All Revelation* (2010).

Acknowledgments

Most chapters of this volume were discussed at a meeting held at the University of Milan on June 20–21, 2019, and we would like to thank the Department of Philosophy "Piero Martinetti" and its director, Luca Bianchi, for financial and organizational support. We would like to thank Katherine Crone for her work in compiling the bibliography. We are pleased to acknowledge the support of the Social Sciences and Humanities Research Council of Canada. Finally, we are grateful to Hilary Gaskin from Cambridge University Press for providing outstanding editorial guidance and encouragement. The editors also thank the Kiel University Library for kindly giving permission to use an image from their copy of the first edition of Fichte's *System of Ethics* for the cover of our volume.

Abbreviations and Translations

References to Fichte appear in the order of abbreviation, volume number, and page number from (1) *J. G. Fichte: Gesamtausgabe der Bayerischen Akademie der Wissenschaften*, 42 volumes, edited by Erich Fuchs, Reinhard Lauth, Hans Jacobs, and Hans Gliwitzky (Stuttgart-Bad Cannstatt: Frommann, 1964–2012), followed by (2) *Johann Gottlieb Fichtes sämmtliche Werke*, 8 volumes, edited by I. H. Fichte (Berlin: Veit, 1845–1846).

References to Kant appear in the order of abbreviation, volume number, and page number from the *Akademie Ausgabe, Kants Gesammelte Schriften*, edited by the Berlin Brandenburg Academy of Sciences. The English translations are taken from the Cambridge Edition of the Works of Immanuel Kant, edited by Paul Guyer and Allen Wood.

FICHTE

A	1790: *Aphorismen über Religion und Deismus* (*Aphorisms Concerning Religion and Deism*)
AP	1799: "Appellation an das Publikum" ("Appeal to the Public"), in Bowman and Estes (2010)
BdG	1794: *Einige Vorlesungen über die Bestimmung des Gelehrten* (*Some Lectures Concerning the Scholar's Vocation*), in Breazeale (1988)
BEIW	1795: "Ueber Belebung und Erhöhung des reinen Interesse für Wahrheit" ("On Stimulating and Raising the Pure Interest Truth"), in Breazeale (1988)
BdM	1800: *Die Bestimmung des Menschen* (*The Vocation of Human Beings*), in Preuss (1988)
EPW	*Fichte: Early Philosophical Writings*, in Breazeale (1988)

ErE	1797: "Erste Einleitung in die Wissenschaftslehre" ("First Introduction to the Wissenschaftslehre"), in Breazeale (1994)
GA	*J. G. Fichte-Gesamtausgabe der Bayerischen Akademie der Wissenschaften* (Reihe/Band: Seite)
GEWL	1795: *Grundriß des Eigenthümlichen der Wissenschaftslehre in Rücksicht auf das theoretische Vermögen* (*Outline of the Distinctive Character of the Wissenschaftslehre with Respect to the Theoretical Faculty*), in Breazeale (1988)
GGW	1798: "Ueber den Grund unsers Glaubens an eine göttliche Weltregierung" ("On the Basis of Our Belief in a Divine Governance of the World"), in Breazeale (1994)
GNR	1796/97: *Grundlage des Naturrechts nach Principien der Wissenschaftslehre* (*Foundations of Natural Right According to the Principles of the Wissenschaftslehre*), in Baur (2000)
GR	1793: "Recension Gebhard" ("Review of Gebhard"), in Breazeale (2001a)
GWL	1794/95: *Grundlage der gesammten Wissenschaftslehre* (*Foundation of the Entire Wissenschaftslehre*), in Heath and Lachs (1982)
RA	1793: "Recension Aenesidemus" ("Review of Aenesidemus"), in Breazeale (1988)
RC	1793: "Recension Creuzer" ("Review of Leonhard Creuzer, *Skeptical Reflections on the Freedom of the Will* (1793)," in Breazeale (2002b)
SL	1798: *Das System der Sittenlehre nach den Principien der Wissenschaftslehre* (*The System of Ethics According to the Principles of the Wissenschaftslehre*), in Breazeale and Zöller (2005)
SW	*Johann Gottlieb Fichtes sämmtliche Werke* (Band: Seite)
VBG	1794: *Einige Vorlesungen über die Bestimmung des Gelehrten* (*Some Lectures Concerning the Scholar's Vocation*), in Breazeale (1988)
VKO	1792/93: *Versuch einer Critik aller Offenbarung* (*Attempt at a Critique of All Revelation*), in Green (2010)
WLnm	1796/99: *Wissenschaftslehre nova methodo* (*Foundations of Transcendental Philosophy*), in Breazeale (1992)
WLnm(H)	1797/98: *Wissenschaftslehre nova methodo*, Halle Nachschrift

List of Abbreviations

WLnm(K)	1798/99: *Wissenschaftslehre nova methodo*, Krause Nachschrift
WM	1794: "Ueber die Würde des Menschen" ("On the Dignity of Human Beings"), in Breazeale (1988)
VM	1796: Vorlesung über die Moral, Kollegnachschrift
ZwE	1797: "Zweite Einleitung in die Wissenschaftslehre" ("Second Introduction to the Wissenschaftslehre"), in Breazeale (1994)

KANT

G	1785: *Grundlegung zur Metaphysik der Sitten* (*Groundwork for the Metaphysics of Morals*). Translation in Gregor and Timmermann (2012)
IaG	1784: "Idee zu einer allgemeinen Geschichte in weltbürgerlicher Absicht" ("Idea for a Universal History from a Cosmopolitan Point of View"). Translated by Allen W. Wood (2007)
KpV	1788: *Kritik der praktischen Vernunft* (*Critique of Practical Reason*). Translated by Mary J. Gregor (1996)
KrV A/B	1781/87: *Kritik der reinen Vernunft* (*Critique of Pure Reason*). Translated by Paul Guyer and Allen W. Wood (1998)
KU	1790: *Kritik der Urteilskraft* (*Critique of the Power of Judgment*). Translated by Eric Matthews (2000)
MS	1797: *Die Metaphysik der Sitten* (*The Metaphysics of Morals*). Translated by Mary J. Gregor (1996)
R	1793: *Die Religion innerhalb der Grenzen der bloßen Vernunft* (*Religion within the Boundaries of Mere Reason*). Translated by Allen W. Wood and George di Giovanni (2018)
WA	1784: "Beantwortung der Frage: Was ist Aufklärung?" ("An Answer to the Question: What Is Enlightenment?"). Translated by Mary J. Gregor (1996)

Introduction

Stefano Bacin and Owen Ware

In the wake of Kant's works on moral philosophy, the *Groundwork for the Metaphysics of Morals* and the *Critique of Practical Reason*, many philosophers entered the ensuing debate on the foundations of morality and the content of its demands. Fichte's voice was one of the most powerful in this regard. From the early stages of his philosophical thought, Fichte felt an especially strong connection with the outlook of Kant's moral philosophy. In a 1790 letter to his close friend F. A. Weisshuhn, Fichte famously wrote: "I have been living in a new world ever since reading the *Critique of Practical Reason*" (GA III/1: 167). At the same time, Fichte's original project of a new systematic account of philosophy, the *Doctrine of Science*, included from the outset a part devoted to moral philosophy. Fichte's programmatic outline of a system accordingly mentioned "new theories of natural law and morality" (GA I/2: 151).

This part of Fichte's project was fulfilled, only three years after the publication of the *Foundations of the Entire Wissenschaftslehre*, when the *System of Ethics* came out in April 1798, for the *Ostermesse* (see GA I/5: 2). The work was anticipated by the lectures on ethics that Fichte had been giving in Jena since 1796. As is witnessed by student notes (published in GA IV/1), he presented in those lectures a first version of the views put forward in the work that he published in 1798. The *System of Ethics* belongs to the core of Fichte's Jena system, along with the two 1797 *Introductions into the Wissenschaftslehre*, the *Natural Right* (1796), and the *Wissenschaftslehre Nova Methodo* (1796–1798). The *System of Ethics* is thus Fichte's last major work before the momentous disruption caused by the accusation of atheism that led to his departure from Jena in 1800. The philosophical significance of such a work can then best be understood by considering the work as a systematic whole.

The high systematic significance of the *System of Ethics* goes in fact well beyond the terms of the post-Kantian debate in moral philosophy. Fichte writes that the subject matter of the work is "our consciousness of our moral nature in general and of our specific duties in particular" (GA I/5: 35; SL 4: 15). However, it is a distinctive feature of the *System of Ethics* that it is not merely a work of ethical theory. An utterly ambitious work, it encompasses (1) a theoretical foundation that supplements the views put forward in Fichte's previous expositions of the "doctrine of science" (*Wissenschaftslehre*), (2) a more specific foundation of moral principles and their authority, and (3) a systematic exposition of moral duties, both general and relative to the individual's role in society. As a systematic work, the *System of Ethics* provides important additions and revisions to the core of Fichte's thought, reflecting his position in the *Wissenschaftslehre nova methodo* that he was presenting in lectures in those years, without publishing it in full. As a work in moral philosophy, the *System of Ethics* enjoys a special priority in classical German philosophy. Kant's own exposition of ethics, the "Doctrine of Virtue" of the *Metaphysics of Morals*, was published only a few months before Fichte's work, in August 1797, and could not play a role in the development of Fichte's view. The *System of Ethics* is thus independent from Kant's parallel work and is without question the main work on practical philosophy between Kant's *Critique of Practical Reason* and Hegel's *Philosophy of Right*. Thus, while Fichte's other Jena works have been investigated more fully than the *System of Ethics* so far, the *System of Ethics* can be regarded, because of its complexity, as "the most mature work of his Jena years, and it easily surpasses in clarity and concision the two versions of the Jena *Wissenschaftslehre*."[1]

In spite of its significance in more than one respect, the *System of Ethics* has been mostly ignored, both from Fichte's contemporaries and from later scholars. Fichte's previous writings had attracted a great deal of attention and had been intensely discussed. Only two years earlier, the *Natural Right*, with which the *System of Ethics* was closely connected for thematic and philosophical reasons, had enjoyed especially positive consideration. Yet, the *System of Ethics* was poorly received. Only five reviews of the work were published, one of which suggested that "there could hardly be a more superfluous work" (see GA I/5: 11). The rapidly growing hostility toward Fichte and the accusation of atheism might have prevented further unbiased appraisal of it. Also some tensions in Fichte's views and the focus of the philosophical debate moving to other issues may have diverted attention from the merit of Fichte's ethics. Whatever the reasons, the *System of Ethics* remains the least appreciated work of his activity in Jena. A survey of its reception bears the appropriate title "Two Hundred

---

[1] Beiser (2002, 324).

Years of Solitude: The Failed Reception of Fichte's *System of Ethics*."[2] The later scholarship has not yet fully rectified the neglect of such a work.

The past two decades have witnessed a steady rise of interest in Fichte in the Anglophone world, with numerous translations, volumes, and monographs devoted to interpreting his philosophy. One cause for this surge of interest is the flourishing of scholarship on Kant and Hegel, which has secured the status of post-Kantian philosophy as an independently valid period of intellectual history. As a result, Fichte has come to enjoy the credentials of an original thinker whose system deserves serious attention. However, Fichte's moral philosophy has not received the same level of engagement, and even the most basic terms of his ethical thought – "freedom," "morality," "drive," "conscience," and "self-sufficiency" – have yet to receive agreed-upon interpretations. Fichte's views on moral philosophy have been considered only in specific investigations. Before the last decade, the scant literature was mainly represented by a few German and Italian monographs.[3] Fichte's moral philosophy has been almost entirely neglected also in recent expositions of the history of ethics, in spite of the great current interest in eighteenth- and nineteenth-century ethics.[4] The present volume aims at calling attention to the *System of Ethics* in its complexity, both as an important part of Fichte's philosophical system and as his key work on moral philosophy, which represents an original contribution to the history of ethics at large.

This volume does not provide a full commentary on Fichte's work, but it aims at a reappraisal of the *System of Ethics* in its entirety, by examining the foundational issues discussed in the first part of the work, its central account of the authority of morality, as well as the normative account of morality extensively presented in the last part of the *System of Ethics*. While this is not a commentary, the volume closely follows the outline of the

---

[2] Zöller (2008). Still in 2017, a review of a recent German commentary of the work stresses that the *System of Ethics* has not received an appropriate amount of attention either by Fichte scholars or moral philosophers more generally. See Jacobs (2017, 235).

[3] See Verweyen (1975), Ivaldo (1992), Fonnesu (1993), and De Pascale (1995, 2003). In the last years, a rise of involvement in Fichte's ethical thought is witnessed by a commentary in German (Merle and Schmidt [2015]), several articles, and three monographs like Allen Wood's (2016a), Michelle Kosch's (2018), and Owen Ware's (2020).

[4] Terence Irwin's three-volume *The Development of Ethics*, which includes extensive chapters on Kant, Hegel, Schopenhauer, Kierkegaard, Marx, and Nietzsche, mentions Fichte only on one page, in passing, with regard to a passage of the *Foundations of Natural Right* criticized by Hegel (Irwin [2009, 139]). The *Oxford Handbook of the History of Ethics* devotes less than one page to Fichte's *System of Ethics* in a chapter on "Kantian Ethics" (Höffe [2013, 470].) The chapter on "Ethics" in the *Oxford Handbook of Nineteenth-Century German Philosophy* (Katsafanas [2015]) passes over Fichte entirely. The only reference work available in English that devotes a part to Fichte is the *Cambridge History of Moral Philosophy* (Wood [2017a]).

work and, after a comprehensive look in Chapter 1, the following chapters engage with key issues discussed in specific sections of the *System of Ethics*. The underlying aim, which has also guided the selection of the topics to focus on, is to highlight the distinctive features of the views presented in Fichte's main work on moral philosophy and promote further discussion with new interpretations.

Fichte's *System of Ethics* was composed when the discussion in moral philosophy was dominated by the debate on Kant's view of morality in the *Groundwork for the Metaphysics of Morals* and the second *Critique*. Fichte shared with many others not only the enthusiasm for the perspective that those works had opened up but also the urgency to consolidate the foundations of morality and complement it with a critical treatment of ethics proper. In his lectures on moral philosophy and the *System of Ethics*, Fichte presented a complete theory of morality in a Kantian spirit almost anticipating Kant's own "Doctrine of Virtue." If the relationship to Kant's thought is crucial to every aspect of Fichte's philosophy, it is here even more significant and complex. A comparison with Kant's outlook goes through the entire *System of Ethics*. Thus, all chapters of this volume will touch, to some extent, upon Fichte's relation to Kant's moral philosophy.

The Kantian background of Fichte's ethical theory, however, is specifically addressed in Chapter 1, by Allen Wood. While the *System of Ethics* was without question inspired by Kant, Wood highlights the fact that this work was composed independently of Kant's systematic account of ethical duties in the "Doctrine of Virtue" (published only a few months before the *System of Ethics*). Both systems ground ethical obligation on a categorical imperative, Wood explains. Kant, however, takes the very concept of such an imperative to have a specific moral content, and to provide us with, first, a formal criterion of moral judgment (universal law or law of nature), second, a substantive value (humanity as end in itself) motivating obedience to duty and capable of grounding specific classes of ethical duty, and third, a conception of an ideal of moral perfection in a community of rational beings (the realm of ends). Fichte's ethics contains all three of these things (or at least analogues to them), but Fichte thinks they need to be derived independently of the concept of categorical obligation, because he regards the categorical imperative as purely formal and empty of content. On Wood's account, then, Fichte departs from Kant's ethics in three crucial ways. The first is Fichte's alternative derivation of the criterion of judgment in a theory of conscience. The second is his alternative conception of classes of duty in a transcendental theory of the embodied, intellective, and intersubjective aspects of human agency. And the third is

Introduction 5

Fichte's alternative account of our communicative and cooperative relations to others in a theory of social perfection.

During the second half of his tumultuous tenure in Jena, Fichte developed two parallel accounts of what he variously called the "instinct of reason" (in the *Wissenschaftslehre nova methodo* lectures, 1796–1798) and our "moral nature" (in the *System of Ethics* of 1798) – that is, our commonsense level recognition of categorical moral demands. He carefully differentiated these accounts from the more concrete project of delimiting actual duties as well as from accounting for our experience of morality as constraining us to act or refrain from acting in a certain way. While Fichte did not explore classical metaethical inquiries along lines we would call metaphysical ("are there moral facts?"), epistemic ("if there are moral facts, how do we know about them?"), or semantic ("what sort of meaning do moral claims have?"), he nevertheless posed foundational questions about morality. The aim of Chapter 2, by Benjamin Crowe, is to arrive at an understanding of Fichte's metaethics that integrates these two parallel accounts. Crowe first characterizes his metaethics as theoretical (i.e., not directly concerned with practical deliberation or action) and idealist (i.e., as avoiding both naturalist and supernaturalist metaphysics along with causal explanation in general). While it is accurate to label Fichte's approach "transcendental," Crowe argues that both accounts ultimately introduce a theological element, namely, the idea of God. On Crowe's account, the role of God turns out to be a "necessary Idea" within Fichte's genetic explanation of our moral nature, without reducing to any form of supernaturalist metaphysics.

Questions of Fichte's metaethics lead naturally to the foundational portion of the *System of Ethics* devoted to a "Deduction of the Principle of Morality" in §§1–3 of Part I. In Chapter 3, Ulrich Schlösser contextualizes these opening moves of the book with reference to Kant's definition of autonomy as the idea of a lawgiving will possessed by all rational beings. According to Schlösser, Fichte objects to this theory of autonomy on two fronts. First, Fichte argues that Kant fails to present a "genetic" account that reveals the inner structure of the legislating subject. From Fichte's point of view, this line of reasoning merely explains that we have to take ourselves as lawgiving, but not how we can understand ourselves to be bound by a law we are giving. Second, Kant argues that the imperative can be applied to sensible incentives, but according to Fichte, he fails to articulate a mediating a priori form that shapes sensibility itself. Schlösser argues that Fichte's conception of striving toward the "entire I" is meant to respond to these perceived shortcomings in Kant's ethics. Because we access selfhood from a first-personal perspective, we do not have an overview of it in its entirety; we always partly objectify it. The striving ascribed to the self, when objectively understood, is what Fichte calls the "formative drive" (*Bildungstrieb*). But that same striving, Schlösser argues, is what Fichte calls the spontaneity of intelligence when it is considered subjectively, and hence these two aspects of selfhood form a complete identity.

Arguably, Fichte's genetic account of agency constitutes one of his most original contributions to the landscape of post-Kantian moral philosophy. It comes to the foreground in Part II of the *System of Ethics* titled "Deduction of the Reality and Applicability of the Moral Law." As Chapter 4, by Owen Ware, shows, what motivates this second deduction is a concern to avoid what Fichte calls "empty formula philosophy," which fails to explain how willing an object is possible. Fichte sets out to avoid this shortcoming by offering a complex theory of the drives, focusing first on what he calls our "lower capacity of desire." Ware argues that the key to understanding this section of the *System of Ethics* lies in Fichte's attempt to derive the character of our "natural drive" (*Naturtrieb*) from how we represent the system of nature as a whole. At the center of this derivation we find Fichte draws upon an organicist model of nature, according to which all the parts of natural systems reciprocally interact for the sake of the whole, and vice versa. While largely overlooked by scholars, Ware shows that this organicist model gives Fichte the resources to present an original theory of desire as an activity of "forming and being formed" by natural objects, in a way that foreshadows what Fichte later calls our "ethical drive" (*sittlicher Trieb*) to unite with others, both cooperatively and reciprocally, in rational community. Even at this most fundamental form of agency, then, the natural drive reveals an original connection to the I and its self-activity.

However, this is just the first stage in a much longer account of the genesis of agency, which Daniel Breazeale shows culminates in Fichte's theory of freedom. One problem of interpretation is that Fichte employs different senses of freedom throughout the *System of Ethics*, and it is not always clear, given the context, what meaning he intends to assign to this word. To complicate matters, Fichte draws an explicit distinction between "formal" freedom and "material" freedom, but scholars to this day have yet to reach any degree of consensus over their exact definitions. In Chapter 5, Breazeale argues that formal freedom is characteristic of the unconditioned, spontaneous activity of the I as such, that is, of the "pure I": It underlies and makes possible both the freedom of conscious reflection and the freedom of practical willing and acting, including the freedom to

Introduction 7

determine not only the means toward one's ends but also these ends themselves. The latter constitutes full material freedom. However, these two senses admit of different degrees, and Fichte himself is committed to the view that reaching full material freedom depends on a process of ongoing cultivation. On Breazeale's account, moral cultivation is a process that begins with a prereflective state of agency and then develops, progressively over the course of one's self-reflective acts, to the height of moral autonomy. In this process, Breazeale argues, one achieves concrete material freedom of choice only by reflecting upon one's own underlying formal freedom as an I.

With these foundational arguments in place, Fichte's next task in the *System of Ethics* is to shed light on the formal and material conditions of morality, first providing a theory of conscience and then, for the remainder of Part III, providing a doctrine of duties. In arguing for the feeling of conscience as a formal absolute criterion for the belief in one's duty, however, Fichte seems to render impossible an account of ethical content. If the individual conscience decides and its verdict cannot be appealed, how can the philosopher claim to give an account of the ethical content that everyone must act upon? Chapter 6, by Dean Moyar, explores Fichte's two arguments for ethical content in the *System of Ethics* and examines the difficulties they raise for the coherence of his overall position. Moyar argues that Fichte has good arguments for deriving ethical content on the basis of the original freedom of the I, but that these arguments put serious pressure on the appeal to formality in the basic argument for conscience as an absolute criterion. The argument for individuality and intersubjectivity later in the *System of Ethics*, in particular, raises questions about whether the methodological individualism of the formal derivation is compatible with the account of content.

Indeed, this perceived tension between Fichte's commitments to individuality and intersubjectivity finds expression in his theory of evil. Chapter 7, by David James, examines this issue in relation to the question of whether Fichte's theory of evil lends itself more to an individualistic reading or a social one. Although James acknowledges that there is textual support for the idea that evil is the product of a morally corrupt society and its influence, Fichte's account of the moral agent's ultimate responsibility for the state of evil in which he or she finds himself or herself implies a moment of radical individualization in his ethical theory. To locate the source of moral evil in social factors, in contrast, would amount to a form of social determination that is incompatible with Fichte's understanding of moral autonomy. James also discusses Fichte's claim that his theory of evil provides the correct interpretation of Kant's theory of radical evil, and how his attempt to interpret Kant generates a puzzle concerning how an individual could ever come to be responsible for his or her evil disposition. Finally, James ties his discussion to an account of how Kierkegaard's concept of sin can be seen to develop some of the implications of Fichte's position.

Scholars have long recognized that Fichte's derivation of content for the moral law comes not from his theory of conscience in Part II but from his theory of the transcendental conditions of I-hood in Part III. But just how this derivation of content is supposed to work remains subject to much controversy. In Chapter 8, by Angelica Nuzzo, Fichte gives us a quasi-phenomenological account of how the I develops through a system of drives in which nature and freedom are constitutively intertwined. In this framework, Nuzzo argues, embodiment plays a crucial role. This is because the body is the locus in which nature and freedom originally intersect: Indeed, it is through the body that the natural drive address itself an agent, and for Fichte it is through the body that one exercises causality in the world. Nuzzo's chapter examines the details of this theory of embodiment by setting it in the larger context of Fichte's confrontation with Kant's formal idea of morality. The quasi-phenomenological setup of the argument is grounded in Fichte's attempt to bridge the gap between the strict apriorism of the ethical law grounded in reason and the experiential dimension of the "original drive" as it is progressively and infinitely actualized in our life.

It might come as a surprise to some readers that Fichte devoted so many pages of his most important ethical work to the state, the church, and even to the learned republic, that is, the learned public opinion. The surprise could be justified, however, when one considers Fichte as the most radical supporter of the separation between law and morality. Chapter 9, by Luca Fonnesu, advances an interpretation of the role and importance of the social institutions (state, church, and learned republic) in Fichte's ethical thought. Almost half of the *System of Ethics* and almost the whole ethics "proper" (*im eigentlichen Sinne*) are devoted to a theory of society that can be understood as a theory of ethical life (*Sittlichkeit*) articulated in different institutions. The exposition of this theory begins with Fichte's theory of intersubjectivity and with his conception of society as a presentation of reason (*Darstellung der Vernunft*) and ends with the doctrine of duties, which has in Fichte's work a different form when compared to the modern doctrine of duties, including Kant's *Metaphysics of Morals*. Fonnesu argues that Fichte's moral theory is a social theory of morality as ethical life, including an objective, that is, social, doctrine of duties, contrasting the subjective, that is, individualist, doctrine of the tradition. Fichte's theory has many features in common with the Hegelian theory of the ethical life, but while Hegel unifies law and morality in a superior space called ethical life (*Sittlichkeit*), Fichte unifies law and morality in an original theory of society.

Like most eighteenth-century writers, Fichte equates "ethics in the proper sense of the term" with a "doctrine of duties." A substantial part of the *System of Ethics* (§§ 19–33) is thus devoted to sketch an account of our main ethical obligations. In spite of its significance for the aims of the work, Fichte's outlines of a normative ethics have scarcely been examined in any detail. The aim of Chapter 10, by Stefano Bacin, is to shed light on some of the most original elements of Fichte's conception of morality as expressed in his account of specific obligations. After some remarks on Fichte's original classification of ethical duties, Bacin focuses on the prohibition of lying, the duty to communicate our true knowledge, and the duty to set a good example. Fichte's account of those duties not only goes beyond the mere justification of universally acknowledged demands but also deploys different arguments than his contemporaries, most notably Kant. Fichte thereby sketches a conception of morality in which the agent is crucially required to contribute to the morality of others. Bacin's chapter explores the contrast between Fichte's view and Kant's thought of an end in itself and suggests that Fichte's view of morality amounts to a form of normative perfectionism that is qualified by the underlying claim of the agent-neutral character of moral demands.

CHAPTER I

Fichte's Ethics as Kantian Ethics

Allen Wood

Fichte himself would be the first to tell you that his ethical theory was inspired by Kant's. In fact, however, Fichte's theory could not have been merely a repetition or imitation of Kant's. This is simply a fact of chronology. Fichte's first works on the topics of religion, right, and ethical theory were all written independently of, and even published earlier than, Kant's main treatise on those same respective topics. The influence of Kant's three critiques, the *Groundwork,* and *Perpetual Peace* is evident in Fichte's writings. But Fichte could not have known the "Doctrine of Right" (1797) at the time he wrote the *Foundations of Natural Right* (1796–1797) or known the "Doctrine of Virtue" (1798) when he wrote the *System of Ethics* (1798).

I suppose it would be possible to write an essay that tries to identify in detail what Fichte knew of Kant's ethical writings, how he understood (or misunderstood) what he found in them, and how the letter of Kant's ethical theory reflects itself in the letter of Fichte's ethical theory. But that would be both myopic and pedantic. The aim of this chapter is to compare the spirit rather than the letter of Kant's and Fichte's ethical theories. In ethics, the foundation of Fichte's system is the same as Kant's: the concept of categorical obligation and its grounding on the unavoidable but also unprovable presupposition of the will's freedom. At the same time, Fichte's development of a theory out of this foundation is in some ways very different from Kant's. I will therefore investigate the common ideas fundamental to their two ethical theories and then the parallel theoretical structures that were the different workings out of the same basic ideas.

1.1   Freedom and Causality

Both Kant and Fichte hold that neither the affirmation nor the denial of freedom can be demonstrated theoretically, nor can we provide any metaphysical account of human freedom. But both hold that we cannot coherently avoid affirming freedom if we are either to represent to ourselves our activity as theoretical judgers or, especially, if we are to commit ourselves to morality as agents (KpV 5: 29; GA I/5: 33, 42 f., SL 4: 13, 25–26; GA I/4: 195–198, ErE 1: 435–439; GAI/4: 261, ZwE 1: 509–510). For both Kant and Fichte, freedom means the absence of causal determination of our actions, which leaves them up to us and presents us with alternative possibilities between which we must decide. But for neither philosopher is the absence of external necessitation mere indeterminacy. For both, freedom consists in the capacity to act for reasons, and especially to follow a basic moral law. Reasons always leave us free to resist them. Freedom therefore involves both the ability to act as reason prescribes and also the possibility of failing to do so. To be free therefore necessarily involves two distinct but necessarily related capacities: first, the broader capacity to choose between right reason and its contrary, and second, the narrower capacity to choose in accordance with it. The latter choice makes us freer in a stronger or more proper sense. The relation between the two means that freedom carries with it a commitment to our *vocation* as free and rational beings. Kant calls the two senses "negative" freedom and "positive" freedom, or *autonomy*. Fichte calls them, respectively, "formal" freedom and "material" freedom. Autonomy or material freedom is what enables us to be self-governing and even self-defining.

For Kant, freedom is a cause operating independently of natural causes, producing its actions "from itself" (*von selbst*) (KrV A534/B562). The free will found in human beings (or the free power of choice, *arbitrium sensitivum sed liberum*) is a kind of cause, which means its concept contains that of a determinate causal law. For Kant, this is the moral law: Thus if we assume the will is free, it follows analytically that it is subject to the moral law (G 4: 447, KpV 5: 29). Kant sometimes represents the law as one that would in fact govern a free will that had no incentives except pure reason. On this account, duty or obligation arises for us only because our will is affected by nonrational incentives, making it possible for us to act contrary to this law (G 4: 449 f.). Freedom is therefore the capacity to be determined solely through pure reason, which might belong to a being (such as God) that had a holy will, and could not act otherwise than according to reason's law. Divine freedom, therefore, is a causal necessity without any necessity of constraint, whereas our freedom involves the possibility of acting contrary to freedom's law. The latter possibility for Kant is not part of freedom itself, but represents only the imperfect power of choice pertaining to the free human will (MS 6: 226–227).

Fichte's concept of freedom is different. Freedom is not the attribute of any *substance, thing,* or *object,* but the self-positing of an *act*. This act is the I, which grounds and unifies experience in the way Kant presents the unity of apperception as doing so. Kant regards this unifying I as some sort of thing or substance that performs the act of unification necessary for experience and cognition, without itself being a possible object of experience or cognition. Instead of grasping the I as such a mysterious "thing," Fichte treats the I as simply the free act itself, and its absolute self-positing is the starting point of transcendental inquiry. This act, to be sure, must have an agent as a condition of its possibility, but that agent turns out to be a lived body in reciprocal causal interaction with its environment.

It belongs to the freedom of the I, as absolutely self-positing that it is capable of resisting any incentive, rational or empirical. Fichte does not, therefore, infer directly from the I's freedom that it must be subject to a law or carry with it an incentive. Here Fichte agrees with Kant's conclusions, but holds that the subjection of the free will to a law (a norm or ought) must be demonstrated. This demonstration takes place in Part I of the *System of Ethics*: The Deduction of the Principle of Morality (GA I/5: 33–72; SL 4: 13–62). The entire system proceeds on the basis of a freely chosen commitment to exercise freedom and draws out of the presupposition of our free agency the concept of a norm or law, a categorical "ought," and also an end or goal of free activity – absolute independence or self-sufficiency (GA I/5: 61–70; SL 4: 48–60). The differences between Kant and Fichte show themselves in the different methods they follow in grounding a system of moral philosophy, which in both cases, however, is equally based on the indemonstrable but unavoidable presupposition of the will's radical freedom.

1.2 Fichte's Synthetic Method, Kant's Analytical Method

Fichte understands the deduction of the moral law as a direct proof, based on the presupposition of freedom, corresponding to the transcendental method he develops as the practical part of his "doctrine of science" (*Wissenschaftslehre*). To put it in traditional Aristotelian-scholastic terminology, Fichte proceeds "synthetically," from first principles, from what is best known in itself (from the standpoint of the philosopher), toward the conclusions of moral science, or what is best known to us (from the standpoint of the ordinary agent). The fundamental principle of morality, as deduced by the philosopher, is nothing but a *concept*: that of a law, a categorical imperative, and an ultimate end (of absolute independence or self-sufficiency). Its deduction leaves open not only how moral duties and intermediate ends can be derived from the principle, but even the question whether the deduced concept applies to human actions at all. To provide a deduction of the applicability of the principle is Fichte's aim in Part II of the *System of Ethics,* while the actual application of the principle is left to Part III.

Kant's approach in the *Groundwork* is strikingly different. Kant describes the method of the first two sections as analytical and only the third as synthetic (4: 392). The first section begins from "common rational moral cognition" and the second from a philosophical account of the will or practical reason. Their goal is to arrive at the supreme principle of morality, which is finally formulated in its systematic completeness in the second section (4: 436). Equally important, the "analytical" procedure is hypothetical regarding the foundation of morality itself. Repeatedly, almost obsessively, Kant reminds us that he is only provisionally assuming that common rational morality and practical reason offer us something real, rather than being a mere illusion, a "cobweb of the brain, overreaching itself through self-conceit" (4: 407). It is only in the third (or "synthetic") section that Kant appeals to the unavoidable (if unprovable) presupposition of freedom and provides a "deduction" of both freedom and the reality of the moral law (4: 447, 454, 463). Kant, in other words, presents us first with a full conception of the moral principle, and only then offers a justification (as he describes it in KpV 5: 8). Application of the principle, the system of duties, is left for the *Metaphysics of Morals,* specifically, the "Doctrine of Virtue" (6: 214–218, 379–382; cf. G 4: 388).

These methodological differences explain other divergences between Fichte's account and Kant's, which are often misunderstood because Kant is so often misunderstood. Perhaps chief among these is Fichte's insistence that the principle of morality deduced in Part I of the *System of Ethics* is limited to the mere thought of a categorical imperative. It is solely the thought of an "ought" and an absolute tendency toward self-sufficiency (GA I/5: 69 f.; SL 4: 59–60). It is nothing but the thought of our own freedom. From it no specific duties can be derived, and even the applicability of this thought to our actions must be separately deduced (GA I/5: 73 f.; SL 4: 63–64).

Kant, however, proposes to derive from the mere concept of a categorical imperative that law which alone can be a categorical imperative. He derives first its form: the formula of universal law (FUL) and the formula of law of nature (FLN) (G 4: 402, 421), then its matter, the formula of humanity (FH) as end in itself (G 4: 427–429), and finally he puts the two together to derive the formula of autonomy (FA) (G 4: 431) and the formula of the realm of ends (FRE) (G 4: 433). Then he presents these formulas as a system (G 4: 436). In the course of their derivation, he relates them to determinate duties, which are apparently to be derived from one or more of them: perhaps FUL (G 4: 421) but more likely FH (G 4: 429–430). It has been controversial in the reception of Kant's ethics whether Kant has been successful in drawing determinate laws and duties from the mere concept of a categorical imperative, and Fichte's procedure is then seen as bolstering the "emptiness" charge against Kantian ethics, which declares this to be impossible.

This way of looking at it, however, badly misunderstands the relation between Kant's theory and Fichte's. It confuses difference in method with a substantive theoretical disagreement. Fichte's synthetic method starts with the bare concept of a categorical imperative as the thinking of our freedom, which of course deliberately abstracts from the content of the imperative and leaves this to be deduced subsequently. Kant, however, begins with the concepts of duty (first section) and categorical imperatives (second section), both considered as belonging to a hypothetically assumed conception of morality whose reality is to be established only later through the deduction from freedom. The concept of morality Kant is assuming hypothetically is either the common sense one based on common rational moral cognition (first section) or that based on a rich conception of the practical use of reason, involving instrumental and prudential as well as moral reason (G 4: 412) (second section). These conceptions of morality are taken to be both contentful and familiar to us both from ordinary moral thinking and given a philosophical account in terms of our entire practical faculty of reason.

The principle Kant presents is an a priori principle, but its formulations are contextualized in relation to empirical human nature, and the content of the formulas depends on contrasting the a priori principle of reason with determinate empirical tendencies in human nature to which morality is the pure rational response. FUL/FLN are a canon of judgment designed to help human beings resist their tendency to corrupt judgment involving partiality to self in the application of duty to particular cases. FH stands in contrast to the human propensity to value the worth of our state or condition (*Zustand*) over that of our person, and to treat other persons as mere means to our discretionary ends. FA commands that we follow a law proceeding from our capacity for rational self-government, in opposition to the historical source of morality in deference to social custom and external authority, from which it is our vocation as enlightened beings to free ourselves. In place of social relations grounded on conflict, antagonism, and "unsociable sociability," FRE commands us to see all rational beings as colegislators in an ideal community whose laws would harmonize all their ends into a single system.

It is in this context that Kant formulates the concept of a categorical imperative. It is from that concept that he derives the system of formulas of the moral law. It is from the unavoidable presupposition of freedom that Kant then proposes to justify the conception of morality expounded hypothetically. The more detailed application of the deduced concept of morality to actions and duties Kant postpones to a *Metaphysics of Morals* (which was published thirteen years later than the *Groundwork* for it).

A common source of error in relating Kant to Fichte is the false picture of Kant's principle – especially FUL/FLN – as a procedure for deriving duties or a discursive criterion of right and wrong. It is instead merely an implicit or intuitive standard of judgment in the application of recognized duties.[1] There is in Kant no procedure of the sort FUL/FLN have often been taken to be. Therefore, there is no issue whether such a procedure has this sort of "content"; Fichte's more abstract presentation of the moral principle should not be seen as a negative answer to the question whether it has one. Once we clear away common invidious misunderstandings of Kant, we should no longer see disagreements where there are differences. Both Kant's and Fichte's methodological choices make sense on their own, irrespective of whether we find their executions successful. Both, however, might also very well succeed. What is essential to the concept of morality they both seek to defend – its basis in freedom, its conception of morality as autonomy resulting in categorical obligation – is virtually identical. Fichte often claims he is simply making Kant consistent. Most of the time he is right.

1.3 Kant and Fichte on Our Human Condition as Moral Agents

There are real divergences, however, between Kant and Fichte when it comes to the way they understand how we apply the a priori moral principle to our situation as agents. Both understand us to have the vocation of being rationally self-governing beings situated in relation to empirical desires that threaten this vocation. But the way they treat this situation is different. Kant understands much of our condition as based on simple empirical contingencies. It is a contingent fact that we finite rational

[1] See Wood (2017b).

beings are also living, embodied beings with biological needs. Consequently, it is also contingent that we are beings of need, whose empirical desires at least potentially come into conflict with the demands of moral reason. It is also a contingent fact that we stand in relation to other rational beings, and that interaction and communication with them play a significant role in the principles of our self-government. For Kant, to be sure, these contingencies are pervasive and crucial to the application of the a priori principle. But Kant accepts them as part of the sensible nature to which our understanding and reason must apply themselves, just as in the theoretical realm our understanding cognizes only through empirical intuition.

Fichte's philosophical method involves the rejection of this way of looking at our condition, both theoretically and practically. Fichte's theoretical philosophy attempts to ground the contrast between sensibility and understanding in imagination and feeling – a deeper unity from which both may be transcendentally deduced. In parallel fashion, his practical philosophy attempts to establish the transcendental necessity of our condition as sensibly conditioned rational beings, confronted by a world that resists our practical striving as free agents while at the same time offering the context for realizing our agency. For Fichte, a holy will is a transcendental impossibility. There is also no coherent concept of an infinite free agent (a divine person) not confronted by a world resisting its free agency or shared by other free agents with whom it stands in reciprocal relation. (Fichte's insistence that God cannot be such fantastic and impossible entity is what led to his dismissal from his professorship in Jena.)

Part II of the *System of Ethics* offers us a transcendental deduction of the fundamental features of our human condition as rational agents. As free agents we are active, and our activity is both situated and limited by the objects on which it can be exercised. Causal interaction with an objective world is possible only if we belong to that world. Free agents are therefore necessarily embodied beings, and their agency can be unitary only if their bodies are organized, internally teleological. We must be living beings standing in relations of dependency and interdependency with our environment. As free agents, our bodily *organization* must assume the form of *articulation*, an organic wholeness that can be freely directed from within. Biological needs cannot be understood merely as natural causal interactions between the living body of the free agent and other bodies. They must therefore assume the form of *drives*. These are present in and to the free agent originally as indeterminate organic striving (*Streben*), experienced as objectless longing (*Sehnen*). *Reflection* gives to this longing the form of determinate *desires*. These are experienced, at the borderline between passivity and activity, as *feeling*.

For Fichte, then, it is not an empirical contingency but transcendentally necessary that our vocation as rational beings must consist in a struggle against a passive or sensible nature. Both Kant and Fichte employ the distinction, derived from Wolffian philosophy, between a "higher" and "lower" power of desire (KpV 5: 22; GA I/5: 126–135, SL 4: 132–142), the higher power involving principles of reason, while the lower expresses only sensible or empirical desires. In both cases, however, moral agency involves both rational and empirical desires. For Kant, reason itself affects our sensibility, resulting in rational feelings without which we could not be morally motivated or be rational agents at all (MS 6: 399–403). True virtue (*virtus noumenon*) can express itself in our lives only as *virtus phaenomenon* – which includes empirical inclinations that harmonize rather than resist moral reason (R 6: 46–47). For Fichte, the positive connection between rational and empirical desire is even more important. Kant thinks that it is possible, and important, to be motivated only by duty, reason, or the moral law. Fichte, however, maintains that there are two basic drives: the pure drive, aiming solely at absolute self-sufficiency, and the empirical drive, arising from our sensuous nature and passivity to external reality.

We might be tempted to think that Fichte would identify the pure drive with Kantian acting from duty, and the empirical drive with Kantian inclination: and then suppose he will insist that morality requires giving absolute priority to the pure drive. If we do think this, we fundamentally misunderstand Fichte's position. He maintains that the pure drive, all by itself, can never produce any action, but could produce only abstention, "continuous self-denial" (GA I/5: 139; SL 4: 147). Moral action thus requires the unification of the pure and empirical drives: "All actual willing is empirical" (GA I/5: 140; SL 4: 148). The ethical drive is therefore a *mixed* drive (GA I/5: 142; SL 4: 152). It must combine the pure drive and the empirical drive. The ethical drive is always mixed with other drives, in particular, the drive for "enjoyment" (*Genuß*), or the satisfaction (*Befriedigung*) of some empirical drive merely for its own sake (GA I/5: 123; SL 4: 128). Fichte insists that action produced in this way may, using Kantian language, have "legality" but not "morality" (GA I/5: 145; SL 4: 154; cf. KpV 5: 71, 81, MS 6: 225). It may be *in conformity to duty*, but is not done *from duty*. Fichte thus preserves that Kantian distinction, but in a different way from Kant. Both philosophers seem to be agreed on two important points: (1) genuine moral volition must in some way involve both reason and empirical desire and (2) within this combination, reason ought to have priority over empirical desire. But the way this combination of views is worked out in Fichte's philosophy has important consequences for his conception of the way moral agents choose which actions they count as conforming to duty.

1.4 Moral Choice

Both Kant and Fichte give an account of how ordinary moral agents make decisions, or at least of how they ought to. Both also have a "doctrine of duties," a theory and even a taxonomy of the ethical obligations to which a moral agent is subject. There is also in both theories a somewhat indirect relationship between these two themes. But the way the two philosophers handle this relationship is different, owing once again to the way their moral theories are structured. Kant and Fichte agree in distinguishing the role of intellect and judgment in making moral decisions from the role of character or moral volition proper, and for both, this distinction shows itself most clearly when we focus on the important role in the moral life that they assign to *conscience*. In discussing this phase of the comparison, I will begin with Kant, whose views on this matter have been grossly misunderstood in their common reception, and then expound Fichte's views by highlighting the parallels and also the differences between his theory and Kant's.

1.4.1 *Kant's Theory of Moral Choice: The Traditional Misunderstanding of FUL/FLN*

Those who know Kant's ethics mainly from the *Groundwork* have commonly ascribed to him the idea that the formula of universal law (FUL) and the formula of the law of nature (FLN) (usually muddled together in people's misconception of his theory) constitute a kind of discursive decision procedure for deciding which subjective principles or maxims are permissible and which are not. This error depicts Kantian agents as beginning their deliberations by proposing a maxim, and then they test it by asking themselves whether they can will it to be a universal law. If they can will this, then the maxim is permissible; if it is not, then the maxim is forbidden. In the reception of Kant's ethics, it has then been controversial whether these formulas can succeed in providing a moral criterion that matches our intuitions or considered moral judgments. This wrongheaded use of FUL/FLN and the controversy over whether they can provide a criterion of moral permissibility have taken on a philosophical life of their own, and it would be foolish to expect to put an end to their discussion. But when it comes to understanding Kant, much good would be done if some pharmacologist could invent a medication which, if ingested, deletes all traces of these matters from the brain of anyone who picks up the *Groundwork*. The same effect, however, might be achieved (less drastically, without science fiction) if someone simply read and understood the "Doctrine of Virtue" from Kant's *Metaphysics of Morals* and took seriously what Kant says in it, and then resolved to understand the *Groundwork* as the product of the same mind. No one who did this could any longer think that Kant's ethics is about proposing maxims and deciding whether they are "universalizable."

Kantian ethics (if we take the outrageous liberty of using that term to refer to *Kant's* ethics) sees the position of the ordinary moral agent as that of someone who does not need a philosophical theory or intellectual deliberative procedure in deciding what he or she ought to do. The *Groundwork* itself is quite explicit about this (if only readers would attend to it):

> It needs no science or philosophy to know what one has to do in order to be honest and good, or indeed, even wise and virtuous. It might even have been conjectured in advance that the acquaintance with what every human being is obliged to do, hence to know, would also be the affair of everyone, even of the most common human being. Here one cannot regard without admiration the way the practical faculty of judgment is so far ahead of the theoretical in the common human understanding . . . . [I]ndeed, [the common understanding] is almost more secure in this even than the [philosophical] because the philosopher has no other principle than the common understanding, but the philosopher's judgment is easily confused by a multiplicity of considerations that are alien and do not belong to the matter and can make it deviate from the straight direction. (4: 404)

We need only look at the work of philosophers who occupy themselves with lifeboat shortages and runaway trolleys, or that of cognitive scientists who theorize about the neurology of moral judgments and feelings, to appreciate the justice of Kant's complaint that philosophy more often corrupts than enlightens ordinary moral agents. Kant thinks ordinary, even uneducated people generally have a better sense of right and wrong than philosophers do. He gives the name "common rational moral cognition" to the capacity he thinks any normal human being has for knowing what is right and what is wrong. And he supposes that from an intellectual standpoint, it is entirely sufficient and in no need of philosophical guidance. This conviction on his part clearly reflects the powerful influence of Rousseau, and we may think (or at least I do) that its democratic impulses, though basically just, are also exaggerated. Kant may have reacted too strongly against the dominant Wolffian position that nonphilosophers would profit from the advice of more intellectually sophisticated minds. But if we are to understand Kant's moral theory, we must face up squarely to the fact that as Kant uses it, FUL/FLN is not supposed to be used in the way the traditional reception (whether "Kantian" or "anti-Kantian") thinks it is to be used.

In the *Groundwork*, FUL and FLN are described as a "standard" or "canon" of judgment (4: 403, 424); in the second *Critique*, FLN is described as a "typic" or "rule" of judgment (5: 67–71). Judgment, for Kant, refers to the capacity or talent of the mind in applying general concepts to particular cases (KrV A132-134/B171-174; KU 5: 179–180 7: 199; 8: 275). Kant argues that this is a special skill, not reducible to any discursive process of reasoning. A standard or canon of judgment is to be used in the correction of moral (not intellectual) errors made by agents through the human tendency toward self-partiality and the indulgence of their own inclinations, which leads them to apply concepts of good and bad, duty and violation of duty in ways that "cavil with conscience" (G 4: 404) and "ratiocinate against those strict laws of duty and to bring in doubt their validity, or at least their purity and strictness, and where possible, to make them better suited to our wishes and inclinations" (G 4: 405). FUL/ FLN, used as a standard of judgment, is supposed to lead agents to look at their situation consistently from the universal standpoint of reason, and expose the corruption involved in using sophistries and excuses to exempt themselves in particular cases from duties of which their common rational cognition makes them aware in general (G 4: 424). It is by no means infallible, but Kant thinks it can help.

Regarded as such a standard or canon, Kant's formulas FUL and FLN represent this standpoint of universality intellectually, but this is not how Kant thinks they function in practice. "Common human reason obviously does not think [the moral principle] abstractly in such a universal form, but actually has always before its eyes and uses as its standard of judgment" (G 4: 403). We should think of FUL/FLN in the same way we might think of rules of logic or grammar, which people seldom or never need to think about explicitly when they perform valid inferences or form grammatical sentences, but which philosophers formulate abstractly for the purpose of giving a theoretical account of the implicit knowledge their skills tacitly represent. This purely implicit and tacit use as a corrective to corrupt judgment is the only one to which Kant ever imagines FUL/FLN being put. It presupposes (and does not derive or justify) the duties being applied through judgment, which are taken for granted. Kant's own justification of the system of moral duties to be applied through judgment appeals to a different formula: humanity as end in itself (FH) (G 4: 429–431 and MS 6: 417–474 *passim*). But this is a philosophical account of these duties. It is significant that the agents whom Kant depicts as employing FUL and FLN as canons of judgment do not even explicitly name or conceptualize the duties whose concepts they are applying (G 4: 402–403, 421–424).

1.4.2 *Kant's Theory of Moral Choice: Duties, Judgment, and Conscience*

The *Groundwork* and *Critique of Practical Reason* are inquiries into the foundations of ethics. They are not works about how everyday moral reasoning is to be carried out or how the principle of morality is to be applied. The one work in which Kant treats of those matters is the *Metaphysics of Morals*, and more specifically the "Doctrine of Virtue." But no one who began the study of Kant's ethics by reading the *Metaphysics of Morals* could possibly think that Kant's theory requires us to choose our actions by formulating our maxims and testing them for universalizability. The Doctrine of Elements in this work presents us instead with a taxonomy of duties, some strict or perfect, most wide or imperfect.

In effect, the "Doctrine of Virtue" offers us a set of concepts of duties, virtues, and vices: Some are concepts of kinds of actions that are morally *prohibited*. The self-regarding ones are killing or maiming oneself, unchastity or self-defilement, excessive indulgence in food and drink (gluttony and drunkenness), lying, avarice, and servility, while the other-regarding ones are arrogance, defamation, ridicule, and the giving and taking of scandal. Some actions and habitual policies are *required*: respect for oneself and others, and the self-examination of conscience. But many of the duty concepts refer to ends, kinds of conduct, or attitudes that are *meritorious*: We have a duty to promote our own perfection and the happiness of others; to behave toward others with beneficence, gratitude, and sympathetic participation; and to value the beauty of nature and to treat nonhuman animals with kindness rather than cruelty. These are not duties to perform or abstain from kinds of actions when these are given some morally neutral description. On the contrary, like the concepts used by Aristotle in his account of virtues and vices, they are concepts whose essential content is moral, and for this reason they can specify duties that hold without exception. They are to be applied to our lives through (determining) judgment, a capacity not reducible to discursive reasoning, through which we decide when particular cases fit a universal concept. In order to emphasize this aspect of his theory, Kant appends to his discussions of most duties a set of "casuistical questions" in which the precise application of the duty concept is discussed, usually in relation to problematic or controversial cases. In relation to the duty not to kill oneself, for example, he lists several courses of actions that might be considered suicide but which some have considered either admirable or permissible, inviting readers to reflect on them and form their own opinion about how the duty applies.

What Kant provides in the "Doctrine of Virtue" is a conception of how we should lead our lives in order to fulfill our moral vocation. (Little or none of our time should be wasted formulating maxims and asking ourselves if they can be "universalized.") We should devote our lives to instances of the ends that are duties: our own perfection (both natural and moral) and the happiness of others. Our own happiness is a permissible end, but our lives have meaning and value through our devotion to the activities, projects, and loving and caring that fulfill these obligatory ends. There is latitude (*Spielraum*) in our choice of which ends to pursue, which to give priority, and how much of our lives we devote to each. The all too common portrayal of Kant as an "absolute deontologist" who insists on constraining our lives by a set of exceptionless moral rules cannot survive even a minimally fair and sympathetic reading of the "Doctrine of Virtue."

Central to our moral life for Kant is *conscience*: the duty to submit oneself, one's life, and one's actions to the inner court in which the human being is accused, prosecutor, and judge all at once. The issue before the court is not directly the objective rightness or wrongness of what we have done, but rather whether we have done our best to determine this, to avoid self-deception and delusion about it, and to fathom our true intentions, aims, and motives. I may be acquitted before this court even if I do what is objectively wrong, as long as I have done my best to avoid error and determine whether the source of my actions is pure. I may be convicted before the court even if I do the objectively right thing, if I have done it for the wrong reasons, in bad faith, or unconscientiously. Kant thinks we cannot avoid pronouncing a judgment of conscience on ourselves, but it is all too easy to be heedless of its verdict or even suppress our awareness of it.

1.4.3 Fichte on Choice, Conviction, and Conscience

If we understand Kant's theory correctly, avoiding the traditional caricatures of it that dominate most discussions of "Kantian ethics," then it is easy to see a strong affinity between Kant's and Fichte's views about how ordinary agents are to live their lives and make their decisions. As we have seen, for Kant conscience plays an important role in our lives as reflective moral agents. But Kant assumes that ordinary moral agents are aware at least implicitly of the duties listed in the Doctrine of Elements portion of the "Doctrine of Virtue" (6: 417–474). Everyday choice is to involve the application of these duty concepts to our particular situation through judgment. Does Fichte make a parallel assumption about ordinary moral agents in relation to the scientific system of duties he derives in Part III of the *System of Ethics*? Perhaps he does, but his distinction between the "applicability" of the moral principle and its "application" gives a different impression. He portrays the individual agent as reflecting on a particular situation and responding to the "ethical drive," which reunites the I's original drive, separated by reflection into the pure drive and the empirical (GA I/5: 125; SL 4: 130). The ethical drive impels the I to form for itself a categorical imperative (GA I/5: 137; SL 4: 145) and a conviction (*Überzeugung*) about what the situation demands of that individual then and there (GA I/5: 146; SL 4: 156). And the decisive role in forming this conviction is played by *conscience*.

Neither in Kant nor in Fichte, however, is conscience a source of information or judgments about what to do. In both, this role is played by *judgment*. Fichte even emphasizes that judgment is a theoretical faculty, which is distinct from the faculty that decides what to do and reaches a conviction about it (GA I/5: 161; SL 4: 173). The formation of this conviction is what involves conscience. Conscience is a feeling of harmony between the pure and empirical I (GA I/5: 158; SL 4: 169). Judgment may err about what is the objectively right thing to do; but conscience, once it has given us the feeling that this is the correct thing to do here and now, cannot err. We have an absolute duty to reach the conviction of conscience, and we cannot be guilty of blamable actions if we follow our conviction, even if the judgment seized on in this conviction is objectively in error (GA I/5: 161 f.; SL 4: 173–174). Kant too thinks that conscience cannot err in the sense that even if our understanding is in error about the objectively right action, following our conscience is all that can be required of us (MS 6: 401). But conscience for Kant is a reflective faculty, "the faculty of moral judgment, passing judgment on itself" (R 6: 186). We make the judgment that something is our duty, and conscience judges whether we have done our best to get that judgment right, and to assess our actions from the standpoint of morality in making that judgment. For Fichte, however, in Part II of the *System of Ethics,* it appears that conscience is fundamental to the process of moral choice. The theoretical judgment that we should do something gains moral force only when it becomes a conviction that we should do it, and this conviction can be achieved only through the feeling of conscience.

1.5   The System of Duties

Kant and Fichte follow Baumgarten in offering us a taxonomy of human duties. In Kant's case, they are derived from the FH. Our duties are ways we treat humanity in the person of ourselves and of others as an end in itself, or refrain from conduct that fails or refuses to do so. Our perfect duties to ourselves divide into our duties as an animal being (MS 6: 421–428) and as a moral being (MS 6: 429–442), with an appendix or "episodic section" on duties to ourselves that appear to us to be duties to other beings (regarding nonrational animals, the beauties of nature, and God) (MS 6: 442–444). These must be duties to ourselves because to have a duty to a being, that being must have a rational will with which we can be empirically acquainted (MS 6: 417–420). Our imperfect duties to ourselves are duties to perfect ourselves both naturally and morally (MS 6: 444–447). Duties to others divide into those of love (MS 6: 448–461) and respect (MS 6: 462–469), and these combine in our duties of friendship (MS 6: 469–473).

Fichte's system of ethical duties is presented in Part III of the *System of Ethics* as a "scientific" account of at least some of what the agent's conscientious convictions will require. On the surface it differs radically from Kant's system, because Fichte holds that we have no duty to treat ourselves as ends, but instead a duty to make ourselves into rational and active tools (*Werkzeuge*) of moral reason in furtherance of its ends, which are summed up in the self-sufficiency of I-hood (GA I/5: 143; SL 4: 152). This looks like a rejection of Kant's FH, which says we should treat ourselves and others as ends, never merely as means. Fichte insists, however, that his doctrine and Kant's are not opposed if only his own view is correctly understood (GA I/5: 230 f.; SL 4: 256): Namely, Fichte argues that I am treated as an end if I fulfill my *moral vocation*, which is to be a means for the realization of the moral law (MS 6: 255–259, 268–270, 277–279, 313–325). Therefore, treating myself as a means to realize the moral end of self-sufficiency is the same as treating myself as an end. Whether this is really consonant with Kant is a larger issue than I can settle here.[2]

---

[2]   See Wood (2016a, 226–236).

How are we to understand the pursuit of the end of self-sufficiency, and ourselves as freely acting tools for its realization? One way to understand this might be to try to identify what the end of self-sufficiency is in such a way that we could choose *actions* directly as means to it. In the nineteenth century, this was sometimes understood as aiming at the maximal control of nature by human beings. Such an interpretation might follow Michelle Kosch, and turn Fichte's ethics into a system of maximizing consequentialism.[3] This is not the place to litigate my disagreement with that interpretation.[4] It is in place here for me to present briefly my own account of the end of self-sufficiency. Fichte denies this end is attainable, and this is not only because it lies beyond human power but because in its very concept the I must be opposed by a not-I or external reality, making complete self-sufficiency a transcendental impossibility. Kosch is quite correct that Fichte favors increasing humanity's control of nature; yet this is not because self-sufficiency consists in this power (which would, in any case, have to be a means to the exercise of that control, and not an end for its own sake). It is rather because Fichte thinks it would release that portion of humanity that must devote itself to menial labor from the servitude to others that this condition involves. Fichte's actual working out of his system of duties in Part III does not involve consequentialist calculations of individual actions in relation to the final end on any conception of it. Instead, it involves the resolution of an antinomy or apparent contradiction between seeking self-sufficiency and the basic transcendental conditions of I-hood. This involves a set of negative, positive, and limitative duties regarding the way the I is to treat (1) the body (GA I/5: 194–198; SL 4: 212–217), (2) the understanding (GA I/5: 198; SL 4: 217–218), and (3) the relation to other I's (GA I/5: 199–204; SL 4: 218–225). It is noteworthy that these duties are not described as ways of achieving or maximizing any determinate ends, but rather as ways of adapting ourselves and our powers to the promotion of the ends of reason, whatever these may turn out to be. They involve prohibitions on certain kinds of actions, the positive promotion of certain specific ends, and limitations on the actions through which these ends may be permissibly promoted.

Kosch is again correct that Fichte's conception of our duties involves teleological thinking. However, the means are not *actions* calculated consequentialistically as means, but rather *things* and *human beings*, which are to be shaped in such a way as to serve the ends of reason, whatever these

---

[3] Kosch (2018, especially 52–68).   [4] But see Wood (2016a, 147–154, 174–184).

might turn out to be. The ends themselves – the content of the self-sufficiency of reason – moreover are ends yet to be determined, through our relation to other I's, which is to be a rationally communicative relation, described by Fichte at length in his account of the social institutions through which we relate to others (GA I/5: 208–227; SL 4: 229–253). Human beings are to communicate with the aim of reaching free, rational agreement among their ends, and the ends on which they agree constitute the standard by which their actions are to be chosen. Fichte's names for these ends are "society" and "perfection" (the perfection of society) (GA I/5: 226 f., SL 4: 253; GA I/3: 40; BdG 6: 309–310).

If the final end of reason, self-sufficiency, is to be seen as an end to be pursued in actions, it would have to be conceived as a condition of human society: *social perfection*; this would include a relation between human beings and nature only to the extent that human society maintains an interaction with nature. Nature's own ends would have to be considered when human beings collectively choose the content of his end; and it would not merely be the imposition of arbitrary human ends on nature. Moreover, because the condition of society constituting social perfection is always provisional, a work in progress, there would be no way that a technical calculus of consequences could be employed in selecting actions toward it. Fichte's actual theory of duties, when we look at its details, concerns the way in which our bodies, understandings, and relations with others should be fashioned by us in a way that enables us to serve the ends of reason – whatever these may turn out to be.

Fichte's end of self-sufficiency, when conceptualized as *social perfection*, in fact looks a great deal like Kant's idea of the realm of ends. Kant's theory too, therefore, has an important teleological side. Both Kant and Fichte ground ethics on a categorical imperative, but both theories also are focused on a human moral vocation that would have us orient our lives to a final end. For both, this end is best conceived not in terms of maximizing human desire – satisfaction, happiness, or control over nature – but instead as the way the community of rational beings should relate to one another. Which further ends people should set for themselves would result from free rational communication between them and from individual choices. It is not the task of moral philosophy to dictate these ends.

1.6 Conclusion

It does no service to philosophical ethics to categorize ethical theories as "deontological," "teleological (or consequentialist)," and "virtue theory." Theories may have different starting points, but no ethics worthy of the name could avoid giving an account of right and wrong action, or the ends we ought to seek or the kind of person we should try to be. All three aspects are prominent in both Kant and Fichte. To use any of these invidious terms to characterize either philosopher is reductive and distorting.

Both Kant and Fichte base their theories on absolute freedom. The starting point for both Kant's and Fichte's theories is with an absolute "ought." Kant's with a categorical imperative, Fichte's with the concept of a moral law. But both also prominently include a doctrine of ends. Kant specifies our own perfection and the happiness of others as ends that are duties, and directs us to systematize our ends in a "realm of ends" and pursue the highest good. Fichte's principle requires us to set the absolute independence or self-sufficiency of reason as an end, and to seek the perfection of society as an end in itself. Kant's theory of ethical duty is entitled the "Doctrine of Virtue," and Kant's taxonomy of duties could more often serve as a taxonomy of virtues, just as he explicitly calls their opposites "vices." Fichte's system of duties prominently includes the way we should try to fashion ourselves, our bodies, intellects, and relations to others, to make ourselves into free and active tools of the moral law. Kant's and Fichte's ethical theories are strikingly similar in spirit, even if in certain respects they develop the same essential ideas in strikingly different ways.

CHAPTER 2

Fichte on Normativity in the Late Jena Period (1796–1799)

Benjamin Crowe

Perhaps because Kantianism is a broad church, Kant-inspired accounts of moral normativity are prominent in contemporary debates.[1] While universally recognized as one of Kant's most innovative readers, J. G. Fichte has mostly been left out of the historical discussion of Kantian ethics.[2] Different groups of questions can be asked about moral normativity.[3] I am interested in Fichte's account of the "rightness" of a moral principle, that is, of its property of holding universally for all agents. It is this part of Fichte's theory of normativity that I want to focus on here.

There are three dimensions of Fichte's account of moral normativity that I will examine. First, his account is *theoretical*; that is, Fichte's theory of moral normativity is not addressed to agents in the thick of action but to philosophers who are interested in explaining what is going on in moral life at a higher order of generality. Second, Fichte's view is *idealist*; Fichte aims at a full account of normativity that makes no appeal to natural or mechanical causes.[4] Finally, Fichte's view is *theological*, in a special sense. Fichte argues that a complete account of the conditions of rational agency requires appeal to what he calls a "pure will." This is because the concept of God (i.e., of absolutely self-determining reason) furnishes the content of

---

Thanks to Owen Ware and his 2018 seminar on Fichte's *System of Ethics* at the University of Toronto, including Michael Morgan, for comments and queries regarding a prior draft of this chapter. Earlier versions also benefited from conversation with Elijah Millgram.

[1] I have found Frederick Rauscher's (2002) to be quite helpful in clearly laying out some of the recent realist and anti-realist approaches to metaethics that claim to be Kantian.

[2] Karl Ameriks's work is valuable in linking Fichte to current debates surrounding metaethical constructivism. See especially his (2000). Charles Larmore (2003), and Daniel Breazeale (2003) challenged aspects of Ameriks's position. For the final round, see Ameriks's (2003).

[3] Robert Stern provides a very helpful schema of the different questions at stake in theories of moral normativity. See his (2012). I rely heavily on the distinctions that Stern draws throughout this chapter.

[4] This is not, of course, all there is to being an idealist; as Fichte himself was well aware, there are a number of distinct views that share this label.

Fichte on Normativity in the Late Jena Period (1796–1799)   29

the law, which he conceives of as a goal or aim that obtains universally and so furnishes a nonarbitrary principle for judging more immediate or particular aims.

My discussion will begin by clarifying the first two aspects of Fichte's theory of moral normativity (i.e., its theoretical and idealist character). I bring out various ways in which, *as* theoretical and idealist, Fichte's account diverges from some prominent contemporary theories in the broad Kantian tradition with particular reference to Christine Korsgaard's constructivism. Next, I will examine Fichte's actual account of normativity as it appears in the "*Wissenschaftslehre* nova methodo" lectures delivered between 1796 and 1798, during the composition of the *System of Ethics* (1798). Working through this and related texts uncovers the centrality of the theological dimension of Fichte's account. This is likely to be the most controversial element of my reading. Discussions in the *System of Ethics* raise problems for my claim that Fichte's metaethics has an indispensable theological component. While I do think Fichte owes us more clarification on certain key issues, I think that the problems I've noted are in no way fatal to my claim that a complete picture of Fichte's view must include this theological element.

2.1   The Basic Character of Fichte's Account of Normativity

Does Fichte have a project in metaethics in the first place? He makes a distinction between philosophically grounded answers to questions about how one should behave and how one should decide what to do, on the one hand, and to philosophical questions about where the principles we use in these situations come from and are justified, on the other hand. The organization of his first major treatise on moral theory, the *System of Ethics* (1798), makes this plain. In Part I and most of Part II, Fichte develops a "genetic explanation" of our "moral nature," that is, of the fact that we acknowledge some things as obligatory, as giving us moral (i.e., noninstrumental) reasons to do things or refrain from doing them. While in an important sense the moral law is the conclusion of the argument of Part I, the formulation that Fichte offers does not look particularly informative from the standpoint of a person trying to figure out what to do, nor is it meant to be so (see GA I/5: 61; SL 4: 52). In fact, Fichte's accent is on the discovery that agency as such is inconceivable without there being some fundamental law of action, and that this law therefore obtains universally of any agent. The justificatory force or normativity of this law stems from our "original determination [*Urbestimmung*]" as rational agents (GA I/5: 62; SL 4: 55).

Fichte's commitment to distinguishing concrete practical questions from properly philosophical ones is a distinctive feature of his approach. This can be seen by way of a contrast with Korsgaard's Kantian Constructivism. In one of the authoritative statements of her view, Korsgaard writes that her primary concern is to answer the "normative question." This is, roughly, the question about *why* a putative obligation actually constrains me as an agent. On her view, this is a question that comes up *within* practice, that is, when a particular obligation makes substantial demands on us and we ask for some justification of the demands.[5] Fichte, too, is struck by the fact that morality *commands*, that it purports to offer overriding practical reasons. Consider his comments from the "Preliminary Remark" that opens Part I of the *System of Ethics*:

> It is claimed that the human mind finds itself to be absolutely compelled to do certain things entirely apart from any extrinsic ends, but purely and simply for the sake of doing them, and to refrain from doing other things, equally independently of any extrinsic ends, purely and simply for the sake of leaving them undone. Insofar as such a compulsion [*Zunötigung*] is supposed to manifest itself necessarily in human beings just as surely as they are human beings, this constitutes what is called *the moral or ethical* nature of human beings as such. (GA I/5: 33; SL 4: 19)

Fichte's talk of "compulsion [*Zunötigung*]" is very similar to Kant's talk about "necessitation [*Nötigung*]" in the *Groundwork of the Metaphysics of Morals* and elsewhere. As Robert Stern has recently pointed out, there are two different questions that Kant asks about the moral law. First, why is a certain principle (i.e., the categorical imperative) a *law* at all, that is, why does it possess universality and necessity? Second, why is it that we experience this universality and necessity as a constraint? Fichte distinguishes these questions as well, and for reasons similar to those adduced by Kant. Fichte holds, like Kant, that our experience of morality as a constraint is grounded in our "mixed" nature, that is, in the fact that we are both rational and natural beings. For a being that is not constituted in this way, that is, for God, the sense of "compulsion" or constraint involved in morality is absent. Such is not our fate; as Fichte makes clear in any number of texts (such as the following from a lecture on ethics in Jena), we are not to expect the relaxation of this moral "compulsion [*Zunötigung*]" any time soon:

> But the I can never become independent of nature since it can never posit itself except as a being of nature [*Naturwesen*], nor [can it posit itself] as

---

[5] Korsgaard (1996, 7–9).

Fichte on Normativity in the Late Jena Period (1796–1799) 31

acting except with a natural power [*Naturkraft*]. Just as certainly as the I should be an I, it is never independent of nature. The final end [*Endzweck*] of a rational being is therefore necessarily infinite, never to be attained, though it should be ceaselessly approximated . . . . The thought [*Gedanke*] that the pure part of the I is God and really a part of the Godhead is indeed sublime. Limitation [*Beschränkung*] constitutes the human being and his essential character. Therefore, only the pure drive strives always to make the human being equal to God. But this task is infinite and never attainable. (GA IV/1: 69)

For Fichte, both the law itself and its character as a law (i.e., as universal and necessary) must be distinguished from moral "compulsion." Note also the connection Fichte draws between the "pure drive" and the idea of God, which will become significant later in the chapter. One takeaway from these discussions is that it is precisely *because* he views our "moral nature" in this way that Fichte is not, as Korsgaard certainly is, concerned about how everyday moral demands raise foundational questions about normativity. For Fichte, one can simply "attach unconditional *faith* to this inner compulsion: i.e., one might decide actually *to think* that one's highest vocation is what is represented to one as such by this inner compulsion and to *act* unfailingly in accordance with this faith" (GA I/5: 33; SL 4: 19–20). This is, according to Fichte, quite "sufficient for engendering both a dutiful disposition and dutiful conduct" (GA I/5: 33; SL 4: 20). Indeed, it would seem that one must have *already* accepted that there are obligations that provide one with compelling reasons in order to face a question about any trade-off in the first place. Fichte suggests as much when he says later that "[w]hen one occupies the ordinary viewpoint, this necessity of consciousness imposes itself immediately" (GA I/5: 36; SL 4: 23). Whatever else Fichte is doing in Part I of the *System of Ethics* (and in related works, as will be seen later), he is not addressing an agent from within the standpoint of agency.

This allows for an important feature of Fichte's position to come into clearer view. Metaethics, or accounting for normativity, is a purely *theoretical* enterprise in Fichte's view; for Korsgaard, on the other hand, it is *practical*. Fichte leaves no doubt about this. In the *System of Ethics*, he writes:

If, as has been claimed [by the deduction], the morality of our nature is something that follows from our rationality according to necessary laws, then for perception itself the compulsion noted above is something primary and immediate, something that manifests itself without any help from us, and we cannot freely change this manifestation in the least. Employing a deduction to gain insight into the grounds of this compulsion does not provide us with any power to change anything about the compulsion, because it is *our knowledge and not our power that extends this far*, and because this whole relationship is necessary; indeed, it is our unchangeable nature itself. The deduction thus produces nothing more than *theoretical cognition*, and one must not expect anything more from it . . .. Even the science of ethics [*Sittenlehre*] is not a *doctrine of wisdom* [*Weisheitslehre*]. (GA I/5: 34–35; SL 4: 21; emphasis added)

Fichte's question isn't Korsgaard's normative question. It is, instead, the *normativity* question, the question of *why* it is that we are creatures that *necessarily* recognize certain claims as giving us compelling reasons to do or to think something. Answering this question is not supposed to change either the fact that or the manner in which we take morality to be reason giving. Instead, the account provides us with theoretical insight into how a noteworthy feature of human nature is the way it is by showing why it *has to be* that way. While Fichte is quite certain that the successful resolution of this inquiry is valuable in many ways, it is ultimately valuable as science, "and science, wherever it is possible, is an end in itself" (GA I/5: 34; SL 4: 20).

In addition to being a strictly theoretical enterprise, Fichte's account of normativity also has a second important feature, its *idealism*. What it means to say that Fichte is an idealist is a matter of continued debate and investigation. What is clear is that Fichte says his system is a system of transcendental idealism, and that his theory of ethics (*Sittenlehre*) as a whole is "according to the principles of the *Wissenschaftslehre*." Thus, Fichte's metaethics is *idealist*. To begin to specify what this means, consider that the explicit goal of Fichte's foundational investigation is to provide "a genetic deduction of what we find in our consciousness" (GA I/2: 159; EPW, 97); for metaethics, this means Fichte isn't after an account of objective moral properties or God's commands. What is further distinctive for Fichte's account is that it is "based upon the nature of the system of reason as such" (GA I/6: 412; Breazeale 1994, 179). In the *System of Ethics*, Fichte explains:

> The path of the deduction will be as follows: we will assign ourselves the task of thinking of ourselves under a certain specified condition and observing *how* we are required to think of ourselves under this condition. From those properties of ourselves that we find in this way, we will then derive, as something necessary, the moral compulsion noted earlier. (GA I/5: 35; SL 4: 22)

Fichte here explicates his idealism in terms of his methodology. This methodology combines three features. First, it is *hypothetical*; that is, we

Fichte on Normativity in the Late Jena Period (1796–1799) 33

propose to think of ourselves in a certain way. Second, it is *subject-* or *agent-centered*; we are proposing to think of *ourselves*, not of other kinds of things, in a certain way. Finally, it is *deductive*; given the hypothesis, certain things follow as a matter of rational necessity. The second feature, in particular, is what makes Fichte's account an idealist one. Fichte makes this quite clear in the *System of Ethics*, where he argues that his account remains "within the region of thinking" (GA I/5: 36; SL 4: 23). He explains what this means as follows:

> That compulsion within us, what else is this but a kind of thinking that forces itself upon us, a necessary consciousness? Or can we here somehow escape from a consciousness of mere consciousness and reach the object itself? Do we know anything more about this demand than this: that we necessarily have to think that such a demand is directed at us? What we derive from our inferences in the deduction is itself an act of thinking; and that which is within us, independent of all inferences, as something primary and immediate: this too is an act of thinking. (GA I/5: 36; SL 4: 23)

Fichte is interested in how we *have* to think about the world, rather than in an individual's psychology. Fichte is not inquiring about how he happens to think about the world, or about how a group of individuals, however selected, happen to do so. Instead, he is interested in the structure of mindedness, or "I-hood," or "intelligence," or "reason" as such.[6] What explains the phenomenon of moral normativity is something that is discovered through a discursive process that involves abstraction, reflection, and inference, rather than being simply invented *or* generalized from observation.

Fichte also wants to exclude any appeal to *mechanical* causation as an explanation of the normative structure realized by minds. In the "First Introduction" to his 1797 *Attempt at a New Presentation of the Wissenschaftslehre*, the reliance on the "principle of causality" characterizes "dogmatism," the philosophical antipode of idealism (GA I/4: 196; ErE, 1: 435). The causality here is *mechanical* causality characterizing objects in a *"real* series" (GA I/4: 196; ErE, 1: 436).[7] For Fichte, idealism commits one

---

[6] This seems to be the clear import of remarks like the following, both found in the "Second Introduction" of his *Attempt at a New Presentation of the Wissenschaftslehre*: (1) that the "I" is "I-hood as such or in general" (GA I/4: 256; ZwE, 1: 503); and that "the concept of I-hood comprises not merely our own specific personality, but our entire mental or spiritual nature" (GA I/4: 257; ZwE, 1: 504). Günter Zöller's exposition of this point is, I think, particularly on target. See his (1998, 28–30).

[7] My reading here closely follows Wayne Martin's (1997) excellent account of dogmatism as a view on which things in themselves play some kind of natural causal role in the explanation of the structure of experience. See especially his (1997, 36–52).

to the view that such causation cannot account for the normative structure of the mind (GA I/4: 198; ErE, 1: 439).[8]

Third, Fichte is committed to the claim that mindedness is fundamentally active.[9] I take this to mean that mindedness is not primarily to be thought of in terms of properties or states but rather in terms of judgment-like acts, or acts of "determination" as he called them. Fichte wants us to think of a thought as something that we *do*, rather than as something we possess in the way that one possesses a certain eye color. That is, to have a cognition is to make a judgment, to take something to be a certain sort of thing.

Fourth, an idealist account of mindedness is meant to uncover the norms or laws that govern these judgment-like acts. Again, these are norms or laws that belong to the structure of "I-hood." As Fichte puts it, "what the intellect feels in this case is not, as it were, an external impression; instead, what it feels when it acts are the limits of its own nature" (GA I/4: 200; ErE, 1: 441). Or, perhaps more clearly, "what idealism presupposes is the following: The intellect acts; but, as a consequence of its very nature, it can act only in a certain, specific manner" (GA I/4: 200; ErE, 1: 441). What makes the structures of these acts of the intellect laws is that they can be shown to be necessary conditions of what it is to be an intellect (i.e., we might prefer to say rational agent) as such. In this way, Fichte argues that there have to be laws that we come to experience as constraining us, including the moral law.

To sum up so far, Fichte's metaethics looks like this: Our "moral nature," that is, taking ourselves to be obligated to do or to refrain from doing certain actions, is to be accounted for on the basis of the nature of "I-hood" or "reason" as such. Such an account explicates ideal laws that are constitutive of mindedness and shows how our moral nature can be exhaustively explained by these laws. Fichte wants to present an alternative to what he often calls a "dogmatic" account, that is, an account that derives a phenomenon from some fact or "being" that is outside of the system of

---

[8] In the "Second Introduction," Fichte briefly revisits this important aspect of his view. He distinguishes between the kind of effect that a philosophical argument can have on another person's mind from "a relationship of mere causality operating through mechanical forces" (GA I/4: 261; ZwE, 1: 509). The difference seems to be that the former involves the recognition of a *norm*, say, a law of inference, while the latter does not. I believe what you say because you have shown me how it follows from some premises; one doesn't need to *argue* a baseball into rebounding off of a bat.

[9] Passages in which Fichte emphasizes this point are too numerous to cite. A fine representative passage, however, comes in the "Second Introduction" to the *Attempt at a New Presentation of the Wissenschaftslehre* (GA I/4: 251–52; ZwE, 1: 498f.).

Fichte on Normativity in the Late Jena Period (1796–1799) 35

"necessary acts" constitutive of I-hood. What is to be shown in the case of our "moral nature" is that, and how, it is a "necessary thought."

2.2 The *Wissenschaftslehre nova methodo* Account

What, then, is Fichte's account of specifically moral normativity? Giving a straightforward answer to this question is complicated by the fact that there is actually no "official" version of the *Wissenschaftslehre*. Scholars continue to debate the degree to which the various revisions represent fundamental shifts or more superficial alterations.[10] In order to simplify matters, I will here avoid taking a position on this issue. Instead, I will focus on the so-called later Jena system of 1796–1799, which contains two of Fichte's clearest and, I think, most important statements of his metaethical position (in the *System of Ethics* and in a key lecture course). In what follows, I reconstruct the account from the lecture series *Foundations of Transcendental Philosophy*, or *Wissenschaftslehre nova methodo*, as it is commonly known. Fichte's stated goal in this iteration of the *Wissenschaftslehre* is to explain the possibility of the "instinct of reason," that is, of the brute fact of our recognition of certain norms as necessary. These "representations accompanied by a feeling of necessity" are the way they are because they reflect conditions of agency, which Fichte conceives of here as self-determination or self-definition. Regarding self-determination, Fichte has this (among other things) to say:

> "I act *freely*": that is to say, "I spontaneously *design* [*entwerfen*] for myself a concept of my action." Therefore, the concept of a goal must always underlie every free action. The product (= some X) is what I am supposed to achieve by means of my own free action. My I, considered as the subject of my practical power (i.e., as forming an image of itself and developing itself accordingly, as self-initiating, and as consciously acting), must therefore always design for itself in advance the concept of this goal. It requires, as it were, a "model," the realization of which is the goal of the activity. (GA IV/2: 48; WLnm, 149–50, translation modified)[11]

---

[10] Frederick Neuhouser, for example, views "the texts of the period from 1793 to 1799 not as representatives of a single, coherent system, but rather as stages in a tumultuous process of insight, self-criticism, and revision" (1990, 33). Others stress the continuity in Fichte's development. See, for example, Zöller (2003) and Dieter Henrich (2003). This issue becomes especially pressing with respect to the direction of Fichte's thought after about 1800. While, for his part, Fichte maintains the continuity of his thought, a reader cannot help but to notice significant differences in style, argumentative strategy, and conceptuality.

[11] This view of the basic nature of rational agency is robust across other writings from this period in Fichte's career. Thus, in the *System of Ethics*, Fichte explains the concept of action: "[W]hat is objective is supposed to follow from what is subjective; a being is supposed to result from my concept

This chapter describes what Neuhouser calls "formal" self-determination. A self-determined action in the "formal" sense is one that depends upon a reason rather than upon a blind impulse.[12] Fichte's point is that an action counts as a *free* action just in case it rests upon a particular kind of concept, namely, that of an end or goal, which serves as a reason to do something. Fichte thinks that these concepts are concepts of oneself, of the one who is acting in a particular case. Agency thus involves envisioning a still uninstantiated self.

To be sure, Fichte recognizes that we are acquainted with action-like processes, or "movements of transition from one state to another," in cases where no concept of a goal is in play. His example is "a tree in winter and in spring" (GA IV/2: 48; WLnm, 150). Elsewhere, he uses the example of a coiled spring (GA I/5: 49–50; SL 4: 38–39). The difference between these processes and an action, according to Fichte, is best conceived of as an activity of self-definition in accord with a previously "designed" or "sketched out" concept of a goal. Finally, following Neuhouser, the concept of a goal can be understood as the concept of something that a person values that gives a person a reason to act.[13] In his example, the goal of health gives me a reason to exercise.

Fichte's next move, having identified the concept of a goal as the *sine qua non* of a free action, is to consider how such a concept can be formed. He first notes that such a concept depends upon a "sphere of what is determinable" (GA IV/3: 374; WLnm, 168). Here, he relies on the idea, found also in Kant, that defining (or "determining") something involves limitation or the exclusion of predicates. Kant makes the point in connection with the transcendental idea of the *omnitudo realitatis*, that is, the totality of all possible predicates that grounds specific judgments. Fichte, of course, is concerned here with *action*, and so he attempts to clarify the notion of this "sphere of what is determinable" by noting that "We are acquainted with what is determinable as a {manifold} divisible into an infinite number of possible actions" (GA IV/3: 374; WLnm, 168). This "sphere" is a further condition of the possibility of rational agency. Thus,

> [t]he I is nevertheless constrained when it engages in this ideal function of concept [formation]. The construction of concept X can be comprehended

---

(the concept of an end [*Zweckbegriff*])" (GA I/5: 22; SL 4: 8). Or again, more clearly, Fichte writes: "I posit myself as free insofar as I explain a sensible acting, or being, as arising from my concept, which is then called the 'concept of an end.' Therefore, the fact presented above – that I find myself to be acting efficaciously – is possible only under the condition that I presuppose a concept designed [*entworfen*] by myself" (GA I/5: 27; SL 4: 14–15).

[12] Neuhouser (1990, 124–26).   [13] Neuhouser (1990, 127).

Fichte on Normativity in the Late Jena Period (1796–1799) 37

only as follows: A manifold is given to the ideal activity, from which it assembles a concept. It ignores whatever it wishes and grasps hold of whatever it wants. Its freedom consists in doing just this, but [in order to do this] it has to intuit what is given as something given, and therein lies its constraint. (GA IV/3: 374, and GA IV/2: 58; WLnm, 168–69; translation modified)

Simply put, "if nothing is given, then nothing can be chosen. The construction of the concept of a goal can be imagined in no other way" (GA IV/3: 374; WLnm, 169).

When Fichte says that the sphere of possibility is "infinitely divisible," he is simply saying that there are no a priori limits that can be established for the kinds of things that people can come to care about. Linking this "sphere" to a person's most basic natural drive (cf. GA IV/3: 380, 374 f.; WLnm 68–69, 172–73) connects the account here with the *System of Ethics*, where Fichte argues that our being part of nature is a condition of agency, as well as the source of the experience of constraint or "necessity" that comprises our moral nature.

This aspect of Fichte's position is notable. On some versions of Kantian metaethics, for example, Korsgaard's, to take some putative concern as giving us a reason to do something requires that, in this instance, we regard ourselves as able to confer value on that concern. In other words, the condition of the value of a concern is our choosing to make that concern valuable. In the account that Fichte is developing here, however, this is not the view. Instead, Fichte thinks that the possibility of self-determination requires a prior awareness that some things are, at least *prima facie*, worth pursuing. This, I take it, is what he means when he says, "if nothing is given, then nothing can be chosen." That is, in deciding to pursue some goal, Fichte thinks we need to already have some sense that this goal is worthwhile.

By itself, however, this condition still does not account for self-determination. As Neuhouser observes, what is required is some nonarbitrary way of determining *which* concern one will take as a reason for doing something.[14] In the *System of Ethics*, Fichte explains his reasoning here more directly. Freedom is, as he points out, "determinable in all possible ways," that is, "[t]he intellect could thus make for itself a great variety of different rules or maxims – for example, rules pertaining to self-interest, laziness, the oppression of others, and other similar rules" (GA I/5: 66; SL 4: 57). The sheer fact that I am capable of formulating a goal does not entail that pursuing this goal is something I am morally required to do. To get to this next stage, what has to happen is that there be another "concept" or

---

[14] Neuhouser (1990, 128).

"rule" that "imposes itself on the intellect, i.e., that the intellect is, under a certain condition, required to think a certain rule, and only this rule, to be the rule governing its own free determinations" (GA I/5: 66; SL 4: 57).

That is, Fichte thinks that a concern becomes a *reason* only when the natural drive is constrained by something further. Some higher-order rationale for endorsing a particular concern as a reason to act is required. As Fichte puts it, a "determinate direction" must be given to freedom (GA IV/3: 437; WLnm, 288). The point is that there must be some further determination that constrains us to determine ourselves in a certain way, otherwise, so Fichte supposes, it is impossible to see how one could move from the general "sphere of what is determinable" to the specific concept of a goal that one takes as a reason to act. This further "determination" must either be another specific concern, in which case a yet higher "determination" is required to make it a reason to act, or it is a determination that does not itself require our reflective endorsement in order to be a reason.[15] In the latter case, what one has is what Allan Gibbard calls a "why-stopper" or a "substantive principle."[16] Indeed, Fichte argues that the determinacy in question here, in order to be a determinacy that is compatible with freedom, must "appear as a determinate, absolute ought, as a categorical demand" (GA IV/3: 439; WLnm, 291).

Next, Fichte scrutinizes the nature of this determinacy:

> This determinacy, which constitutes my basic character, consists in the fact that I am determined to determine myself in a certain way. For this reason, it assigns me only the task of acting in a certain way; it assigns me an "ought." Man's determinate nature or "vocation" is *not something he gives himself*; instead, it is that through which a human being is a human being. (GA IV/3: 444; WLnm, 300)

This is an important passage that brings out another distinctive feature of Fichte's view. Again, other views in the Kantian family provide a helpful contrast. For example, according to Korsgaard, the "source of the normativity of moral claims must be found in the agent's own will."[17] Fichte is saying here that self-determination is only possible if there is a norm that does not depend on anyone's endorsement for its normative status.[18] It is

---

[15] Neuhouser outlines this kind of regress (1990, 158).   [16] See Gibbard (1999).

[17] Korsgaard (1996, 19). As she puts it later on, "The reflective structure of human consciousness requires that you identify yourself with some law or principle which will govern your choices. It requires you to be a law to yourself. And that is the source of normativity" (1996, 103–4).

[18] Fichte's argument, at least in this text, seems to be closer to D.H. Regan's (2002) "Moorean transcendental argument" for realism. It also seems rather close to Thomas Nagel's (1970) view of the relation between moral constraints and the will in *The Possibility of Altruism*. Fichte's position

Fichte on Normativity in the Late Jena Period (1796–1799)

hard to understand what Fichte is saying here about "that through which a human being is a human being" in any other way. Human beings are agents; for Fichte, an action in the proper sense of the term is something that a human being performs. But then, what it is to be a human being cannot itself be something that depends upon what a human being does. Action, for Fichte, is a process of self-selection, and the structure of "reason as a whole" (GA IV/3: 445; WLnm, 302) is what governs this process. This structure is something that is given, not produced (cf. GA IV/3: 503; WLnm, 435). Fichte writes:

> This is a determinacy that we ought to produce; but that one ought to do this is itself something one discovers. Accordingly, this is a task that necessarily has to be thought of, {an Idea} . . .. This task, however, is not one that is left to our own free choice, and it does not depend upon whether we want to impose it upon ourselves or not. We must necessarily impose this task upon ourselves, just as surely as we discover ourselves to be rational beings at all. (GA IV/3: 503, and GA IV/2: 239; WLnm, 436)

What Fichte takes himself to have shown is that we cannot conceive of rational agency without there being a "determination" or law that obtains universally. This relation between conditioned (agency) and condition (a law) is what explains the normative force of the latter. The law is not something we can choose, it is not something that holds some of the time for some agents, but rather it is something that holds for rational agency as such. To put it another way, Fichte wants to resist the inference from:

1. A self-determined action is one that is based on a reason, that is, on some concern that I take to justify my intended course of action.

To:

2. The normativity of my judgments depends *entirely* on my taking something to be a reason.[19]

---

also resonates with what R. Jay Wallace calls "factive" moral realism more than with Korsgaard's constructivism. See Wallace (2006). The position worked out here in WLnm seems to clearly entail the thought that moral discourse, as well as our moral deliberations, are answerable to what Wallace aptly describes as a "set of facts about what is the case" (2006, 197). Of course, Fichte would balk at the language of "facts" here. In his own immediate context, "facts" are the explananda of transcendental philosophy. Nevertheless, it is clear that Fichte thinks that there is something that is the case, that is, our "vocation," that is not so because of our willing it to be.

[19] Terence Irwin (2004) argues that there are good reasons to think that Kant avoids a similar slide, and for similar reasons; namely, that a regress threatens if there is not a principle that holds independently of our endorsement. In his words: "[W]e can still legitimately ask for the moral credentials of the constituted or constructed principles. If these depend on the actions that constitute or construct the principles, we can ask the same question about these actions. To avoid an infinite regress, we

Fichte's resistance to this move shows up quite clearly in a number of other places. For example:

> Answer to the question, "Who am I?": {I am the person I make of myself; my determinacy depends upon my own free decision, which follows from the task of limiting oneself.} But what ought I to be? {This lies in my individuality.} Individuality is not determined by any being; it is determined by a law: what I should become is something that is prescribed for all time. {This, as was already said above, is the ethical law.} (GA IV/3: 461, and GA IV/2: 168; WLnm, 337–38)

Fichte crucially identifies this original determinacy as a "pure will" that is distinct from and explanatorily prior to any "empirical willing." The latter, again, is a process of deliberation in which a goal is constructed, selected, and pursued (GA IV/3: 447; WLnm, 293). The "pure will," on the other hand, is antecedent to this process. Fichte emphasizes this point when he remarks that "this act of willing determines my entire being and essence, once and for all, for all eternity" (GA IV/3: 449; WLnm, 311). It is plain that some decision that I make is not what determines me to be the kind of thing that I essentially am; rather, what I essentially am provides an explanation for the sorts of decisions that I should make. The "pure will," which Fichte also calls "reason as such or the realm of reason in its absoluteness," expresses itself in "absolute," that is, nonderivative, practical concepts (GA IV/3: 464; WLnm, 341). That is, the process of goal-formation and pursuit is governed by an antecedent set of rules that are expressive of "reason in its absoluteness." The content of this law is "*the concept of absolute self-sufficiency*" (GA I/5: 70; SL 4: 61), or "self-sufficiency as a norm, in accordance with which the intellect charges itself to determine itself freely" (GA I/5: 63; SL 4: 54). Similar formulations are found throughout the *System of Ethics*, with the addition that the ideal end of a rational agent is unification with God, which is at once the attainment of absolute self-determination (GA I/5: 139; SL 4: 140; GA I/5: 142; SL 4: 143; and GA I/5: 231; SL 4: 245). As noted in a previous passage, this norm has the status of an Idea, something that must necessarily be thought (GA I/5: 74–75; SL 4: 67). That is, "reason in its absoluteness" is "an infinite end, which can never be achieved" (GA I/5: 126; SL 4: 125).

It is in working out this account of the pure will that Fichte articulates a *theological* dimension to his theory of normativity:

must recognize some non-constructed principles. This is just a variation on Kant's argument about positive law presupposing natural law" (2004, 162).

Fichte on Normativity in the Late Jena Period (1796–1799)

> Though we have tried hard {for many §§} to explain the origin of our concept of a goal, our attempts to do so {always} involved us in {the same familiar} circle: . . . . Now, however, we have succeeded in answering this question, for it is not a difficult question to answer in [the context of] the ongoing process of reason. All we have to do is indicate the first concept of a goal. But this first concept of a goal is {not something we ourselves construct; it is} something we receive. To be sure, it is not given to us as a particular determinate goal; instead, what is given to us is simply the overall form of a goal as such – something from which we can make a selection. {This is the summons to engage in a free action.} . . . . No individual is able to account for himself on the basis of himself alone. *Consequently, when one arrives – as one must – at [the thought of] a first individual, one must also assume the existence of an even higher, incomprehensible being.* (GA IV/3: 469; WLnm, 352; emphasis added)

An alternative version of this passage runs:

> This assertion is very important because of the consequences derived from it in the *Theory of Right*, which states: The individual cannot develop himself. One individual can be developed only by another one, and the development of the first individual is something that can be accounted for only by assuming a higher, absolute reason. (GA IV/2: 177 f.; WLnm, 352)

Here, Fichte introduces God in a manner comparable to Lessing's famous account of divine revelation as the progressive education of the human race.[20] Fichte's lifelong interest in providing a rational reconstruction of the traditional Christian concept of revelation is a topic that deserves treatment in its own right.[21] What I want to focus on here is the fact that Fichte uses the phrase "absolute reason" to explicate his conception of God. This suggests that it is the concept of God, as an Idea, that furnishes the content of the moral law in a way that resists reduction to the will of any particular individual.

This claim can be filled in somewhat by considering remarks found throughout Fichte's writings on religion. In a manuscript from the summer of 1796, Fichte argues that the distinction between idolatry and genuine theism lies in the fact that the former deifies "blind choice [*Willkühr*]" and lawless power. Rather than kowtowing to the arbitrary dictate of a cosmic toddler, a true theist, on Fichte's view, is best understood as

---

[20] See Lessing (2005).
[21] Initial steps toward an account of this important element of Fichte's thought are taken in Hansjürgen Verweyen (1995). Verweyen also cites the connection to Lessing, as well as the comments to in the *Foundations of Natural Right* to which Fichte refers in the passage quoted here.

[o]ne who raises himself to morality, whose determination of will no longer depends upon blind choice, on obscurity, or on accident – he does not will this or that because he simply happens to will it [*weil er nun einmal will*], but rather [because] he simply must will the final end of the moral law. (GA II/4: 297)

The genuine religious standpoint essentially involves the recognition of a norm that transcends particular interests and that therefore provides a nonarbitrary constraint on which interests a person might pursue. Similarly, in one of his poorly received responses to charges of atheism, the *Appeal to the Public*, Fichte contrasts a "higher existence, which is independent of nature as a whole and is simply grounded in ourselves" with a life shaped wholly by "accident" (GA I/5: 425). Fichte argues that such a "higher existence" requires a conception of the "pure will," and which he describes in explicitly theistic terms.[22] The "pure will" is explanatory bedrock. It is, he writes, "something *purely intelligible*, but it can express itself through a *feeling of 'ought,'* and in this way it becomes an object of thought" (GA IV/3: 447; WLnm, 72). The "feeling" of ought is itself only fully explicable on the condition that there is present a desire that runs opposed to "pure will," a condition that is absent in the case of God (GA IV/2: 145; WLnm, 295). "God" and "pure will" are interchangeable terms. The pure will is "the explanatory ground of consciousness" (GA IV/3: 440; WLnm, 293), and so cannot be located within the psychology of a particular person or persons. That God or the "pure will" is the ultimate condition of rational agency does not entail that this condition is therefore located only within my *particular* instantiation of rational agency.

The manner in which Fichte is conceiving of God here is very important to understanding the theological dimension of his account of normativity. "God" is a term that Fichte deems entirely suitable for the nonempirical law to which his account of the conditions of rational agency commits him. That there is such a law is a nontrivial claim, given that there are all sorts of other accounts that can be and, indeed, have been, offered (e.g., that moral obligation bottoms out in rational self-interest). But is there any reason to think that calling it "God" makes any important difference to Fichte's account? A letter of August 1795 to Jacobi is suggestive on this issue. Fichte

---

[22] This resort to theistic language to describe the "pure will" has echoes in some of Fichte's other writings from this period. For example, in the "Legal Defense," he describes his conception of God as "pure acting" (GA I/6: 46–7). In lectures dating from throughout the 1790s, which take Ernst Platner's *Philosophical Aphorisms* as their text, passages suggesting a similar point can be found in abundance.

writes that, from the common sense point of view, "the pure I, which does not completely vanish even for this point of view, is posited outside of us and called God" (GA III/2: 392). He goes on to ask rhetorically: "[h]ow else could we have arrived at the properties that we ascribe to God and deny of ourselves if we had not found them in ourselves and then only *denied them of ourselves in a certain respect (as individuals)*" (GA III/2: 392, emphasis added). Similar comments are found in the *System of Ethics*. Agents assume that there is a "spiritual and intelligible being outside of themselves; and if they understood 'themselves' to mean *their empirical I*, then they would be entirely correct" (GA I/5: 188; SL 4: 195). For Fichte, the normative structure of "reason as such" is something that is certainly immanent to us as agents; at the same time, it is not reducible to an empirical fact, nor to any individual human being. This irreducibility is the primary feature that Fichte wants to bring out by identifying it with God. Thus, elsewhere, Fichte identifies God with "the absolutely pure form of reason" (GA I/5: 142; SL 4: 143), the "*reason* upon which ours is *rooted [aufgepflanzt]*" (GA II/4: 289), the "highest, ultimate ground of all things; the truly absolute being" (GA II/4: 322).

Is this theological aspect of Fichte's account compatible with his idealism? A proper idealistic explanation does not locate the necessity of a representation within the psychology of an agent. Instead, it is precisely the psychology of an agent that needs to be explained.[23] What explains it is, on an idealist account, "I-hood" or "reason as such," which is itself a system of laws. These laws do not obtain because some agent endorses them, nor because they possess empirical adequacy; rather, any agent's endorsement of any claim, practical or theoretical, *presupposes* the independent lawful domain. At the same time, because this basic source of normativity is an explanation of why *I* feel the force of moral obligations, there is a sense in which this structure is immanent to my nature. As Fichte says, "The task of limiting myself in a certain way is present within me" (GA IV/2: 169; WLnm, 339). Put in Fichte's preferred religious language, a kind of paraphrase of Paul's famous address at the Areopagus in Acts 17:28, God is that "without which I neither live nor move" (GA II/4: 303). My individual agency instantiates, in a partial or limited way, an ideal structure that is, to this extent, normative for me. God, for Fichte, just is this ideal structure.

---

[23] Fichte's most explicit and direct clarification of this important point can be found in his polemic essay "To the Philosophical Public," first published in the winter of 1800 in the *Intelligenzblatt der Literatur-Zeitung* (GA I/6: 457–60).

BENJAMIN CROWE

2.3 A Complication

Many of Fichte's contemporaries – and, doubtless, many readers today – would find my insistence on a theological dimension to Fichte's metaethics questionable, as the "Atheism Controversy" of 1798–1799 shows.[24] More troubling for my reading, however, are comments that Fichte himself makes at the end of Part I of the *System of Ethics*, in which he indicates the advantages of his approach:

> The [categorical imperative] no longer appears to be some sort of hidden property (*qualitas occulta*), which is what it previously appeared to be, though of course no positive pretext for such an interpretation was provided by the originator of the critique of reason. Thanks to this derivation, that dark region of sundry, irrational enthusiasm [*Schwärmerei*], which has opened itself in connection with the categorical imperative (e.g., the notion that the moral law is inspired by the deity) is securely annihilated. (GA I/5: 62; SL 4: 52)

Fichte wants to deny that the moral law has a "ground" other than itself, picking out the notion "that the moral law is inspired by the deity" as particularly problematic. This is a pretty general thesis to deny, and it is worthwhile to contextualize Fichte's discussion within the immediate reception of Kant's ethics. One important stream of Kant reception with which Fichte engaged was the so-called Old Tübingen school of theologians, familiar to scholars on account of their role in educating Tübingen's idealist triumvirate of Hegel, Hölderlin, and Schelling.[25] The most prominent members of this group were Gottlob Christian Storr (1746–1805), its leading light, Johann Friedrich Flatt (1759–1821), and Friedrich Gottlieb Süskind (1767–1829). While Flatt was an early and powerful critic of Kant, the feature of this school that has come to define their position is the deployment of skepticism (based on Kantian premises) to support the rational tenability of traditional theological claims. Perhaps more to the

---

[24] To be fair, Fichte's critics probably meant different things by "atheism" when they accused him of it. Some, such as J. A. Eberhard, a prominent defender of Wolffianism, object to Fichte's denial that God is a substance. See *Ueber den Gott des Herrn Professor Fichtes und den Götzen seiner Gegner: Eine ruhige Prüfung seiner Appellation an das Publikum in einigen Briefe* (1799). Others, like Jacobi, seem to have found the impersonal nature of Fichte's "moral world order" puzzling. Neither, apparently, took Fichte to be saying that God, in some sense of "God," does not exist. Herder, in a late but important piece, argues that the problem with Kantian moral theology as such is that it makes God an abstraction, an Idea, rather than a living force that expresses itself in nature and history. See his 1798 *Vom Religion, Lehrmeinungen, Gebrauchen*, available in Jacobi (1994).

[25] Henrich has examined the "Old Tübingen" position and its influence in the formation of German Idealism quite extensively in two informative works: (1992) and (2004). See H. S. Harris (1972) for another helpful account of this context.

Fichte on Normativity in the Late Jena Period (1796–1799)   45

point here, Süskind was also an early critic of Fichte. In 1794, Süskind published a translation, from the Latin, of Storr's work on Kant's moral theology, to which he added a critical review of Fichte's *Versuch einer Critik aller Offenbarung*. Süskind explicitly defends the claim that one of the "epistemic grounds [*Erkenntnißprincip*]" for accepting "practical truths" about God is "a particular fact [*Faktum*]" or "appearance [*Erscheinung*]" that is brought about "through the supernatural causality of God in the sensible world."[26] In connection with this claim, he later accepts the application of the categories of the understanding, specifically causality, to the "intelligible world."[27] His chief claim is, roughly, that the conscience is a product of God's influence on the human mind. This feature of Süskind's position is likely reflected in Fichte's use of the phrase "*qualitas occulta*." In natural philosophy, someone is charged with invoking a *qualitas occulta* when there is a suspicion that one is appealing to an *ad hoc*, mysterious, causal power that cannot be strictly inferred from the phenomena. Fichte's worry in this passage is that people like Süskind are doing just that when they attribute the moral law to divine causation.

Understanding the likely polemical context of Fichte's remarks about the categorical imperative in the *System of Ethics* helps to alleviate the suspicion that these remarks explicitly commit Fichte to rejecting the kind of theological account of normativity that I attribute to him. Fichte's idealism, it will be recalled, asserts a complete, theoretically satisfying account of normativity without appeal to any mechanical causes. The kind of noumenal or intelligible causation that Süskind explicitly defends, and which Fichte seems to be rejecting in the passage from the *System of Ethics* quoted earlier, is, if anything, simply a more mysterious and theoretically inert kind of mechanical causation. That, at any rate, is what many of Kant's early critics alleged when they attacked his doctrine of the thing-in-itself. Moreover, as Fichte makes clear in a number of places, the only sort of causation that he countenances is mechanical causation; hence, noumenal causation, if there is any, must be a species of it. What Fichte objects to is the vestigial dogmatism that lurks in the views of people like Süskind. Rejecting a mechanical explanation of the normativity of the moral law, however, does not commit Fichte to rejecting *any* explanation. Indeed, he clearly thinks that there is another type of explanation on hand, namely, the kind that a transcendental idealist can provide.

Taken within the context of transcendental idealism, a theological explanation of the normativity of the moral law need not present Fichte

---

[26] Süskind (1794, 135).   [27] Süskind (1794, 202).

with any difficulties. Recall what such explanations involve: situating a particular norm within the "system of reason." There is no reason to think that what he says about God in the *Wissenschaftslehre nova methodo* lectures and elsewhere should be understood as incompatible with idealism. Fichte's position is just that a *complete* account of the normativity of the moral law requires appeal to another "necessary thought," that is, that of God. There is no danger of this move being accused of importing a *qualitas occulta*; this is because the "necessary thought" is not a *mechanical cause*, and because it is not *ad hoc* (at least by Fichte's lights), but is rather based on a fairly transparent transcendental deduction of the conditions of self-determining agency.

By way of conclusion, what I have attempted to do in this chapter is set forth the basic commitments that comprise Fichte's distinctive account of moral normativity. The moral law is a law (i.e., is universal and necessary) because it is a condition for the possibility of rational agency. This account is idealist because it does not appeal to anything outside of "reason as such" or "I-hood" as part of its explanation. But it is theological, in a nontrivial way, because "reason as such" is not any *particular* instantiation of rational agency. Instead, it is a supra-empirical, or "intelligible," ground for the structure of our experience. "Reason as such" is not determined by anything other than itself, and it cannot be said to overlap completely with any particular entity that instantiates it. For Fichte, these features add up to an idealist rendering of the attributes traditionally ascribed to God.

CHAPTER 3

Fichte on Autonomy

Ulrich Schlösser

There are many ways to deal with freedom of action in the architecture of a philosophical system. One may reinterpret freedom in such a way that it fits into the compatibilist image. Another option is to introduce two irreducible layers of reality. One of them would be the causally ordered world of appearances in nature, the other a noumenal realm. Both realms would be taken for granted in order to secure different philosophical aims – the intelligibility of nature and the possibility of self-determination that can be effective. Action would have to be described under two perspectives. Fichte's philosophical orientation is different. In his Jena period, Fichte becomes convinced that the question "What shall I do?" is not one question among many. Philosophy has to treat it as the most fundamental one. Accordingly, autonomy is the most basic starting point for deriving a philosophical system and assigning subsequent aims in the first place. Whether following this strategy is a good idea is an open question; but if one tries to understand the implications of attributing such a proud place to autonomy, Fichte is the right author to look at.

This chapter focuses on the essential cornerstone of his approach: The chapter addresses the question of how Fichte conceives of autonomy itself in paragraphs 1–3 of his *System of Ethics*. In order to sharpen his conception of autonomy, I will use the introduction of my chapter to draw a contrast to other (potential or actual) considerations on this topic. In his *Groundwork of the Metaphysics of Morals*, Kant guides the reader to autonomy through the following three steps: Firstly, he introduces the categorical imperative as formal and therefore universal, because (unlike a hypothetical imperative) it does not depend on a material condition. Secondly, he claims that every reasonable being posits ends and is also an end in itself. In combining these two elements, the universality of the law on the objective side and the reasonable being on the subjective side, Kant reaches the idea of the will of every reasonable being as universally lawgiving, that is, the basis for autonomy.[1] From Fichte's point of view, this line of reasoning merely explains *that* we (as reasonable beings) have to take ourselves as lawgiving, but not *how* we can understand ourselves as bound by a law we are giving. What is missing is a "genetic" account of this consciousness and, in particular, an account which reveals this consciousness as an aspect of our most general characteristic, namely, being a self in the first place. There is a further shift from Kant to Fichte. In Kant's step-by-step compositional procedure, it seems prima facie as if the universality of the law and the self-relatedness in lawgiving were distinct and had been established by different lines of reasoning. Fichte wants to avoid the impression of such a duality; he does so by introducing the idea of the self as free-standing in the *content* of the imperative, too.

This move impacts Fichte's stance on two further issues that are related to the topic of autonomy. These issues do not derive directly from Kant. They have been made explicit in debates inspired by him.[2] It has been argued that in self-legislation, the governing will is either not yet determined by the law – and therefore genuinely free – or the will is already oriented towards the law. In the first case, there is always a gap between the will and the law as the alleged outcome of his self-determination. In the second case, a further act of self-determination which gave the will its orientation would have to be postulated and a regress follows. Considered from Fichte's point of view, this dialectic is mistaken. There is not first a completely indeterminate self and then a transition by mental action. Following the alternative description, the law is the only possible *expression* of freedom. Fichte's tendency to include the self in the content of the law supports this alternative description.

The second issue is the following: It is a widespread opinion that acting according to the moral law is merely acting on the basis of reasons.[3] One may worry that this opinion does not sufficiently differentiate between rationality and morality. However, even if this approach does pick out the (morally) right actions on the ground that the reasons have to be reasons for everyone, it could still be correct in an extensional sense only. From Fichte's point of view, there is an aspect of understanding missing: namely, to understand the action as a case of a law expressing our own freedom and thereby as itself manifesting autonomy.

---

[1] Kant 4: 420ff.
[2] See Pinkard (2002, 50f., 59, 121f.), Pippin (2008, 71) and the criticism of this line of reasoning in Rödl (2007, 110ff.).
[3] See, for example, Pippin (2016, 59).

Fichte acknowledges further criteria his conception of autonomy has to meet. Even though Fichte aims at grasping the inner structure of autonomy, he cannot offer a speculative derivation of the moral law starting from a merely theoretical model of the self, because such an endeavour would rob the moral law of its dignity. Nor can he step behind the spontaneous activity involved in autonomy in order to point to a further ground that accounts for its being active. Whereas these criteria are oriented backwards and concern the possibility of stepping behind autonomy, others are directed forwards and relate to the applicability of its results: Even though the content of the moral law includes already the concept of a self, there still must be a clear distinction to us insofar as we are the creatures the law is applied to. In addition, the law must indeed be applicable and be a biting law as Fichte believes it should be.

Because the applicability of autonomous self-legislation is at stake, it is worthwhile to complement the profile of Fichte's position by having a brief look at its objective side, too. Unlike what is the case in Kant's theoretical philosophy, we learn in his ethics very little about the form of our sensibility as a condition for applying the demands of reason. However, inclinations should not be too heterogeneous to reason, nor should they be given to us like shots out of the dark, dissociated from a more general idea of nature. In Fichte, there is an a priori constraint on sensibility. Similar to the orientation towards the self in the imperative, there is also a drive to ourselves given on the objective, bodily side. It is not shaped by concepts and thus geared towards being a self as universal, but it is present in feeling. This drive provides the structural setting of our sensibility. It allows for both a difference and a structural homogeneity to the demand and thus grounds its applicability. The drive has a correlate in our first-personal access to nature more broadly: Fichte alludes to the *"Bildungstrieb"* (a term originating from Blumenbach)[4] as a striving to maintain the organization of one's parts. Thus, nature is not primarily considered as a causal mechanism completely different from spontaneity in self-legislation – such a two-layer approach would lead to doubts about whether autonomy can indeed be efficacious. Because nature outside of us is disclosed in a way that corresponds to our action guided by our tendency to the self, how we conceive of it cannot contradict these premises. However, elaborating on these last considerations is beyond the scope of this chapter.

---

[4] See Kosch (2018: 13ff.).

3.1 The Will as Given

In order to understand Fichte's way of integrating these targets into his position, we have to pay close attention to how he himself organizes his complex line of reasoning. He does not start with the actual foundation of his position at the outset; instead, he offers at the beginning a dialectical presentation moving from one standpoint to its opposing counterpart. The content revealed is not wrong. We need it for the correct position. However, the standpoints in isolation also turn out to be fundamentally incomplete. Fichte establishes his genuine, systematic starting point only through this reasoning. It is a position organized around a blind spot which introduces the building blocks of autonomy in a platonic second-best journey[5] given this presupposition. They are derived all as elements of one single structure.

Fichte gets his reasoning going by articulating the following claim:

> I find myself as myself, only as willing. (GA I/5: 37; SL 4: 18)

It is implied in articulating the claim at the beginning that even from a pre-theoretical point of view one is likely to endorse it. If someone were responding: "I do not find myself as willing at all," Fichte would probably stop the dialogue. Familiarity with having a will is presupposed; it cannot be demonstrated to anyone: I have already to take for granted that I am in a situation where the orientation of my will matters. It is up to me. The orientation of the will shapes the way in which I am engaged in the situation. However, when emphasizing that we find ourselves *only* or primarily as willing, Fichte *does* offer a preliminary argument for why this is the case. The argument is less directed to the pre-theoretical person but rather to someone who already has a philosophy: Firstly, I assume that mental states have a bearer, an underlying substance as their subject entertaining them. Secondly, they can be broadly divided into representational states such as conscious perception or thought and volitional states. But we are not directly or immediately aware of ourselves as substances. We don't see the substance, we merely add it in thought or – depending on the background theory – in imagination. This claim would have been hardly controversial in the late eighteenth century. It is present in Hume's sceptical turn against Locke.[6] There is also a parallel to Fichte's claim in Kant: Inner sense, the organ for what is given within ourselves, does not provide us with the intuition of a soul as an object (Kant, KrV B 37/A 22).

---

[5] See Plato's *Phaedo*, 99c-e.   [6] Hume (1888, 15ff.).

If we turn to our states, Fichte argues, we realize that conscious representation is what we as consciousness *immediately are*. In being conscious, our attention is directed to the object first; being conscious of objects is usually not one of them. Here, one may illustrate Fichte's claim by referring to the contemporary thesis of a "transparency" of mental states. We don't see them. We see the object through them. Thus, the volitional states come to the foreground: It is conceivable that they are a way of how I *find* myself.[7]

Even if it is conceded that I encounter myself originally as willing, it is still an open question what it is I thereby encounter. The willing is not at all like inclinations pushing me. This holds even though inclinations also seem to be given to me – and they are part of my objective side in the sense that they are aroused by and related to objects. But for that very reason, they can belong only to what I find *in* myself rather than to finding myself. Note that in Fichte, inclinations are not separate entities anyway but modifications of an underlying self-organizing activity of us humans. The inclination may become a modification and thereby a limitation of willing, depending on the direction of the latter. The willing itself – our topic – has to differ from them in structure.

As is the case in Kant, the will is self-active. It is self-active from the very beginning and throughout the development of Fichte's conception. In order to underline his point, Fichte draws surprisingly on the comparison to a steel spring. Illustrating the will as self-active by relying on a mechanical object is certainly an unusual move. We have to focus on both the common aspect in the comparison and the divergence of the will. The relevant aspect in the steel spring's pushing the object away is not the external impact the object has on the spring by its weight or movement. Fichte is interested in the fact that given this condition, the spring can express itself in the movement only when it is acting on itself. Focusing on the aspect of acting on itself and abstracting from the external influences fits well to Fichte's search for a starting point. The spring acts on itself through its inner tension. Its capacity to act on itself thereby depends on its nature; but in this respect, Fichte has to modify his image, because in the will, there is no fixed nature that precedes and regulates the enactment; its nature consists *in* the self-enactment. Because we cannot (strictly speaking) be forced into that activity from outside, Fichte also uses reiterated formulations, for example the "absolute tendency toward the absolute" (GA I/5: 45; SL 4: 28). Thereby, he

---

[7] For an alternative, theoretically much more demanding reading of these passages, see Schmidt (2015), where the implications of Fichte's address to the reader are explored.

52 ULRICH SCHLÖSSER

takes from the very beginning the criterion into account that we cannot step behind spontaneity.

3.2 The Will Appropriated

The structure of spontaneity Fichte sketches while elaborating on the principle of § 1, namely "I find myself as myself only as willing," is of particular interest for Fichte's overall project. However, the reader should not be misled here. The starting principle itself is certainly nothing like a first principle or a highest proposition similar to the one Fichte articulates in the 1794–1795 version of the *Wissenschaftslehre*. So far, we are dealing merely with a fact of consciousness Fichte relates to primarily for didactic purposes. At this point, a reader familiar with Fichte is likely to argue as follows: Because it is a fact about consciousness that we take ourselves immediately to be given that way, the philosopher is entitled to tie his reasoning to this principle; but he also has to stand back and step behind that fact, that is (articulated in the terminology of the early *Wissenschaftslehre*), he has to abstract further and perform an act of reflection. From the standpoint of the transcendental philosopher of consciousness, facts are to be explained genetically. Note that this demand does not relate to the will itself as a topic. Even as philosopher, Fichte wants to stick to the will's absoluteness and ground his philosophy on it. The demand relates to its mode of being present, that is, to the fact of consciousness of how we initially take up willing.

However, in the given context of the *System of Ethics*, there is a still more pressing concern: The mode of presence assigned to the willing – being altogether objective, independent from our thought, merely found – seems even to contradict what the principle explicitly says: namely that it is myself. For how could anything that is so independent from my thought and the first-personal perspective underlying it actually *be myself* as a spontaneous being? Even if we assume that there is something that acts upon and something being acted upon and both are identical, calling it "I" may still be just a name. Consider the following worry in the background: Suppose there is not only a mechanism pushing myself behind my back – a mechanism would do so in a way which is at least predictable – but there is also an objective spontaneity. The latter would be within myself, but it would not yet be appropriated by myself. This means that we would have to *foresee* its enactment in us, but for all we know so far, we couldn't do so. If this were all we know, the outlook would be rather worrying and a source of self-alienation. Fichte has worked hard to even offer *arguments* for why we find ourselves only as willing according to the principle in § 1, but now he has to concede that the insight achieved on that ground cannot but be very incomplete. In order to complement it, we need no less than a radical shift in standpoints. We have to transcend the natural attitude. It is an attitude according to which consciousness is transparent for itself like glass. It is prima facie object-directed. Furthermore, in accepting this attitude, we treat the structure just mentioned as a mere fact we do not surpass. The attitude blocks a full understanding of ourselves as autonomously willing persons.

Fichte accomplishes the aim of stepping back and transcending the natural attitude by taking up an insight from the *Wissenschaftslehre* which is more fundamental than the *System of Ethics*. He takes up an insight on the nature of selfhood and applies it to the still missing self-consciousness aspect in willing. The turning point in the line of reasoning is located at the beginning of § 2. According to this insight, I cannot be a self behind my back. Being a self implies an awareness of that fact. Earlier, Fichte postulated an underlying subject of willing following the grammatical pattern of a proposition. A self, in contrast, cannot be like a substance preceding acts of consciousness of it or existing irrespective of them. It is only there in and as self-consciousness. If I am self-conscious, on the other hand, the question whether there is a self at all as if this were an independent issue makes little sense. Fichte expresses this claim in a striking way: "One does hear the question proposed: What was I before I came to self-consciousness? The natural answer is: I was not at all, since I was not an I" (GA I/2: 260; GWL I: 97). There is no intelligible point of view prior to or behind self-consciousness. If I were following the invitation to take up such a perspective, no addressee for the question would be left.

How can this radical idea of selfhood be introduced into our consciousness of willing in such a way that it can offer a deeper and more accurate understanding of it? If I start by taking myself (including my willing) as a given I have to take a stance towards, then there can be no direct or linear transition to the self-conscious point of view from the inside. This is true, because it is hard to see how I could evolve gradually into this point of view similar to a gradual mixture of gases or liquids – and how I could grasp myself doing so. There is not just a gap between these two aspects, either. Fichte chooses intentionally a more dramatic, active formulation: I have to tear myself away from myself (GA I/5: 48; SL 4: 32), whereby the latter self is the one previously described: a real willing characterized as independent from my referring to it in thought or theory. The key concept of "tearing oneself away" is, of course, a metaphor, but it is well-chosen. The metaphor stands, once again, for an unavoidably self-induced activity of striving for one's independence or free-standing status. One can get there only by doing it oneself, one cannot be put or posited in that position from outside. Tearing oneself away is an analogue to the self-positing in the *Wissenschaftslehre* transferred into the practical or existential sphere where we are always already embedded in contexts.[8] Note that thereby one of the key topics of the previous reasoning is still present – namely that there is an element of absoluteness in willing, distinguishing it, for example, from mere inclinations forced on us by nature according to an organic striving. The difference in how the topic is treated now consists in the willing's being moved from the objective to the subjective side and in its being tied to features of self-consciousness.

This, however, should not be the only change. Willing is not a neutral topic that could be placed at different theoretical locations without further modifications. In order to explain the implication of the change, Fichte goes back once again to the example of the steel spring, this time with the aim of reaching the bottom of its inadequacy. Certainly, we can conceive of the steel spring as acting upon itself. In focusing on this aspect, we can abstract from external effects such as forces operating on it. These forces push the spring and account for its state of being tense. Within this state, the spring does exercise a force upon itself. However, it does so due to its own fixed nature. What happens is that on that ground, there is the transition from one state of being to another state of being. Fichte claims, in contrast, that self-determination located on the subjective side is not at all like that model. We determine ourselves by means of *concepts*; this is a frequently overlooked but crucial difference. In particular, Fichte has cases of concept application in mind in which we do not apply the concept with the understanding that the entity to be determined had the property corresponding to the concept previously and independently from applying it. The entity receives its determination through our applying the concepts. As Fichte says: A real activity "is brought under the sway of the concept (*kommt unter die Botmäßigkeit des Begriffs*)" (GA I/5: 48; SL 4: 32). On the subjective side, the origin of applying the concept is not like a fixed state from which the application follows necessarily, but it is the exercise of our intellectual capacity. We cannot understand our own intellectual capacity according to the model of a mere mechanism – this time, a mechanism of

---

[8] "Tearing oneself away from oneself" has here the methodological function of isolating the aspect of selfhood that was missing in willing described as merely objective and "given." Throughout the *System of Ethics,* the metaphor is also used more broadly, for example for transcending our drives in everyday life and becoming accessible to moral self-determination in the first place.

the mind. For us, it is the source of orientation. We rely on it, for example, when we step back in order to find out whether a mechanism suggested to us, e.g. that of a computer or a robot, does lead to correct results in the first place. Our intellectual capacity is the origin of thought and critical deliberation. Taking it to be bound to a clearly fixed entry point and a rigid procedure would undermine our trust in it. These intuitions help to explain Fichte's quite forced formulations: For us, intelligence is agility and that means it is not bound by a given nature, not even its own. Prima facie, these features introduced in Fichte's considerations are not unfamiliar to us: From the legislation of the parliament to the New Year's Resolutions, there is determination through concepts – and there is a complex debate of creative minds in the first case and in respect of the result open consilium with oneself in the latter case. We have to focus, however, more closely on the self-relational structure of that process and its tendency to critical independence.

Because we are dealing with an original starting point, a situation of genuine independence, neither thinking and thus applying the concept nor the content of it can derive from outside. The thought is actualized by myself, and it is the thought of myself as a self-active and therefore independent being. Thinking this thought cannot be induced from outside because no one outside of myself can literally force myself into thinking the thought "I." I can only do it myself. Applying it cannot be deduced from previous thoughts either, for in that case, applying it would become rationally necessary rather than spontaneous. The content of the concept is nothing but the mirror of this self-activity. It contains the structure of a free-standing self. Therefore, it is strictly general, that is, it is not tied to any empirical characteristics of a person. This last aspect conforms to my remark in the introduction that in Fichte, there is not the universality of the law as constraint on content on the one side and spontaneous activity on the other. The universality is already in the structure of self-relation.

3.3 The Problem of Mere Potentiality

Fichte has argued that self-determination properly speaking is a determination by a concept whereby the most fundamental way of grasping that concept is not to take it as a vehicle for universalization. It is the concept of myself as a free-standing being. Its application goes back only to intelligence as a potential or capacity to move to a determinate state. Note what kind of modality Fichte has in mind. He does not refer to something like a firmly specified logical sphere of possibilities, for setting up such a sphere would have to start with an actual case of successful concept application plus its context and draw an inference back to prior or other possibilities. We have recognized from the very beginning that Fichte is not fond of this type of top-down reasoning post factum. Nor does he believe in the intellectual capacities' having a firm nature like natural dispositions which act in a certain way given this or that circumstance. Intelligence is therefore a state of latency, more real than logical possibility, but not yet actualized in a determinate way. Intelligence merely leads to or enables a determinate state. It is like a moment of the so-called potencies Schelling sketches many years later.[9] However, if we conceive of intelligence that way, we certainly cannot say more than the following: It can actualize itself, but maybe it does not do so. Following Fichte's program, this is not enough. He believes that we are actually engaged in the process of self-determination. Moreover, he wants to show how self-determination can be efficacious and thus make a difference in the world. Certainly, intelligence as mere potential or as an ultimate source of what may happen cannot explain that either. Fichte's second, subject-centred approach to self-determination seems to have reached an impasse. Determination through the intelligence by means of the concept of myself as a free-standing, judging subject does not fare better than finding myself endowed with a genuine will, that is, a volitional capacity that is not just pushed by nature, but acts onto itself.

One response to the predominance of potentiality and the merely intellectual character of what is happening in conceptual determination may be just to go back to the initial approach closer to a natural attitude. Insofar as I took having a will and therefore the will itself as given, it is actual. Because I treated it as a fact independent from my theorizing about it, I assigned one important feature of reality to it. Shall we complement one approach with the other? However, given the move of reflection Fichte has introduced in the second approach, can we simply go back to the unquestioning, matter-of-fact attitude of a natural consciousness? Even if we did so, the resulting conception may still not be successful. It has been argued that the application of the concept of myself as free-standing subject cannot be directed by anything outside of the self-relation. The will, considered as given and in need of being appropriated in the first place, would have to count as coming from outside. Thus, just adding the first approach to the second in an unreflecting way will not solve the problem. We are ready for a second revolution of standpoints within the first three

---

[9] See, for example, Schelling (1856-, 13: 204ff.).

paragraphs of the *System of Ethics*. Only thereby can we reach the systematic starting point of Fichte's deductive line of reasoning.

3.4 The Elusive Entire Self as Starting Point

Fichte's systematic starting point is not any longer directly accessible from a non-philosophical pre-understanding; but it can be made intelligible through the previous dialectical line of reasoning. We have to overcome too much of mere potentiality in the model of conceptual self-determination. We cannot do so by going back to a will as something objective we refer to as found in us. Nevertheless, a form of self-activity will have to fulfil the task. It has been a topic throughout Fichte's line of reasoning and will continue to be one; but it should not be characterized in any one-sided way. This is why Fichte introduces the "drive towards the entire self" (*Trieb auf das ganze Ich*) (GA I/5: 54; SL 4: 39) at the centre of his conception. There is no alternative left.

Firstly, I would like to point to some possible misunderstandings concerning associations the term is meant to inspire. Fichte's key term should not be identified with any established notion of self-preservation – neither a modern nor an ancient one. This holds even though it does allow to capture the self-preservation as living being in its relative value, that is, as something one may override. Accordingly, the tendency to the self's free-standing independence is not meant to be in tension with a strict form of moral orientation. As we will see, it is a condition for the moral demand as demand on us and also for our being able to fulfil it.

Even more important than the notion of striving is the other term Fichte uses: The entire self. In a preliminary way, it can be introduced as follows: The self is not only the basis of a take on something from a subjective point of view but always and unavoidably the moment of being an object belongs to it as well. In looking through the entire *System of Ethics*, one will realize that the respective side of being an object can even be considered as successively unfolding on several layers moving from the centre of the self outwards: If we start from the subjective angle, it is firstly the activity as transparent for itself in the performance of spontaneity as a form of self-knowledge. It is secondly the willing as real both directed by the intelligence's concept of self and pointing to action. There is a further continuity. This very willing is constantly in relation with the drives and in touch with the living body, whereby the latter, in turn, is organized by a *Bildungstrieb*. The reasoning of the *System of Ethics* started from willing, that is, the middle layer of objectivity. It was first considered in isolation. We know now that it is also self-governed and efficacious through embodiment.

Note that Fichte endorses a quite pointed formulation: We as human beings ultimately *are* the *identity* of both sides – the subjective and the objective one. It is not the case that first we exist and then we are conscious and have thereby a relation to ourselves, as if the latter moments were an external addition. On the other hand, we are as that self-relation always already real, that is, life in its actual performance. In reference to the "inner circle" of the self – the sphere of thought – Fichte emphasizes that putting the sides apart and trying to establish a consecutive order is inadequate and will fail:

> Consequently, we never think the two together but only *alongside* each other and *after* each other; and by means of this process of thinking of *one after the other* we make each of them reciprocally dependent on the other. This is why one is unable to avoid asking, *Am* I because *I think of myself*, or do *I think of myself* because I *am*? Yet there is no such "because" in this case; you are not one of these two because you are the other. You are not twofold at all, but are absolutely one and the same; and you are this unthinkable unity (*Eine*). (GA I/5: 56; SL 4: 42)

However, the passage also indicates that in our conscious existence we can't help proceeding that way. This has a dramatic consequence for the set-up of Fichte's conception: The striving refers to the entire self as identity of the sides whereby the latter becomes our systematic starting point; but it is nevertheless unintelligible to us. Fichte's conception of the basis of autonomy is organized from a blind spot. The argument why the entire self is elusive is not of the following type: I cannot grasp the entire self in its inner identity, because the subjective side is always behind my back. It is behind my back precisely because it is what I in a narrow sense am in grasping. If I try to grasp it, too, I objectify the subjective side. That means it is really slipping to a higher level and is thereby elusive again. Because the subjective side is inaccessible, the entire self remains opaque. Fichte has argued against such a line of reasoning at other places.[10] It would render self-consciousness impossible. His characterization of the subjective side in § 2 rules out this reasoning as well. Fichte's actual reasoning implied in the text differs from it. It allows for grasping the subjective side in the mode of reflection, but not for grasping the original identity. We are always already within the relation of cognition. The object of cognition is merely an element within it. Thus, the differentiation between subjective and

---

[10] GA IV/2: 30; WLnm, 113.

objective has been actualized. The object has been set over against the cognizing subject. We are already "too late" for grasping the original unity. It is not only true that a relationship of opposition has been established, but it is also difficult to avoid that through the application of the form of judgment, the object presents itself as already determinate. The last aspect hinders us from appreciating the element of openness Fichte assigns to performance in conscious life. Finally, the discursive form of thought forces us to dissolve an original identity into a successive order where we move from one element to another and even tend to bind them together in a grounding order without being able to stabilize it.

This critical turn limiting the scope of cognition may be surprising in the context of Fichte's Jena period. On the one hand, it can be read as an indicator of Schelling's influence on Fichte. In his early paper on the I[11] that oscillates between the terminologies of Fichte's *Foundation of the Entire Science of Knowledge* and Jacobi, Schelling introduces the unconditioned. It should not be confused with the self as the subjective side of a subject–object relationship; it precedes the latter. Thereby, it eludes every effort to objectify it. A similar tendency to accommodate Schelling's thought into his early writings can be found in Fichte's adding a footnote on subject–object identity to the third edition of the *Foundation*.[12] On the other hand, the critical turn may also be explained by an internal development of the *Wissenschaftslehre*. In 1794–1795, Fichte moves from the fact (*Tatsache*) of consciousness to the deed-act or fact-act (*Tathandlung*), but he still believes that the internal structure of the latter can be captured and thereby "domesticated" by the corresponding logical form. His stance in the *System of Ethics* can be read as a more critical assessment of this possibility. In this respect, Fichte's reasoning in 1798 is a precursor of the *Wissenschaftslehre 1804*, which focuses entirely on comprehending the incomprehensible as incomprehensible.[13] The *Wissenschaftslehre 1804* uses our being too late in relation to the absolute starting point itself as the ground for a deduction of our multi-faceted relation to the world.

In a second step, we must explore our cognitive situation and spell out what it means for composing autonomy. We endorse an original identity, but within consciousness and, in particular, thought we have already entered a situation of differentiation. In relation to ourselves, Fichte even claims that the aspect's being actually distinct has been *established* only by

---

[11] Schelling (1976-, I/2: 87ff.).   [12] GA I/2: 261.
[13] GA II/8: 54ff.; SW 10: 115 and Schlösser (2001).

means of consciousness or thought. The overall situation leads to an inherent ambivalence in the reading of the subjective side and the objective side. Let us start again with the objective side: Following the differentiation, it appears itself as something independently given to me, and that means I cannot be certain of its coincidence with the original identity of the entire self. Of course, there are further reasons for being sceptical about that. The objective will stands for real efficacy, and thus for our influence on the world. The world is a determinate sphere of individual entities. If the objective side of willing is meant to influence it, it has to take up a similar degree of determinacy. This cannot happen without the still more objective, bodily side of ourselves. As mentioned earlier, this does not mean that we have the will on the one hand and particular inclinations pushing us from a natural basis on the other hand. The determination becomes a determination of the objective side of the will and is therefore a modification of our spontaneity. However, the potentially finite willing in its apparent independence still belongs to the scope of those tendencies we have to tear ourselves away from. We do so by means of the subjective side of performance. It is not outwards/object-directed but inwards/self-directed. It points towards the unity of the self to be re-established. Its task is to bring the other side we cannot deny the status of belonging to us "under the sway of the concept" of ourselves. The realization of the task is not any longer given in mere potentiality as something which may happen. It has now a backup in our striving for the entire self. Only thereby does it become actual – not by objective willing or by other concepts.

We have to move on and trace the other aspect of this ambivalence. The two sides do not only appear in their relative independence. It must also still be recognizable that they are both modifications of the original identity of the self. In order to be an expression of the whole, each of the sides has to include from the very beginning the functional determination of the other. Fichte unavoidably presents this thought in a complex box-in-the-box structure. He does not try to point out the original identity directly but refers to our thought in self-determination. After all, the thought does not relate merely to the subjective side but should be able to map or picture the entire self from its point of view. Fichte writes that absoluteness is the *form* of the thought – it is not generated or deduced from anywhere else. Its *content* is characterized through mutual determination. The latter is the stand-in in thought for the elusive unity of the self. How does Fichte build up his model of mutual determination in the self as represented in its concept? A preliminary consideration is the following: The objective side as including its other cannot be a mere object – a thing for us; nor can it be

Fichte on Autonomy 61

a thing fully under the constraints of external connections regulated by determinate laws of nature – something primarily described as not living. Even though it is objective, it still must be such that it is endowed with self-activity as it has been the case with objective willing at the beginning of Fichte's text. If we move one step further outside from the centre of the self, it is the will as governing the associated body. How the subjective side is also meant to be determined by the objective side is harder to state. Understanding Fichte's thought certainly demands some charity. In taking up several meanings or applications of the term "objective" we can say: In the *Wissenschaftslehre nova methodo*, Fichte has already argued that the I, considered from the first personal point of view, cannot be like a substance, thus a thing *underlying* all processes of the intelligence.[14] Nor can we objectify the intelligence itself and treat it as a fixed capacity, like the acorn, which – as an objective entity – includes already the set-up of the entire tree to be actualized given adequate circumstances. What other notions associated with objectivity are available and how could they be applied to the subjective side as an aspect singled out in the whole of the self? We are certainly entitled to say that the form of lawfulness belongs to objectivity. Once again, the lawfulness cannot relate to a law that regulates external impact. It can be applied to the subjective side only insofar as it relates to a law for the self and a law of the self, that is, a law to direct us by the concept of ourselves as free-standing subjects. Fichte comes close to the concept of autonomy. He uses the idea of the mutual determination of the sides in the entire self in order to play with formulations from the beginning of section 3 in Kant's *Groundwork*.

The mutual determination of the subjective side and the objective side as derivative from the entire self has so far been presented as a stable, unmoving relationship, but Fichte also presents it as dynamic. Thereby, the tendency of our thought post factum to always establish and follow a uniform direction gets a hold on us. Starting from the subjective side, Fichte offers a striking formulation:

> We now have to think of what is objective as determined by what is subjective. What is subjective is the positing of an absolute but completely undetermined power of freedom, as described in the previous section. What is here described as objective is determined, produced, and conditioned thereby; the thought indicated is possible only on the condition that the I thinks of itself as free. Finally, each determined by the other: the legislation in question manifests itself only on the condition that one thinks of oneself

---

[14] GA IV/2: 29; WLnm, 112.

as free, but when one thinks of oneself as free, this legislation necessarily manifests itself. (GA I/5: 61; SL 4: 48)

There are several layers in this formulation. At the first layer, the passage is to be read as follows: First, there is a free capacity, thinking the concept of itself. In doing so, it is not yet bound. However, if it thinks itself and thereby establishes a reference to the objective side, the principle kicks in and a necessity is established: If you think yourself, necessarily, you have to do it in this particular way (that is, the intelligence can only grasp itself as free-standing). Note that there is most likely another layer in Fichte's thought. So far, we only know that if the capacity thinks of itself, it can only do so in this particular way, which leaves the question open whether it thinks of itself or not. The basic performance in the antecedent of the conditional is merely factual. The second claim potentially involved in that passage is more demanding: If the self is independent according to the content of the already actualized thought of itself, it can have this very status only through and by means of itself. Because it is intelligence, this cannot happen behind its back or by means of nature. As intelligence, it can only be independent if it has the concept of itself, that is, if it is in intellectual possession of itself. From the content of the thought it follows that this very thought has to be thought. The necessity in question is a necessity post factum, because we start from the already actualized thought and focus on its content. Because it is the content of the *already actualized* thought, we can present the very thought also from the subjective side by referring to the performance of it: If it has been thought, we then know that it has been thought necessarily. The necessity here does not only concern how the self has to be thought as it has been the case before, but that it is thought.

The second layer of Fichte's passage bears similarities with metaphysical speculations in his later *Wissenschaftslehren*:[15] Does the absolute – being – exhibit itself in a representation or does it not do so, remaining enclosed into itself? Starting from the very idea of the absolute and aiming at a deductive reasoning, we cannot answer this question; but because we have its exhibition or revelation at hand, we can conclude that, given the absolute, its exhibition must have been necessary. In this example, too, the necessity is post factum.[16]

---

[15] See, for example, GA II/13: 57ff.; SW 10: 333.

[16] Schmidt (2015) grounds his striking reconstruction of §3 on the necessitation involved in any form of rational assent. This solution, however, is too independent from the particular thought in question – thinking myself as independent – and its textual environment.

Fichte on Autonomy

Only if we move to the second layer, there is indeed a contradiction between the freedom of a performance and the necessity of a lawful connection as Fichte argues in an additional commentary to his conception. This can be illustrated by drawing again on the parallel to the expression of the absolute: If the expression were a free performance, it could not conform to necessity. This holds even if the necessity has been established only post factum. It is not surprising that such a tension arises because the subjective and the objective are equally primordial in the all-encompassing structure of unity. We cannot expect that the tension can be fully dissolved by moving to a consecutive order. Fichte can't help introducing a further modification. Because he has insisted throughout on the importance of self-activity, the modification will have to concern the necessity with which the determination gets a hold of the performance. It is not strict necessity but necessity as a "norm" – Fichte uses here a more modern term than the Kantian "*Nötigung*" (necessitation) (GA I/5: 63; SL 4: 52). On the basis of our thought we know that we are obliged to entertain it. In doing so, we determine ourselves. Without this modification, Fichte's structure of unity would fall apart.

We are now in a position to articulate the result of Fichte's reasoning about freedom and the law in a context that has been inspired by Kant. Freedom is understood as the "capacity for independence" (*Vermögen der Selbstständigkeit*) (GA I/5: 64; SL 4: 51). In its processual character, it has an impact on itself as objective. In this very impact, lawfulness as necessitation in the normative sense points the activity to a concept or principle whereby the content of the latter includes again the idea of independence or being a free-standing person. Fichte's approach does not include the claim that there is freedom first and then a transition to the law; nor does it include the claim that in being free we determine ourselves to accept the law in a second step. In that case, freedom would be the unique basis and a regress would follow – for what would guide our freedom towards the law if it were not determined by it in the first place? Rather, in the unintelligible point of identity, freedom and lawfulness are literally meant to be one, mere facets of the same. Because we are as cognizing beings already in the state of differentiation, we have to consider each moment always already under the perspective of its correspondence to the other. Fichte's idea can also be expressed as follows: Being bound by a principle is not the result of a free act of self-determination; rather it is the expression or manifestation of the latter. It is the only expression in which freedom can find itself.

Fichte draws two further conclusions from this starting point: Due to my status as an *entire* human being, including both subjective and objective aspects, the willing I find in myself is inevitably related to the demand of the moral law. There is no room for questions such as: Am I really a citizen of the realm of self-determination? All beings of this type are in an intelligible way within the scope of the law. Some formulations suggest that Fichte probably wants to draw an even stronger conclusion. He starts again from the entire self and our striving to it and claims that this entire structure, including the law that partakes of it, is also the basis of why I am *capable to follow* the law. According to Kant, the insight into the moral law and its obligatory character leads to treating myself as free, and thus taking myself to be able to follow the law. Fichte concedes this formulation, granted the posterior status of the claim which is revealed in the unilateral direction of its reasoning. However, as it stands, it is still merely an epistemological claim. The law is the antecedent in the order of cognition (*ordo cognoscendi*). Fichte aims at moving beyond that limitation:[17] The inner ultimate unity and thereby the necessitation of the law depending on it also provide the ground for the reality of our capacity to act in accordance with it. The situation is not such that there is the moral law on the one hand and in addition, an independent fact of human essence or nature on the other hand. Of course, Fichte has to further elaborate on his conception in order to stabilize this last claim: There can be overwhelming forces of nature, but nature as such cannot contradict the possibility of our following the moral law. In order to argue for this claim, Fichte has to show that nature is disclosed in the first place in the context of the self actualized in a will and its embodiment. If that is true, we can't help understanding nature in a way that does not contradict these preconditions.[18]

In looking back to Fichte's approach, a concern about his strategy still has to be addressed. In respect of Kant, I was referring to a line of reasoning which leads from the formality of the law via the idea of reasonable beings as end in themselves toward the fact *that* the will of every reasonable being

---

[17] In this respect, I disagree with Owen Ware's illuminating paper (2019, 13–15), which seems straightforwardly to identify Fichte's stance with the Kantian strategy of epistemically deriving our acceptance of our own freedom from the moral law. Of course, Fichte does not believe that Kant is wrong. What he does is good at its place. But the Kantian strategy does not yet reach the most fundamental level of considering the relation between moral law and freedom of will. Its limitations become apparent in its one-directedness and in the fact that he offers an epistemic claim only. The difference to Fichte's stance is revealed in the fact that he starts the passage Ware quotes by boldly asserting that freedom and the law are not two thoughts at all, but literally one – "a complete synthesis." (This is also meant to relativize the original status of the so-called reciprocity thesis in §§ 5 and 6 of the *Critique of Practical Reason*.) Fichte's assertion points to the original self which is the backup even of the relation Kant establishes.

[18] Fichte's actual reasoning is more dialectical: At GA I/5: 108; SL 4: 109–110, Fichte argues that my nature has to be grounded on the entire system of nature. However, the subsequent reasoning shows that without projecting the drive onto nature or synthesizing it with nature in the first place, this project could not succeed.

has to be conceived of as a (universally) self-legislating will. At the beginning, it seemed as if Fichte wants to move beyond a mere claim *that* we have to think of the will in a certain way towards a genetic account of the consciousness in question. He would thereby aim at strengthening the intelligibility of ethics. However, choosing the unintelligible unity of self as a starting point (or the at least partially unintelligible striving for the entire self) seems straightforwardly to contradict this aim. Fichte tries to avoid this contradiction in a way that anticipates the set-up of his *Wissenschaftslehre* 1804. There is a derivation, but it is based on the implications of the insight that we do unavoidably miss the starting point we nevertheless have to presuppose. The actual starting point is to be found in the dualistic consciousness of an elusive unity. In this reasoning, we do not step behind the spontaneous performance in order to look for another ground of why it is happening, nor do we undermine the dignity of the law by offering a merely speculative derivation. In the dualistic model, both are made intelligible as mutually related aspects of one structure. Nor are they undermined in their status by our assuming the basic unity, because the latter is not a third entity but the identity of both.

CHAPTER 4

Feeling, Drive, and the Lower Capacity of Desire

Owen Ware

> If one considers only the higher capacity of desire, then one obtains a mere metaphysics of morals, which is formal and empty. The only way to obtain a doctrine of ethics, which must be real, is through the synthetic unification of the higher and lower capacities of desire.
>
> – Fichte (GA I/5: 126; SL 4: 131).

4.1 Introduction

Worries that Kant's theory of ethics reduces to an empty formalism emerged just after the publication of his major works in moral philosophy, long before Hegel made this a famous point of criticism in the *Phenomenology of Spirit* (1807). To this day it remains one of the most hotly contested issues in the scholarship surrounding Kant's formulations of the categorical imperative. One need only browse a recent issue of *Kantian Review* or *Kant-Studien*, for instance, to find the question "Is moral content derivable from a universal law?" commented upon, discussed, and debated. In this chapter, I shall turn to one early post-Kantian thinker who was not only attuned to the threat of empty formalism but also made a rigorous attempt to avert it: Fichte.

My central claim is that Fichte's response to the problem of empty formalism clarifies a novel but largely misunderstood aspect of the *System of Ethics*: namely, its theory of drives. In particular, I shall argue that this problem explains why Fichte finds it urgent to guide the reader, in Part II of the book, from the most basic elements of agency (drive, feeling, longing, desire, and pleasure) to their transformation in the space of reflection, of which one's conscience is a unifying power. One payoff of this reading is that it offers evidence for a robustly transcendental reading of Fichte's drive theory, according to which the most basic elements of agency require a connection to the I and its free activity. Another payoff is

Feeling, Drive, and the Lower Capacity of Desire 67

that this reading serves to shed light on Fichte's oft-repeated claim that a system of ethics must have a real, applicable principle. As we shall see, Fichte's commitment to a drive theory and his commitment to rescuing ethics from reducing to a set of empty formulas turn out to be two sides of the same coin.

4.2 Empty Formula Philosophy

One can see that much of Fichte's early work was shaped in response to the skeptical worry that Kant's system offers no resources to justify the applicability of its concepts. Indeed, his first attempts to present a new "doctrine of science" (*Wissenschaftslehre*) bear the mark of this concern. "I believe," Fichte writes in the 1794 *Foundation of the entire Doctrine of Science*, "to have found the way in which philosophy must rise to become an evident science" (GA I/2: 109; GWL 1: 86). Soon afterward Fichte tells the reader where this path must begin: "We have to *search out* the absolutely first, the absolutely unconditioned principle of all human knowledge" (GA I/2: 112; GWL 1: 91). By way of elimination Fichte argues that only the self-positing activity of the I satisfies the criteria of such a principle, and the rest of the *Doctrine of Science* unfolds as a series of deductions from this starting point, first in the domain of theoretical philosophy (Part I) and then in the domain of practical philosophy (Part II).

Given this aim to provide a new foundation of human knowledge in a first principle, it is not surprising that Fichte characterizes his subsequent writings on political and moral philosophy as branches of a general system. Both the 1796 *Foundations of Natural Right* and the 1798 *System of Ethics* bear the subtitle "*nach Principien der Wissenschaftslehre*" ("according to principles of the Doctrine of Science"). The goal of these texts is not to lay down the foundations of a system of human knowledge as such, but rather to derive a specific "science" (*Wissenschaft*) from the principle of the I and its self-positing activity. It is also noteworthy that Fichte organizes each text around the same three-fold structure: Part I offers a "deduction" (*Deduktion*) of a concept, either of "right" (*Recht*) or of "morality" (*Sittlichkeit*); Part II offers a deduction of the concept's "applicability" (*Anwendbarkeit*); and finally, Part III offers a "systematic application" (*Systematische Anwendung*) of this concept, leading to either a doctrine of rights or a doctrine of duties.

This division of labor shows that a concern with questions of applicability was never far from Fichte's mind during the 1790s, nor was it an isolated topic of investigation. One example of this concern appears in the

68   OWEN WARE

Introduction to the *Natural Right* titled "How a real philosophical science distinguishes itself from mere formula philosophy." Whereas the formula philosopher, Fichte explains, analyzes the facts of consciousness as they appear in introspection, the transcendental philosopher reproduces the activity of the I underlying these same facts. For this reason "the first procedure gives concepts without an object, an empty thinking; only in the second manner is the philosopher a spectator of the real thinking of his spirit."[1] Continuing further, Fichte writes:

> The first is an arbitrary imitation of the original acts of reason [one has] heard from others . . . . The latter alone is the true observation of reason in its procedure. From the former arises *an empty formula philosophy*, which believes it has done enough if it can show that one can think of something, without being concerned about the object (about the conditions of the necessity of this thinking). A real philosophy [*reelle Philosophie*] holds concept and object together simultaneously, and never treats one without the other. The aim of the Kantian writings was to introduce such a philosophy and to abolish all merely formal philosophizing. (GA I/3: 317; GNR 3: 6)[2]

Of course, Fichte is not claiming that Kant had presented the correct solution to the problem of "real philosophy" – that of grounding all human knowledge in the absolute activity of the I. Yet Fichte believed Kant had set up the task in the right way, referring to his well-known tenet from the *Critique of Pure Reason* (1781–1787) that "Thoughts without content are empty" (A51/B75). What motivates Fichte to preface the *Natural Right* around the problem of an empty formula philosophy is a misunderstanding he saw threatening this tenet at the time. In Fichte's view, defenders of Kantian philosophy had produced nothing more than "empty thinking" by analyzing the facts of consciousness given to introspection. And Kant's early critics had then concluded that Kantian philosophy

---

[1] The distinction between a real and mere formula philosophy first appears in the 1794 *Wissenschaftslehre*. Fichte writes: "In a doctrine of science facts will certainly be established, upon which a system of real thinking distinguishes itself from all empty formula philosophy; but *that* it is a fact is something not to be postulated, but rather to be arrived at by way of proof, as we have done in the present case" (GA I/2: 363; GWL 1: 220).

[2] "Das erstere ist ein willkürliches Nachmachen der von anderen vernommenen ursprünglichen Handelsweisen der Vernunft ... [D]as Letztere allein ist wahre Beobachtung der Vernunft in ihrem Verfahren. Aus dem ersteren entsteht *eine leere Formular-Philosophie*, die genug gethan zu haben glaubt, wenn sie nachgewiesen, dass man sich irgend etwas denken könne, ohne um das Object (um die Bedingungen der Nothwendigkeit dieses Denkens) besorgt zu seyn. Eine reelle Philosophie stellt Begriff und Object zugleich hin, und behandelt nie eins ohne das andere. Eine solche Philosophie einzuführen, und alles bloss formelle Philosophiren abzuschaffen, war der Zweck der Kantischen Schriften."

itself amounts to empty thinking, unable to justify the applicability of its central concepts (GA I/3: 317; GNR 3: 6). But the way past skepticism about applicability, Fichte's argues, lies in the doctrine of science or *Wissenschaftslehre*, of which the doctrines of right and ethics are meant to bring to completion.

But how is the method of *reelle Philosophie* supposed to work in the case of these particular systems? Fichte speaks to this question when he describes what the philosopher must do to secure a deduction of a concept. If the concept is original to reason, then its deduction will consist in showing that it is a necessary condition for the self-activity of a rational being in general. The philosopher, Fichte writes,

> has to describe this action itself according to its form, as well as what arises for reflection in this manner of acting. By doing this he delivers at the same time the proof of the necessity [*Nothwendigkeit*] of the concept, determines it, and shows its application. None of these elements can become separated from the rest, otherwise the individually treated parts will be handled incorrectly, and that is a merely formal philosophizing. (GA I/3: 319; GNR 3: 8)

By Fichte's own lights, any mode of philosophizing will be empty if it cannot bring together a concept with its object. That is why, in the context of the *System of Ethics*, Fichte's deduction of the moral law's applicability in Part II commences with a theory of the lower capacity of desire. For, in order to show that the moral law is a required concept for actual willing – that is, for willing an object – he must first present the most basic elements of agency itself (including the "natural drive"), something that Kant neglected to do. As we shall see, one of the more surprising results of this theory is that it locates a form of primitive reciprocity in the very heart of desire, according to what Fichte will call a "formative drive" (*Bildungstrieb*).

4.3 The Question of Applicability

Fichte draws attention to the problem of empty formalism in the *System of Ethics* when he stops to consider the path of Part I:

> All the principles established in Part I are merely formal, without any material meaning. We see *that* we should do something; but we grasp neither *what* we should do nor *where* we should do it. This was the result of how all merely formal philosophizing occurs: we set up abstract thoughts, which are in no way concrete, and we described a reflection in general without determining it, i.e., without showing the conditions of its possibility. (GA I/5: 83; SL 4: 76)

As he goes on to explain, "there was never any intention of concluding our investigation after merely setting forth these purely formal propositions, as if everything had already been accomplished" (GA I/5: 83; SL 4: 76). The strategy of Part I is to show that when we consider our willing in the abstract, separated from a world of objects, our willing appears to be free, and this is a "fact of consciousness" (*Thatsache des Bewusstseins*). When we then ask what grounds we have to assent to this fact, to believe that we really are free, Fichte argues that our conviction turns out to have a moral basis. That is to say, the concept of morality, understood as a law of self-sufficiency, gives us grounds to assent to the appearance of freedom. In this respect, Part I shows that the concept of morality is necessary for securing freedom as what Fichte calls an "item of faith" (*Glaubensartikel*), and this gives proof "*that* we should do something," namely, strive for self-sufficiency. Nevertheless, Fichte draws attention to the fact that this law on its own is merely formal and empty because it leaves two further issues unaddressed: What should I do in striving for self-sufficiency? and where should I strive for it?, each of which, he claims, bear upon the question of its applicability.[3]

As Fichte defines his terms, a deduction of the necessity of a concept need only show that it is a required condition for determining an object, whereas a deduction of a concept's applicability must go further. "The concept of *morality*," he explains, "has already now been derived in and for itself as a determinate form of thinking, as the only possible manner of thinking of our freedom" (GA I/5: 73; SL 4: 64). What Fichte adds in this "Preliminary Remark" to Part II is that consciousness of freedom "has only been determined immediately. The concept of freedom might also determine several other things mediately or indirectly, and that is here the question" (GA I/5: 74; SL 4: 64–65). This suggests that the question of the moral law's necessity and the question of its applicability are both transcendental – that is, they concern the connection of

---

[3] As I hear these questions, Fichte is saying that in the course of transcendental reflection I can distinguish the insight *that* (*dass*) I ought absolutely to do something from the insight *what* (*was*) I ought to do and *where* (*wohin*) I ought to do it. The first insight is what secures the deduction of the concept of morality in Part I of the *System of Ethics*: when I see that I ought absolutely do something, I have grounds to assent to the appearance of freedom, which (like all appearances) is susceptible to doubt. That I ought not to go beyond morality and rationalize away its authority is what gives me a footing to say "I *am* actually free" in place of "I *appear* to myself to be free." This is the *Glaubensartikel* mentioned earlier: "Belief in the objective validity of this appearance is therefore derivable from consciousness of the moral law. *I am actually free* is the first article of faith" (GA I/5: 65; SL 4: 54). That I am warranted to think of myself as free, as capable of determining myself, is only secure on the basis of my consciousness of a law to strive for self-sufficiency, the moral law. This makes the concept of morality the sole ground for accessing my freedom as a real possibility.

Feeling, Drive, and the Lower Capacity of Desire 71

a concept and its object – but they differ in scope.[4] The question of necessity only concerns the general determination of my consciousness of freedom in *abstract* willing (i.e., in willing without an object), but the question of applicability, of which Fichte plans to secure over the course of Part II, concerns the specific determination of this consciousness in *actual* willing (i.e., in willing an object).

Framing Fichte's second deduction in these terms might not seem helpful at first. But I believe it throws light on the text of the *System of Ethics* when we consider how Fichte structures the remainder of Part II. Instead of moving straight to the task of enumerating a set of duties we ought to perform in striving for self-sufficiency, Fichte ventures upon what may seem like a long detour: §§4–9 examine questions of activity, causality, drive, feeling, longing, desire, pleasure, and nature, leading up to a deduction of our "lower capacity of desire" (*niedere Begehrungsvermögen*) (GA I/5: 122; SL 4: 127). Yet it is only in the latter half of Part II, after introducing the concept of freedom and securing a deduction of our "higher capacity of desire" (*oberes Begehrungsvermögen*), that Fichte announces the "Principle of an Applicable [*Anwendbaren*] Doctrine of Ethics" in §§12–13, almost 100 pages after first formulating the problem of applicability. On my reading, Fichte's plan becomes clear when we remember that consciousness of freedom in general concerns a rational being in the abstract, separate from a world of objects (and that is the path of *formal philosophy*). But the specific

---

[4] To elaborate on this, I am proposing that the deductions of both Parts I and II are transcendental because they seek to exhibit a *synthetic connection* between a concept and an object. The difference is one of scope: The connection that marks the deduction of Part I concerns the concept of morality and abstract willing, whereas the connection that marks of deduction of Part II concerns the concept of morality and actual willing. For this reason, my reading differs from Wood's (2016a), which characterizes Fichte's first argument in the *System of Ethics* as a metaphysical deduction. Wood writes: "Any new concept that is introduced in this way, and shown to be necessary to avoid a contradiction, is thereby given (in Kantian terminology) a *metaphysical deduction*. That is, its origin is seen to be transcendental rather than empirical, since the concept is needed if the possibility of experience, grounded on the self-positing I, is to be coherently conceived at all. At the same time, it is provided also with a *transcendental deduction*. That is, its objective instantiation in experience is shown to be necessary as a requirement for coherently conceiving the conditions under which the I can be, and be aware of itself as, active" (2016a, 64). "The principle of morality," Wood continues, "receives a *metaphysical deduction* – a demonstration of its *a priori* transcendental grounding – in Part One of the *System of Ethics*, and then its applicability (in Kantian terms, its *transcendental deduction*) is supplied in Part Two" (2016a, 64). As Kant draws this distinction in the first *Critique*, a metaphysical deduction of the categories aims to exhibit "the origin of the *a priori* categories in general . . . through their complete coincidence with the universal logical functions of thinking," whereas a transcendental deduction aims to exhibit "their possibility as *a priori* cognitions of objects of an intuition in general" (B159–160). Viewed in this light, Fichte's deduction of Part I clearly aspires to be more than a metaphysical deduction, since it seeks to show that the concept of morality is *required to determine* our consciousness of freedom.

form this consciousness takes in actual willing concerns a rational being engaged in this world (and that is the path of *real philosophy*).

4.4 The Original Drive

Without losing sight of this bird's-eye perspective on the *System of Ethics*, let us now examine the drive theory making up the deduction of Part II. If one had to summarize the basic thrust of this theory in a single sentence, one could say: all the activity of a finite rational being proceeds from a fundamental "drive" (*Trieb*). This fundamental drive, which Fichte calls an *Urtrieb*, can be further analyzed in terms of a "natural drive" (*Naturtrieb*), a "pure drive" (*reiner Trieb*), and a mixture of the two, the "ethical drive" (*sittlicher Trieb*). One point I wish to highlight from the beginning is that every element of willing Fichte discusses over the course of Part II is an abstraction of single ground of activity. An equally important point to call attention to is that no basic difference separates the lower and higher expressions of this activity. All the elements of the lower capacity of desire (such as drive and longing) make up the nonself-conscious expression of the *Urtrieb*, and all the elements of the higher capacity of desire (such as reflection and conscience) make up its self-conscious expression. The *Urtrieb* is nothing more than pure activity as such, the pure striving of the I considered in its original wholeness (GA I/5: 125, 126, 136, 137, 189; SL 4: 130, 131, 143, 144, 206). For Fichte, what distinguishes the lower and higher expressions of this drive is not agency or a lack thereof but self-reflection or a lack thereof. The capacity of deliberation that we designate with "free choice" is nothing more than the lower capacity transformed in the space of self-reflection.

This is, I think, the key to understanding Fichte's drive theory. On a basic level his claim is that when I reflect upon an object, I limit myself in relation to what I posit, and I thereby divide myself from it. I posit my I in contrast to a not-I. If I now reflect upon myself, then the same activity of limitation and division occurs: I limit myself, as the subject of reflection, in relation to the object of reflection, and thus I become self-conscious. While Fichte wants to characterize the pure I[5] in terms of an original wholeness – a unity of subject and object – his point is that reflection is the activity of breaking up this original wholeness. This explains why he thinks all activities of the I, all doing and willing, are mere manifestations of

---

[5] Not to be confused with the "pure drive," of course.

Feeling, Drive, and the Lower Capacity of Desire 73

a single, fundamental drive, the *Urtrieb*, which we break up through acts of limitation and division. In the *System of Ethics*, we therefore find the striking claim that acts of reflection break up an original wholeness at the heart of the self, the original wholeness of the I considered as sheer activity, sheer striving. And what Fichte wants to claim is that, qua drive, this fundamental striving at the heart of the self is a striving *for* something. It is not an abstract striving, but a striving for an object. But if that is the case, then we must ask: How does reflection separate the lower and higher expressions of this striving, and is this consistent with Fichte's commitment to the original wholeness of the I?

As the following passage shows, Fichte is attuned to these questions:

> Are my drives as a natural being and my tendency as pure spirit two separate drives? No, from a transcendental viewpoint both are one and the same fundamental drive which constitutes my being, simply viewed from two separate sides. That is to say, I am subject-object, and my true being lies in the identity and inseparability of the two. If I regard myself through the laws of sensible intuition and discursive thinking, then I am a completely determined object, which in fact my drive is as a natural drive, since in this regard I myself am nature. If I regard myself as subject, then this same single drive becomes for me a pure, spiritual drive, or it becomes the law of self-sufficiency. (GA I/5: 125; SL 4: 130)

What Fichte goes on to say is equally helpful to consider:

> All phenomena of the I rest solely upon the reciprocal interaction of these two drives, which is, properly speaking, only the *reciprocal interaction of one and the same drive with itself*. – This immediately answers the question concerning how things as opposed to each other as these two drives can occur in a being that is supposed to be absolutely one. The two are in fact one, but I-hood in its entirety rests on the fact that they appear to be different. The boundary separating them is reflection. (GA I/5: 125; SL 4: 130–31)

I have cited these passages to support the suggestion that, for Fichte, the pure I is an original wholeness that we can characterize in terms of a single drive whose various divisions, limitations, and levels (from low to high) are the product of reflection. What we regard as a dualism at the root of our nature as sensible and rational beings is nothing more than a difference of perspectives. My natural drive and my pure drive are expressions of one and the same activity, either considered before or after the boundary line of reflection. Yet the fundamental drive is not an abstract activity, as we noted above. Rather, it is a real ground of activity, a striving for something determinate. Our question now becomes: What is the object of this

74 OWEN WARE

fundamental drive? Or better, how can we comprehend this object as philosophers reflecting upon it?

4.5 Drive, Longing, and Desire

The answer to this question brings us to the core of Fichte's deduction of applicability in the *System of Ethics*. But in order to understand this step, we must first get clear on the key elements making up Fichte's drive theory in the *System of Ethics*:

- *Drive.* For Fichte, a drive is a real ground of activity and is therefore directed toward something. This is the *essence* of the I, he claims: it is "absolute activity and nothing other than activity: but activity taken objectively is *drive*" (GA I/5: 104; SL 4: 105; cf. GA I/2: 418; GWL 1: 287). Now by what mode does one originally relate to this activity? Or how does it originally manifest itself to consciousness?
- *Feeling.* Fichte's answer is that the drive of the I originally manifests itself to consciousness in the form of "feeling" (*Gefühl*), what we might call the nonself-conscious mode by which we relate to the activity of the drive. It is through feeling that I relate to my striving immediately, without yet being conscious of myself as distinct from this striving, and so without yet being divided from myself in reflection.
- *Longing.* If we isolate this sheer feeling of my drive in its nonself-conscious state, then what can we say about this feeling itself? Fichte introduces a new term to capture its character: "longing" (*Sehnen*). Longing is a "sensation of a need," but an indeterminate one: it is a sensation of a need without any concept of the need's end (GA I/5: 106; SL 4: 106). Longing is indeterminate because it is not yet mediated by what Fichte calls a "concept of an end" (*Zweckbegriff*), which he defines as a "*Vorbild* für etwas ausser uns" ("*pre-figuration* for something outside us") (GA I/5: 79; SL 4: 71). Longing captures the feeling of a drive, understood as a real ground of activity directed toward an end, prior to the conceptualization of that end – that is, prior to any act of reflection.[6]
- *Desire.* What happens if reflection upon longing occurs? Fichte's answer is that reflection makes it possible for me to posit a *Zweckbegriff*. When I divide myself in reflection from the activity of my drive, I can consider

---

[6] Longing, Fichte writes, is "the feeling of a need with which one is not oneself acquainted. We feel that something – we know not what – is missing" (GA I/5: 106; SL 4: 125).

Feeling, Drive, and the Lower Capacity of Desire

the aim of my drive: I can *prefigure* an object that would, if attained, satisfy my longing.

- *Pleasure/Displeasure.* This reflective act of prefiguration is what gives rise to "desire" (*Begehren*), whose goal Fichte calls "enjoyment" (*Genuss*) (GA I/5: 123; SL 4: 128). What I am seeking in positing an object for my longing is the satisfaction of my longing, the attainment of which produces "pleasure" (*Lust*) and the frustration of which produces "displeasure" (*Unlust*). We can then speak of desire as the activity of prefiguring ends for the satisfaction of the natural drive, all of which would not be possible, Fichte adds, without reflection.

Insofar as desire requires reflection, then, Fichte has shown that desire requires the free activity of the I, and this amounts to a deduction of our *Naturtrieb* as a lower capacity of desire. This is consistent with Fichte's nonnaturalism about action (there are no brute elements of desire)[7] and is of a piece with his nonnaturalism generally (there are no brute elements of consciousness). Yet Fichte does not think this deduction suffices to prepare for his account of the higher capacity of desire, which will occupy the final sections of Part II (§§10–13). In addition to a preliminary deduction of desire, Fichte thinks it is also necessary to derive the natural drive from a more general concept of "nature" (*Natur*). The nature of a finite rational being, he argues, "must be explained originally; it must be derived from the entire system of nature and grounded in the latter" (GA I/5: 108; SL 4: 110). In the course of this new derivation in §§8–9, we find Fichte introducing an important but rarely discussed concept in the *System of Ethics*, the concept of nature as an "organic whole" (*organisches Ganzes*), to which I now turn.[8]

4.6 Nature and Organicism

At this point in Part II, the reader is liable to forget the problem Fichte posed to motivate this transition of the *System of Ethics*: the problem of the moral law's applicability. Even if the concept of morality is necessary to

---

[7] On this picture, what is represented as brute in desire requires a connection to free reflection to become an instance of agency proper: "Sonach äussert sich schon beim Begehren die Freiheit; denn es fällt zwischen dasselbe und das Sehnen eine freie Reflexion" ("Freedom is therefore already manifest in desiring, for an act of free reflection intervenes between longing and desiring") (GA I/5: 122; SL 4: 127). Even what we might consider the lowest expression of human agency, our desiring of a natural object, bears a necessary link to freedom, which is more evidence that Fichte's system of ethics unfolds, as he explicitly says, according to the idealist principles of the *Wissenschaftslehre*.

[8] For exceptions to this neglect, see Fischer (1869), Burman (1891), and Schick (2015).

determine my consciousness of freedom, the question remains whether this concept is applicable when I reflect upon the conditions of actual willing, which involves an object to-be-attained. One way to frame the project of Fichte's deduction of applicability is to say that he is seeking to illuminate the structure of agency itself, first by breaking down the most elemental conditions of drive, longing, and desire, and then by presenting their higher expression in deliberation, choice, and conscience. Ultimately, Fichte will argue that the concept of morality is a required condition for the latter as a higher faculty of feeling. Yet his point is that the affective conditions of conscience are already built into the structure of action in its expression as nonself-conscious desire. And that is why the "principle of an applicable doctrine of ethics" Fichte introduces at the end of Part II – to follow one's own conscience – does not impose a law foreign to the structure of action, which would raise the specter of applicability anew, but is instead a law that arises wholly internally from the conditions of actual willing.

Still, the question remains: After the deduction of the lower capacity of desire, why does Fichte find it necessary to provide a further derivation of the natural drive from the "entire system of nature"? The answer, I believe, speaks to the end of the natural drive – that of prefiguring objects for the sake of enjoyment. As we know, enjoyment is the *Zweckbegriff* that orients the activity of the natural drive, which Fichte later equates with the "maxim of one's own happiness" (*die Maxime der eigenen Glückseligkeit*) (GA I/5: 167; SL 4: 180). But it is unclear from the discussion so far what the matter of this end contains, and so it is unclear for what and to what end the natural drive strives, given that Fichte has yet to clarify the concept of enjoyment itself. On my reading, this is the lacuna he seeks to fill in by providing a derivation of the natural drive from the system of nature as such. The claim Fichte goes on to develop in the remainder of §§8–9 is that the concept of nature considered as an organic whole reveals the end of the natural drive, which in turn reveals the *Zweckbegriff* of enjoyment. As we shall see, what makes this organic model so pivotal is that its more common alternative, the mechanistic model, does not give us resources to understand for what and to what end the natural drive strives, which Fichte maintains is a distinctive kind of harmony.

To start with, what is it about the law of mechanism that is insufficient for the task at hand? According to this model of explanation, we only have the law of cause and effect at our disposal, and so we can only posit the connection between parts of nature in heteronomous terms. "Every member of such a series has its activity communicated to it by another member

Feeling, Drive, and the Lower Capacity of Desire

outside itself" (GA I/5: 109; SL 4: 111). Fichte points out, however, that this law cannot make sense of the character of a drive as an internally motivating force: "A drive," he explains, "is something that neither comes from outside nor is directed outside; it is an inner force of the substrate, directed upon itself" (GA I/5: 109; SL 4: 111). By its very character, a drive conveys a form of "self-determination" (*Selbstbestimmung*), not in the sense of rational self-legislation, but in the sense of internally generated activity striving for a determinate end (GA I/5: 109; SL 4: 111). But how can we make sense of this? Fichte's point is that we need a new model for explaining the system of nature "outside" us – a new way of positing the connection between parts of nature in autonomous terms – if we are to understand nature "inside" us, the natural drive. The alternative he pursues is organicism.

According to this alternative model of explanation, we do not posit the connection between parts of nature in heteronomous terms, with one part subordinated to the other in a causal series. Rather, organicism gives us a framework for thinking of parts and their whole standing in a connection of mutual determination, with each part relating to the whole and the whole in turn relating to each part. The operative category of explanation here is not cause and effect but "reciprocal interaction" (*Wechselwirkung*) (GA I/5: 111, 113, 114, 115, 118, 119; SL 4: 113, 117, 122, 125, 129, 130), which permits us to think of a community between parts of nature and their whole.[9] The reason why this model is attractive to Fichte is that it makes room to explain two unique features of a *Trieb*: (a) its character as an internally motivating force, on the one hand, and (b) its character as a motivating force directed to something outside of itself, on the other. What is unique about a drive is not just its autonomy, the way in which it strives *from itself*, but also what we might call its teleology, the way in which it strives *for something*. Organicism gives us an appropriate model to understand these two features because of the way it frames the part–whole structure of nature: parts are not subordinated to each other but are coordinated. According to organicism, the system of nature as such is represented as a system whereby each part is what it is through its relationship to the whole, and vice versa (GA I/5: 111; SL 4: 113–114).

In another work Fichte gives the example of a tree to illustrate this holistic structure (GA I/4: 14; GNR 3: 203). If we represent a tree as

---

[9] The category of "reciprocal interaction" (*Wechselwirkung*) plays a central role in Fichte's doctrine of science, too, as I have argued elsewhere. See Ware (2019b).

possessing consciousness and powers of will, he explains, we can imagine that each of its individual parts would strive to preserve itself and maintain its own being. At the same time, we can also imagine that each of its individual parts would also will the preservation and maintenance of the tree itself. The striving for self-preservation in each part would be coequal to each part's striving for the preservation of the whole. The same cannot be said, Fichte adds, with the example of a pile of sand, "where each individual part can be indifferent to whether any other part is separated, trampled upon, or strewn about" (GA I/4: 14; GNR 3: 203). What is special about the holistic structure of a tree is in fact common to all living organisms, whereby every part stands in a relation of reciprocal interaction to the whole. Living organisms are not mere aggregates but self-organized systems in which each part works coordinatively with all others. Fichte hints at this idea in the *System of Ethics* when he speaks of the inner dynamics of plants, adding: "Here there is everywhere harmony, reciprocal interaction, and not, as it were, mere mechanism" (GA I/5: 120; SL 4: 124).

What exactly do we learn from viewing the natural drive through this organicist lens? Fichte's answer is that it gives us a unique way of seeing the autonomy and teleology of our original striving, which is consistent, he claims, with a more general law of striving that we can posit in the system of nature outside of us. This is what he calls the "formative law" (*Bildungsgesetz*) of nature:

> *Formative Law of Nature*: "every part of nature strives to unite its being and efficacy with the being and efficacy of every other determinate part of nature." (GA I/5: 119; SL 4: 121)

On the assumption that nature operates according to this *Bildungsgesetz*, that all parts of nature strive to unite their being and efficacy with all other parts, it is possible to determine the character of the natural drive more precisely. We can say that what the natural drive strives for is a kind of unification, a unification that is, Fichte argues, both active and passive in character. It is a striving "zu bilden und sich bilden zu lassen" (to form and to be formed) and hence a striving for mutual "formation" (*Bildung*), or what Fichte now terms the "formative drive" (*Bildungstrieb*) (GA I/5: 119; SL 4: 121).[10] Hence, the concept of a *Bildungstrieb* helps fill in the gap from his previous discussion of desire insofar as it specifies the end of the natural

---

[10] Fichte also calls it a "drive for self-preservation" (*Trieb der Selbsterhaltung*) (GA I/5: 118; SL 4: 122). For an illuminating discussion of this concept in Fichte's ethics, see Loewe (1862).

Feeling, Drive, and the Lower Capacity of Desire

drive. What the natural drive strives for is enjoyment, but enjoyment understood in terms of the Formative Law, that is, enjoyment as the reciprocal interaction of shaping and being shaped.

The far-reaching implication of this claim, I want to suggest, is that it brings a novel view of desire to the foreground. When we characterize the activity of the natural drive in terms of a striving for mutual *Bildung*, it follows that reciprocity is built into the most elemental structure of agency, prior to its higher expression in deliberation, choice, and conscience. Fichte calls attention to this when he says that what the natural drive seeks is not to *absorb* an object (which would result in its elimination) but rather to *relate* to it:

> There is in me a drive, one that has arisen through nature and that relates itself to natural objects in order to unite them with my own being: not to absorb them into my being outright, as food and drink are absorbed through digestion, but to relate them as such to my natural needs, to bring them into a certain relationship with me, concerning which we will learn more in the future. (GA I/5: 119; SL 4: 123)

As Fichte explains a few pages later, this view of desire can be thought of in two ways. My natural drive seeks a connection to objects as natural things, and this connection can be either immediate or mediate:

> My desiring has as its object things of nature, with the goal either of unifying these things with me immediately (as in the case of food and drink) or of placing them in a certain relationship with me (as in the case of clear air, an extensive view, good weather, and the like). (GA I/5: 122; SL 4: 127)

At the heart of desire, then, we find an activity of prefiguring a connection of mutual formation, either by unifying an object with the natural drive immediately or by unifying an object with the natural drive mediately. And this is what we learn when we view the natural drive through an organicist lens: the *Zweckbegriff* of desire is not the elimination of its object, even if that happens to occur in the case of food and drink. The *Zweckbegriff* of desire is coordinative and – to anticipate Fichte's concept of the ethical drive – nondominating and noncontrolling.

But how does any of this bring us closer to demonstrating the moral law's applicability? The concept of a *Bildungsgesetz* sketched earlier allows us to understand what I previously called the teleology of the natural drive, its directedness to objects. We can now say that the natural drive aims at the mutual formation between itself and objects rather than one-way consumption. The novelty of this claim, as I hinted at, is that it posits a form of primitive reciprocity in the act of desiring: When we prefigure an object to satisfy the natural drive, it is a prefiguration structured around the end of unification – that of bringing together an object with the drive. In this respect, we can say that a fundamental form of harmony orients the activity of desire even in its lower capacity. In my view, the significance of rethinking desire as mutual *Bildung* becomes clear later in the *System of Ethics* when Fichte argues that the natural drive supplies the moral law with its content. Without understanding the model of organicism Fichte lays down in §§8–9, we risk overlooking the fact that the matter of morality stems from our original striving for harmony.

Let me review the main steps of our discussion so far. After separating the concept of willing from its object in Part I, Fichte faces the task of bringing the two back together with the aim of demonstrating the role of morality in their connection. That is the overarching goal of his deduction of applicability, which is why Part II of the *System of Ethics* devotes so much space to examining the original conditions of willing (drive, longing, feeling, desire, and pleasure). To understand these conditions better, I had us turn to a largely overlooked section of the *System of Ethics*, where Fichte attempts to derive the character of the natural drive from the "entire system of nature" in §§8–9. These sections show that while Fichte is an idealist in positing the activity of the I as fundamental to all experience, he nevertheless embraces an organicist model when considering how we represent nature outside of us. As we have seen, Fichte argues that the natural drive we represent as internal to us must be in accord with the same explanatory law of the system of nature we represent as external to us, according to what he calls the "formative law" (*Bildungesetz*), where all the parts of a system exist for the sake of the whole, and the whole, in turn, exists for the sake of all the parts. Accordingly, the natural drive within us exhibits what I have called a form of primitive reciprocity: to relate to objects both actively and passively in a relation of coordination rather than subordination. And that is why, I have argued, Fichte defines the natural drive as a "formative drive" (*Bildungstrieb*).[11] But now we must ask: How does the original reciprocal activity of the formative drive help bring Fichte's argument in Part II to completion? How does this establish the right kind of connection between willing and its object, such that the concept of morality is required for their connection? The answer, I believe, lies in Fichte's concept of the ethical drive.

---

[11] For further discussion, see Angelica Nuzzo's contribution in this volume.

4.7 The Ethical Drive

Allen Wood has observed that if we read Fichte's distinction between a natural drive and a pure drive according to Kant's distinction between a lower (or empirically conditioned) and a higher (or pure) exercise of practical reason, "then we are in for a big surprise."[12] This is certainly true. For Kant, the higher faculty of desire, which is equivalent to pure practical reason, is the very locus of moral worth. This is not the case for Fichte's pure drive. In the theory of action he goes on to develop in §§10–12, the pure drive arises through a second act of reflection.[13] When I bring my longing under reflection, I can posit an end for my longing, and that end is already an instance of my free agency: It is a conceptually mediated object to-be-attained. Were I then to reflect on this activity of prefiguring an end for my natural drive, I would become aware of myself in a different light: I would see my I, which had previously been absorbed by the concept of an object, as distinct from that object. I would, in a word, become self-aware of my free activity, the activity already contained in my original act of prefiguring an end for my natural drive. What Fichte now wants to claim, in developing this next part of his theory, is that a new drive emerges from this act of self-reflection, a striving to be independent of the natural drive itself and its object. This is what he calls the pure drive (GA I/5: 139; SL 4: 141).[14]

What is surprising is that Fichte does not locate the source of moral worth in actions that accord with the independence now demanded by the pure drive, as we might have expected in light of his concept of self-sufficiency. Instead, Fichte locates the source of moral worth in actions that accord with the ethical drive, which he defines as a "mixed drive" (*gemischter Trieb*) (GA I/5: 143; SL 4: 152). Regarding this drive, he writes:

> It obtains its material, toward which it is directed, from the natural drive; that is to say, the natural drive that is synthetically united and fused with the ethical drive aims at the same action that the ethical drive aims at, at least in part. All that the ethical drive obtains from the pure drive is its form. Like

---

[12] Wood (2016a, 156).

[13] For further discussion of this "genetic" account of freedom, see Ware (2019c) and Daniel Breazeale's contribution to this volume.

[14] Fichte anticipates this claim in the 1794 *Wissenschaftslehre* when he describes the pure drive as "an absolute drive, a drive for the drive's sake," whose formula would be "a law for law's sake, an absolute law" (GA I/2: 450; GWL 1: 327). In this context, too, Fichte identifies this law with the categorical imperative, writing: "The *indeterminacy* in such a drive is easily located; for it drives us out into the indeterminate, without an aim (the categorical imperative is merely formal, and has no object whatever)" (GA I/2: 450; GWL 1: 327).

82   OWEN WARE

> the pure drive, it is absolute; it demands something purely and simply, for
> no end outside of itself. (GA I/5: 143; SL 4: 152)

As I read this passage, Fichte is saying that the ethical drive is a striving for wholeness in a self divided by reflection. Just like the natural drive, it strives for a kind of relationship between an object and the drive, a relationship of mutual formation. Yet, unlike the natural drive, the relationship in question is not restricted to objects of nature (food, drink, good weather, etc.). As a striving for wholeness in a self divided by reflection, the ethical drive seeks a relationship of mutual formation between the conditions of the entire I and its original being as an *Urtrieb*. This is the extent to which the ethical drive maintains the end of the pure drive, because the *Zweckbegriff* of the former, the complete reunification of all my drives back to their primordial root, is formally equivalent to complete independence and self-sufficiency. The difference is that complete independence and self-sufficiency is, as Fichte tells us time and again, an empty concept. It is precisely the concept of the moral law with which we began in Part I by separating the will from its object. Only the ethical drive contains the principle of an applicable ethics, then, because it draws upon the matter of the natural drive, whose inner dynamics foreshadow the striving characteristic of what now Fichte calls our "ethical vocation" (*sittliche Bestimmung*) (GA I/5: 141; SL 4: 150).[15]

But why does Fichte now locate the principle of an applicable ethics in one's "conscience" (*Gewissen*)? While I can only sketch an answer here, the following is worth noting.[16] For Fichte, conscience is the higher capacity of feeling by which we have immediate access to the ethical drive and its striving for wholeness. In the same way that the attainment of an object for my natural drive produces a feeling of harmony, Fichte says that the attainment of an object for my ethical drive produces a feeling of harmony as well. It is not a feeling of simple pleasure, however, but a "feeling of approval" (*Gefühl der Billigung*) or self-respect that comes in the wake of aligning my actions with my deeper drive for wholeness (GA I/5: 137; SL 4: 145). Conversely, a failure to bring my actions into alignment with the ethical drive produces a feeling of pain – not simple pain, but a "feeling of disapproval" (*Gefühl der Misbilligung*) or self-contempt. All of this provides

---

[15] Later in the *System of Ethics*, Fichte specifies this vocation further in terms of striving for "universal moral cultivation" (*allgemeine moralische Bildung*) on the basis of reciprocal communication with all rational human beings (GA I/5: 213; SL 4: 235).

[16] See Ware (2017) for further discussion of the importance of "feeling" (*Gefühl*) for understanding Fichte's theory of conscience.

Feeling, Drive, and the Lower Capacity of Desire 83

strong evidence for reading Fichte as a philosopher for whom the feelings of *Gewissen* express (at a pretheoretical level) the content of morality.[17] We have seen that the content of morality comes from the natural drive, whereas the form comes from the pure drive. As a synthesis of the two, the power of conscience gives immediate expression to my striving for wholeness, and only through such a union, Fichte argues, "ist Sittlichkeit in der wirklichen Ausübung möglich" ("is the actual exercise of morality possible") (GA I/5: 142; SL 4: 151).

What conscience expresses as a higher capacity of feeling helps to brings this last point into sharper focus. The higher pleasure of self-respect arises when my actions accord with the end of the ethical drive, the complete reunification of all my drives back to their primordial root. Self-respect is a feeling of harmony between my current striving and the fundamental *Urtrieb*, which precedes the fracturing of my faculties in the space of reflection. All pleasure has this quality, for Fichte, because a feeling of harmony also arises when I bring objects into relationship with my natural drive, even objects I do not consume like good weather and an extensive view. What makes the feeling of harmony unique in the case of conscience is that it arises not in relation to the goal of my natural drive (which is limited to my lower capacity of desire), nor in relation to the end of my pure drive (which is limited to my higher capacity of desire), *but in relation to my entire being*. It is a feeling of harmony between my striving and my fundamental drive considered as a unity of subject and object. And it makes sense that I can only relate to the original unity of my being through a *Gefühl*, because feeling (unlike reflection) does not divide subject and object. Feeling is the only mode by which I can, for Fichte, access the primordial unity of my original I, the very object of my ethical vocation.

By way of conclusion, let me repeat that even the lower capacity of desire requires an act of reflection to posit an end, the *Zweckbegriff* of enjoyment. When I reflect upon the activity of prefiguring an end for my natural drive, I become aware of my independence from it, and this gives rise to my pure drive for freedom. The key to Fichte's deduction of applicability, I have argued, lies in his claim that even the ethical drive requires an act of prefiguring an end, whose *Zweckbegriff* combines both the form of the pure drive (that of freedom) and the matter of the natural drive (that of mutual formation). The conceptually mediated product of this synthesis yields a determinate imperative to act upon the natural drive, with its inner

---

[17] I have discussed these aspects of Fichte's theory of conscience at greater length elsewhere. See Ware (2017) and Ware (2020).

dynamic of mutual formation, but without limiting this inner dynamic to objects of nature. It is, Fichte says, an imperative that commands unconditionally and for its own sake, and it applies across all times and situations. In a word, the *Zweckbegriff* that emerges internally from the union of the pure and natural drives is precisely the concept of morality, but morality now understood in its material significance as a principle of action. In the case of abstract willing, then, Fichte was able to derive a principle of self-sufficiency in Part I, but this principle remained merely formal and empty. Having shown that this same principle emerges as the only possible *Zweckbegriff* of the ethical drive in Part II, Fichte has finally demonstrated its applicability.

CHAPTER 5

Fichte and the Path from "Formal" to "Material" Freedom

Daniel Breazeale

One should never have said "the human being *is* free," but rather "the human being necessarily strives, hopes, and assumes that he is free." – The proposition, "the human being *is* free" is not true.

– J. G. Fichte[1]

5.1 Preliminary Efforts (1793–1796)

The 1790s were an especially fertile period for reconsiderations of human freedom and its relationship to morality. A dominating influence upon these conversations was Kant's recent work on practical philosophy, which was continuing to appear even as disputes over its interpretation raged. As an erstwhile, if reluctant, proponent of rationalist determinism and an enthusiastic convert to "the Critical philosophy," Fichte paid close attention to these debates. Indeed, as the self-proclaimed author of "the first philosophy of human freedom,"[2] he could ill afford *not* to. Accordingly, the second edition of his first book, *Attempt at a Critique of all Revelation*, included a substantial new second chapter devoted to "theory of the will."[3] Like Kant, Fichte here recognizes different *kinds* of freedom, while at the same time, like Reinhold, resisting Kant's identification of practical reason and will. The result is the first statement of a genuinely new, "Fichtean" view of the relationship of freedom (including freedom of choice or *Willkür*) to practical reason and morality, an account couched in terms of the basic *drives* of the I.

---

[1] *Eigene Meditationen über Elementar-Philosophie/Practische Philosophie*, GA II/3: 183. All English translations in this paper are the responsibility of the author.
[2] Draft of a letter to Jens Baggesen, April/May 1795; GA III/2: 298; EPW, 385.
[3] "§ 2, Theorie des Willens, als Vorbereitung einer Deduction der Religion überhaupt" (GA I/1: 135–61; VKO 5: 16–39). This chapter was composed in late 1792 and early 1793 and appeared in the spring of 1793.

Fichte defines willing or volition (*Wollen*) as "determining oneself to produce a representation while conscious of one's activity," and, following Kant, he calls the capacity to engage in volition "the faculty of desire (*Begehrungsvermögen*)" and identifies the "form" of this same faculty as "absolute spontaneity."[4] This, I suggest, is the first reference to what Fichte will later call the "formal freedom" of the I.

The content of a representation – that is, what is actually willed through the practical power of desire – can either be empirically given or spontaneously produced by the agent. This is what distinguishes nonmoral from moral volitions. Yet even in cases of volitions motivated entirely by sensible *Neigung* or inclination, Fichte insists that it is not the sensible or natural drive itself nor one's representation of what may satisfy it that actually determine one's volition. Instead, this is determined by the agent's free *judgment* concerning what will or will not produce happiness or pleasure. There is thus an all-important gap between drive and will, because even empirically motivated volitions presuppose the absolute spontaneity of the I, insofar as it possesses the capacity to suspend willing and to reflect upon the objects of the same.

In the case of *moral* volition, however, spontaneity is present not only as the *form* of volition as such but also as the *content* or *material* of the same. This is just what distinguishes a moral from a nonmoral volition. In the case of the latter, the content is first *given* to the agent, who then must spontaneously "will" it. In contrast, the *content* of a moral volition is not supposed to be *given* to the agent at all; instead, it is spontaneously *produced*. From this Fichte concludes that the content in question must itself be somehow grounded in the *form* of the pure faculty of desire, that is, spontaneity. Following Reinhold, though without mentioning him by name, he still maintains that it is an *allgemeingeltend* or universally recognized "*fact* of consciousness" that we possess such a supersensible power of volition.[5] (Five years later, in the *System of Ethics,* he will offer a *proof* that we possess such a power, in the form of a transcendental-genetic derivation of the same from the original self-positing of the I.)

For an *actual* moral volition, however, more is required than the idea of what is right. In addition, we require "an action of spontaneity in our consciousness." Like Reinhold, Fichte distinguishes the essential spontaneity of the higher power of desire (practical reason) from what he calls "the freedom of choice (*libertas arbitrii*)" of which we are conscious whenever we are aware of *choosing* anything. Unlike Reinhold, however, Fichte claims that

---

[4] GA I/1: 135 and 140; VKO 5: 16 and 23.   [5] See GA I/1: 140; VKO 5: 23.

Fichte and the Path from "Formal" to "Material" Freedom

this same freedom of *Willkür* is also present in nonmoral volition and is not confined to choosing between moral and immoral actions.[6] Accordingly, he distinguishes explicitly between *two kinds* of "freedom": the freedom of choice (*Willkür*) and what he calls that "absolutely first expression of freedom through the practical law of reason." In the former case, freedom is understood *negatively*; it signifies "complete liberation from the coercion of natural necessity." In the latter, Fichte writes, "freedom does not mean choice at all, since the [moral] law allows us no choice but rather commands by necessity."

It is precisely the confusion of these two very different "expressions of freedom" that makes it so difficult to conceive of "moral necessity," of a law that is supposed to "command freedom." By this point, however, Fichte was convinced that the only way to defend freedom against skeptical attack would be by appealing to what he calls the "only correct concept of transcendental freedom," according to which reason is capable of giving itself a categorical law through its own *spontaneity* and hence *freely* – a law that commands "precisely *because* it is *law*, necessarily and unconditionally." In this case, he concludes, "no *Willkür* is present, no choosing between various determinations by means of this law, since it determines matters in only *one* way."[7]

A similar distinction between two very different *kinds* of freedom is also a prominent feature of two important book reviews Fichte composed immediately following the second edition of his book on revelation: the first, a review of Leonhard Creuzer's *Skeptical Observations on Freedom of the Will* and the second a review of F. H. Gebhard's *On Ethical Goodness as Disinterested Benevolence*.[8] In the Creuzer review, Fichte reiterates his distinction between two types of freedom and commends Reinhold for recognizing that "one must carefully distinguish between *those* manifestations of absolute self-activity by means of which reason is practical and assigns a law to itself, and *those* manifestations through which a person (in his function as *will*) determines himself to obey or not to obey this law."[9] We are, according to Fichte, conscious of the former (that is, of the moral law), but he disputes Reinhold's contention that we are also immediately conscious of the latter: of our free act of self-determination or *willing*, which he then proceeds to identify with *Willkür*. He concludes this review by accepting Creuzer's challenge "to invent a new faculty of free choice

---

[6] See GA I/1: 150; VKO 5: 35.   [7] GA I/1: 147; VKO 5: 32.
[8] GA I/2: 1–14; RC 8: 411–17. For English translations, see Daniel Breazeale (2001a, 2001b).
[9] GA I/2: 8; RC 8: 412.

(*Vermögen der Willkür*), tear it from its natural context, and thus set it up as an isolated indeterminacy."[10]

All in all, the Creuzer review raises more questions than it answers, and the reader is left wondering just how the power of free choice is supposed to be related both to the original spontaneity of the I and to the morally necessitated will.[11] Some of these issues are clarified in the more substantive Gebhard review. Rejecting the position of both the moral sense theorists, namely, that what determines the will in the case of moral actions are feelings of a disinterested, benevolent drive, and the so-called Kantians, who contend that what determines the will in such cases is practical reason, Fichte proposes that the will might instead by determined "by a third factor: namely, an absolute self-activity or spontaneity (*Selbsttätigkeit*)."[12]

After agreeing that "reason is practical" – that is, that the I is spontaneously capable of practical self-legislation – Fichte cautions that "it is not a *fact* that reason is practical, nor that it has the power to produce the feeling of what is simply right."[13] Instead, this is something that must be *proven*. (Note that in the Creuzer review Fichte says what needs to be proven is that we possess the power of free choice or *Willkür,* whereas here, in the Gebhard review, he states that what needs to be proven is that we possess the power of spontaneous practical legislation (i.e., that reason is indeed "practical").) He soon came to realize that he could prove neither of these without proving the other and that the only way to do this would be by deriving *both* from that unconditioned self-positing with which the *Wissenschaftslehre* commences.

In the draft of his review, Fichte proposes that any proof that reason is practical must proceed as follows: "There must be something unconditioned – if the human being is to possess personality, then this unconditioned something must not be given to him; he *must give it to himself, by means of his own spontaneity*."[14] Accordingly, the feeling of what is absolutely right cannot be *given* by anything but must instead be "*produced* by absolute self-activity," inasmuch as "reason cannot consider anything to be absolute that it has not produced through its own activity."[15] Hence, the only way to "prove that reason is practical" (i.e., that the I can legislate for

---

[10] GA I/2: 14; RC 8: 417.

[11] For a careful analysis of the Creuzer review and Fichte's departure therein from Reinhold's view of freedom, see Wayne Martin (2018).

[12] GA I/2: 34; RG 8: 42.   [13] GA I/2: 26; RG 8: 423; emphasis added.

[14] GA II/2: 256, emphasis added.

[15] GA II/2: 264. "In order to arrive at an absolute, practical reason has to be assumed" (Draft of RG, GA II/2: 256).

Fichte and the Path from "Formal" to "Material" Freedom   89

itself a law governing its own freedom of choice) is to *begin with freedom*. But, cautions Fichte, "the unconditioned spontaneity of practical reason must not be confused with that freedom of choice which must also be recognized as essential to human action."[16] Hence the formidable challenge facing the system he was just on the verge of constructing: both to *distinguish* the original spontaneous self-determination of the I from empirical choosing and individual moral volition and to *connect* it to both. This is a task he would finally accomplish in 1798 in the *System of Ethics,* where it would be articulated in terms of the distinction between "formal" and "material" freedom.

In fact, this distinction was first introduced in 1796, in Part One of *Foundation of Natural Right.* As Allen Wood has noted, however, these terms (especially the term "material" freedom) are here assigned a rather different meaning than they will acquire in the *System of Ethics* and other works.[17] In the *Natural Right,* formal freedom is described as an *apodictically valid, qualitative* category, which applies to free beings "in general" or "as such."[18] In other words, "formal freedom" seems to be a new name for what Fichte had previously called the "absolute self-activity" or "original spontaneity" of the I, which is broadly consistent with what he will have to say about formal freedom in the *System of Ethics.* In contrast, in the *Naturrecht* – but *only* there – "material" freedom is understood as a *quantitative* concept concerned exclusively with the extent of the *empirical domain* within which an individual can exercise practical efficacy.[19]

In the *System of Ethics,* "formal freedom" remains a purely *qualitative* category and continues to designate that original spontaneity without which, according to Fichte, no potential or actual agent could be an "I" at all. This is the kind of *freedom from* external determination that distinguishes the I from the Not-I, or mind from nature. But "material freedom" now refers to a specific kind of formally free act; namely, one in which the spontaneity of the I is responsible not merely for determining the *means* one will employ to achieve some end but for determining the *end* of one's actions as well. This remains a *quantitative* category, however, because

---

[16] See Fichte's criticism of Gebhard for confusing "practical reason" with "the will proper" (GA I/2: 28; RG 8: 426). Note that in this case, Fichte appears to mean by "the will proper" *Willkür* or freedom of choice with respect to what one will will.

[17] See Wood (2016a, 70 n).   [18] GA I/3: 404; GNR 3: 113.

[19] Hence, according to the new account of the relationship of right proposed in this same treatise, such a relationship first arose only when an individual "materially limited its freedom through itself; that is, it limited the sphere of those actions that were possible by virtue of its formal freedom . . .. It has therefore limited its freedom through the concept of the subject's (formal) freedom" (GA I/3: 350–51; GNR 3: 43).

90   DANIEL BREAZEALE

there are, on Fichte's account (or at least on my account of his account), various *degrees* of material freedom.

In what follows, I shall do my best to explicate the notions of "formal" and "material" freedom within the contest of the *System of Ethics*. My remarks are bound to appear controversial, because my interpretation differs profoundly from that offered by other recent commentators on this topic, including Michelle Kosch and Frederick Neuhouser, though I do not here intend to discuss these differences.[20] And with this, we can finally turn our attention to the *System of Ethics* in the hope of illuminating what Fichte there describes as his "genetic concept of freedom."[21]

5.2   Formal Freedom

Formal freedom is a defining feature of the spontaneous activity of I-hood as such, that is, of the I understood simply as an unconditioned

---

[20] Kosch defends a very "thick" or concrete notion of formal freedom as "a complex empirical psychological characteristic of social beings, involving component capacities whose products and maintenance require the right sort of interaction with the right sort of human and natural environment" (Kosch 2015, 351). She describes "Fichte's positive characterization of formal freedom" as "self-determination through concepts of ends" and hence argues that formal freedom requires "deliberative rationality" (Kosch 2018, 16). She also asserts that "formal freedom, briefly stated, is the disposition to form intentions spontaneously on the basis of concepts of ends" (2011, 155) and maintains that "Fichte's core notion of moral agency ('formal freedom') is the disposition to form intentions spontaneously on the basis of concepts of ends" (2015, 351). The term "material freedom" does not even appear in Kosch's paper on "formal freedom," which is unsurprising, since she annexes to formal freedom the very features that are supposed to characterize material freedom and distinguish it from formal freedom. This is all quite bewildering, as when she writes that "formal freedom varies together with excellence in reflection, which is itself moral excellence in the formal sense" (2018, 150) and insists that "formal freedom itself comes in degrees" (2015, 354), a claim that is impossible to reconcile with Fichte's understanding of formal freedom as a qualitative rather than quantitative category.

Neuhouser (1990) also seems confused about formal freedom, for he maintains that "what Fichte has in mind here is close to Kant's conception of 'practical freedom' or *Willkür*. To say that a subject's action is self-determined in this [formal] sense is merely to say that it is freely chosen, which further implies for Fichte that it is chosen in accord with a practical maxim" (1990, 122). Like Kosch, Neuhouser also thinks that explicit, voluntary reflection is a necessary ingredient in formal freedom (1990, 125). Moreover, in a note on p. 125 he asserts that Fichte developed a characterization of formal freedom "as requiring purposive concepts and some degree of reflection." Once again, this seems to get things backwards, inasmuch as Fichte claims that the "reflection" in question accounts for the possibility of actions that are materially (and not just formally) free. Neuhouser also (mistakenly, in my view) agrees with Kosch that formal freedom is subject to degrees (see e.g., his reference in the note on p. 128 to "full formal freedom"). Again, this seems to be a much thicker conception of formal freedom than is warranted by Fichte's own remarks; indeed, it is directly contradicted by his explicit assertion that "freedom of choice" applies only to material and never to formal freedom (see GA IV/2: 58; WLnmH; and GA IV/3: 374; WLnmK).

[21] GA I/5: 52; SL 4: 37.

Tathandlung or F/Act – along with all that this entails. The foundational portion of the *Wissenschaftslehre* purports to demonstrate that this is what underlies and makes possible both the freedom of conscious reflection and the freedom of practical choosing, willing, and acting. "Formal freedom," insists Fichte, "is the root of all freedom."[22] One could describe such purely formal freedom as the "innate" or "external" freedom of the I, in the sense that every I is – as such and just because it is an I – to that extent "free" from all external causation or determination.[23]

Though the term does not appear in the *Foundation of the Entire Wissenschaftslehre*, it is easy to see that the various spontaneous acts of self-assertion and self-reflection deduced in the course of Fichte's elaborate, genetic analysis of the conditions for the possibility of that unconditioned, spontaneous act of self-positing with which this treatise begins are all "free" in the relevant, purely formal sense of the term. That is to say, they are neither *caused* nor *determined* by anything external to the I itself, including its own "original limitations," as revealed through a check or *Anstoss* upon its outgoing activity. Instead, all such constitutive acts – including the I's spontaneously produced, but involuntary and necessary, "reflections" upon its own limits and actions – are described as springing spontaneously from the I alone.[24] In such cases, the I is never *required* to reflect, inasmuch as nothing *outside* the I itself is responsible for the "reflections" in question.[25] Such an act, writes Fichte, "occurs because it occurs and simply for the sake of acting; i.e., it occurs with absolute self-determination and freedom. Such an action contains within itself its entire foundation, along with all the conditions for such acting."[26]

It follows that all the constitutive acts of reflection described in the foundational portion of the *Wissenschaftslehre* can be described as "formally free," because they all occur "spontaneously" – even if they may, in another

---

[22] GA I/5: 129; SL 4: 135.
[23] In his first public mention of the term "formal freedom" (namely, in 1796, in Part I of *Foundations of Natural Right*), Fichte maintains that formal freedom pertains to every I whatsoever, just because it is an I, but he does not elaborate on this somewhat opaque definition. Instead, he simply describes formal freedom as an apodictically valid, qualitative category, which applies to free beings "in general" or "as such": "What is at issue here is only that the person be free in general, but not the extent to which he must be free . . .. Each person is supposed to be free without qualification" (GA I/ 3: 404; GNR 3: 113).
[24] See GA I/3: 172; GEWL 1: 366.
[25] See GA I/2: 338 and 379; GEWL 1: 189 and 240, as well as GA I/3: 173 and 178; GEWL: 1: 367 and 373.
[26] GA I/2: 450; GEWL 1: 327.

92   DANIEL BREAZEALE

sense, also be described as "necessary."[27] "The I," says Fichte, "reflects simply because it is an I."[28] But it also follows that, unless one is a transcendental philosopher, one will lack any explicit awareness of such formal freedom and will instead remain "lost in objects."

Though Fichte does not explicitly do so, one could easily distinguish between the "theoretical" and the "practical" spontaneity (or formal freedom) of the I. The first is manifest in the I's spontaneous reflection upon and positing of its own limits, the second in its endless striving to expand those same limits and assert its own radical self-sufficiency (which is the source of what will later be identified as the "pure drive" of every I). It must be emphasized that such "formal freedom" is, in both cases, quite *involuntary* and involves no *choices* on the part of the I; yet it is still "free," in the Spinozistic sense that nothing *outside* the I compels it either to cognize or to act. Hence, as Fichte concludes in his lectures on *Wissenschaftslehre nova methodo*, "formal freedom is postulated along with immediate consciousness; or rather, it is identical with it. Formal freedom is immediate self-consciousness itself."[29]

5.3   Material Freedom

Material freedom is the freedom of a self-conscious *agent*; hence, material freedom is the freedom of *willing*. "The will is free in the material sense of the term. When it wills, the I provides itself, as an intellect, with the object of its willing, and it does this by choosing among several possible objects."[30] Unlike formal freedom, material freedom involves conscious *choice*,[31] first, with respect to the *means* for accomplishing naturally

---

[27] See GEWL, where Fichte declares that those acts of "reflection," by means of which the I posits for itself is own limits and posits them in the form of external objects, occur "necessarily and with absolute spontaneity" (GA I/3: 175; GEWL 1: 369).

[28] GA I/3: 186; GEWL 1: 384.

[29] GA IV/3: 374; WLnmK. Though this is certainly how Fichte generally construes formal freedom throughout the *System of Ethics*, on a single occasion (in § 22, "Duties Regarding the Formal Freedom of All Rational Beings") he offers the following, eccentric definition of formal freedom: "The formal freedom of an individual consists in the continuous reciprocal interaction between his body, both as a tool and as a sensory organ, and the sensible world – an interaction that is determined and determinable only through the individual's freely sketched concept concerning the character of this reciprocal interaction" (GA I/5:263–64; SL 4: 276).

[30] GA I/5: 148; SL 4: 159.

[31] According to Fichte, "willing" involves an absolutely free transition from indeterminacy to determinacy, accompanied by a consciousness of this transition. This is why formal freedom cannot involve willing, and hence cannot involve any free choice: because no indeterminacy is present in the case of merely formal freedom. Hence, Fichte concludes that "the will is free [only] in the material sense of the term. Insofar as it wills, the I gives the object to itself, inasmuch as it selects one of several

Fichte and the Path from "Formal" to "Material" Freedom

assigned ends and then with respect to one's ultimate *ends* themselves. Unlike formal freedom, which every I must possess in full, material freedom exists in *degrees*, though Fichte himself does not always sufficiently emphasize or even acknowledge this point.

So what is material freedom? It is "the capacity for choosing" (*das Vermögen zu Wählen*); hence, "there is no will without free choice [*Willkür*]."[32] Material freedom is thus concerned with the *content* of one's representations and hence of one's choices and actions, either by choosing one among several naturally possible ends or by positing an end not given by nature at all. On Fichte's scheme, one first exercises one's freedom of choice almost unconsciously and then with ever greater self-awareness, which is to say, with consciousness of one's own original spontaneity or formal freedom, until, finally, "full material freedom" is obtained or at least approximated – at which point, as we shall see, *Willkür* disappears from the picture once again (or rather *would* disappear were one ever to obtain complete material freedom, that is, total independence from the Not-I).

In order to obtain material freedom, the individual I must first "tear itself away from itself," that is, from its ordinary thrall to objects; it must instead emulate that self-reverting activity that is the identifying feature of I-hood as such and consciously turn its attention back upon itself, thereby explicitly positing its own *activity* – indeed, positing *itself* as originally active or *formally free*. This, says Fichte, "is how the absoluteness of real action first becomes freedom proper, the absoluteness of absoluteness, the absolute power to make itself absolutely."[33] "Freedom proper" in this context means complete material freedom.

Unlike formal freedom, material freedom presupposes consciousness, and the reflection involved must be voluntary – that is, freely undertaken. It is obvious that only an *intellect* can be free in the material sense, because freedom of choice demands the ability to weigh options as well as some evaluative norm, concept, or idea, which can be grasped only cognitively. But *from where* is the materially free I supposed to obtain such a norm? On this point, Fichte is clear: it must generate it *from itself*, more specifically, it can obtain it only by means of voluntary *reflection* – first upon its own natural desires and then upon its own absolute being or formal freedom as

---

possible objects or facts. Insofar as the I intuits and comprehends indeterminacy, it elevates itself to a thought-of determinacy. In this way the object can still be given by the natural drive, i.e., as an object of longing, but not as an object of willing" (GA IV/1: 75).

[32] GA I/5: 148–49; SL 4: 159.   [33] GA I/5: 48 SL 4: 32.

an I, which is thereby transformed into "a norm, in accordance with which the intellect charges itself to determine itself freely."[34]

But intellect is not enough, because an intellect without practical power or *drive* cannot act efficaciously at all. Hence, even as the intellect imposes a rule upon itself and thus aspires to material freedom, "actual acting," notes Fichte, "always remains dependent upon absolute freedom [i.e., formal freedom]; and the acting of the free intellect is not actually determined by the rule or norm in question; and it is never mechanically necessary, since this would destroy any freedom of self-determination. Instead, all that is determined is the necessary concept of the intellect's acting."[35] We can, after all, always *fail* to act in accordance with a norm we have recognized. Or can we? This is a point to which we shall return.

5.4 Degrees of Material Freedom

Let us now consider what I will be referring to as the several "degrees" of material freedom, an account assembled in part from Fichte's examination of formal and material freedom in Parts One and Two of the *System of Ethics* and in part from his discussion of "the will in particular" in § 16 and of "the history of an empirical rational being" in § 17.[36]

1. *The Sub-Human Individual. Potential Material Freedom.* Where to start such a history? On the one hand, Fichte seems adamant that all human beings are at least indirectly aware of their formal freedom to some degree and thus are materially free as well; indeed, he insists that everyone has the capacity as well as the obligation to *become* materially free in what I will be calling the "full" sense of that term. On the other hand, he often laments that many – perhaps most – human beings are not actually free in the full material sense and some are not materially free even in the subordinate senses of that term. The solution to this puzzle is to conceive of human beings as inherently *capable* of full material freedom, while recognizing how far short of this goal most of us fall. Here, in any case, we will begin with what is, perhaps, a purely imaginary first stage of merely *potential* material freedom.

An individual at this first stage must at least be *conscious,* because that is a necessary condition for being a rational being or an individual I. At first,

---

[34] GA I/5: 63; SL 4: 42.   [35] GA I/5: 66; SL 4: 55.

[36] Though the following account adheres closely to Fichte's texts, it nevertheless conflicts with a few passages in which he appears to limit material freedom to the final stage of the series described here, that is, to the standpoint of morality or full material freedom. See, e.g., GA I/5: 132; SL 4: 139.

Fichte and the Path from "Formal" to "Material" Freedom 95

suggests Fichte, such an individual is conscious only of his natural drive and the objects thereof. Nevertheless, he remains free. As Fichte explains, "in the world of objects, I act only with natural force; this force is given to me through the natural drive and is nothing other than this natural drive itself within me – the causality of nature upon itself, a natural causality that is no longer under the control of a dead and unconscious nature, but a causality that I have brought under *my* (the intellect's) control by means of an act of free reflection."[37]

Though such a person may be described as "free" in a certain respect, he himself is entirely unaware of this and is, therefore, in his own eyes "no more than an animal."[38] Unlike all the other animals, however, this one has the *potential* to become more than an animal. This is because he is formally free, and because material freedom arises from consciousness of formal freedom, and because, as we shall see, every formally free I possesses an original "drive to freedom." It is therefore reasonable to expect that no "human being" could actually occupy this first standpoint – or at least, not occupy it for long.

2. *The Intelligent Animal. Actualization of Material Freedom.* A person at this level exercises his freedom of choice (and hence his material freedom) but without being explicitly aware that he is doing so or of the norm guiding his choice (the maxim of enjoyment or self-interest). The transition to this second stage occurs when an individual, in one of Fichte's favorite phrases, "*tears itself loose* from all that lies outside it and brings itself under its own control and thereby posits itself as absolutely self-sufficient."[39] He explains this difficult thought as follows: Because the *subject* engaged in this act of reflection is formally free, it is self-sufficient and dependent only upon itself. By reflecting upon a naturally given *object* of consciousness – namely, upon *itself* as a natural being – the reflecting subject takes up into itself this naturally given object, which thereby becomes something *for* the I, a *representation*, an object of *cognition*.

At first, the self-consciousness in question is simply an explicit awareness that one is, in fact, engaged in *making choices*.

> I can become aware of formal freedom just as well as I can become aware of material freedom. To be sure, I am not originally conscious of formal freedom ..., yet I can still become conscious of formal freedom after my self-consciousness has developed and after I have gained some experience. It

---

[37] GA I/5: 139; SL 4: 148. See too, GA I/5: 129; SL 4: 135. [38] GA I/5: 165; SL 4: 178.
[39] GA I/5: 128; SL 4: 133; emphasis added.

is simply by becoming conscious of formal freedom that I, as an intellect, first obtain the power to postpone natural satisfaction. The natural drive, however, will continue to express itself while its satisfaction is being postponed, and it will express itself in various ways. For this reason, I also acquire at the same time *the* specific ability to reflect upon the natural drive in the different ways it presents itself to me and to *choose among several possible satisfactions of this drive*. I choose to satisfy only one need, and I choose this with complete freedom of the will, for I choose with the consciousness that I am determining myself.[40]

Even if it is always the case that the stronger natural drive will prevail in such situations, Fichte insists that this drive would not exist *for me* at all if I had not exercised enough self-control to be able to reflect upon it and compare it with others. By forgoing immediate satisfaction and then comparing these competing desires, maintains Fichte, "I have still conditioned the object by my will through self-determination, and *my will remains materially free*."[41]

A clear description of the act of reflection that first makes possible material freedom occurs in Fichte's lectures on morality from the summer of 1796. Here he begins by distinguishing the spontaneous reflection of the I upon "objects" characteristic of what I have called the first level of material freedom from a new, second reflection upon that first reflection – a new reflection that has as its object the spontaneous activity of every I as such, that is, formal freedom. But he concludes that these two reflections are in fact, inseparable, a conclusion based upon his understanding of I-hood as a "self-reverting activity."

> By means of absolutely free reflection the I obtains mastery over itself. – Reflection is an action grounded purely and simply in the I; whereas the natural drive, which is what is reflected upon, is a passive state, something given and present without any contribution from free activity. *In order to arrive at a consciousness of freedom, therefore, a second reflection is required.* This second reflection, which is directed at the reflecting subject, abstracts completely from the object; nothing appears within this second reflection but pure activity, and this alone is posited as the genuine I. (These two reflections are not separate in nature; on the contrary, they are one and the same action; for this self-reverting activity is precisely what is required [by the *Wissenschaftslehre*].) Here subject and object coincide, and thus there arises an intuition.[42]

The intuition in question is, presumably, one of the I's own formal freedom. But *how* and *why* such a reflection occurs is, on Fichte's account,

---

[40] GA I/5:151; SL 4: 162.   [41] GA I/5: 151; SL 4: 162; emphasis added.
[42] GA IV/1: 59; emphasis added.

Fichte and the Path from "Formal" to "Material" Freedom   97

quite inexplicable. In other words, this is something that occurs spontaneously, "through absolute freedom"; "it happens because it happens."[43]

In the preceding case, the stronger desire always prevailed over the weaker ones, but this need not always occur, for we sometimes employ our power of reproductive imagination to recall desires not currently present and add them to our reflective mix. At the same time, we may also become clearly aware of the maxim guiding our choice among these desires – the maxim of happiness or enjoyment (a.k.a. "the maxim of self-interest"), now raised to the level of *enlightened* self-interest. In this way, one becomes capable not merely of choosing but of choosing *prudentially*.

Such a person has become, according to Fichte, "an intelligent animal."[44] Such an intelligent animal is unquestionably free in the material sense of the term, because he is clearly engaged in making free *choices*. One of the chief advantages of this new account of freedom over Reinhold's, according to Fichte, is its explicit recognition that "freedom of will – which is not the same as self-sufficiency – is present without morality."[45]

3. *The Rebel Without a Cause. Blind Material Freedom.* A person at this third level of material freedom has consciously reflected upon his formal freedom and, unlike those at the lower levels, has become aware of the connection between his formal freedom and his own "pure drive" for self-sufficiency, which is the *original expression* of the former. Once again, transition to this third level is supposed to be accomplished by a new act of reflection, one in which one becomes aware for the first time of oneself as possessing an original drive for independence. As Fichte puts it:

> If a human being is left to himself and is fettered neither by the example of his age nor by a ruinous philosophy, it is then to be expected that he will become conscious of this drive to absolute self-sufficiency, which is always enduring and active within him. He then raises himself to a completely different kind of freedom; for though he [was] formally free within the domain of the maxim just described [viz., the maxim of happiness or self-interest], materially he [was] wholly and completely dependent upon the objects of nature. He [had] no other end than the enjoyment they afford.[46]

For the person we are now considering, this is the extent of his "new reflection." Hence, the only standard of choice and behavior he can infer from his newly discovered drive to self-sufficiency is that he should actively *resist* being determined by anything except his own will. Hence, as Fichte

---

[43] GA I/5: 165; SL 4: 178–9.   [44] GA I/5: 167; SL 4: 180.   [45] GA IV/1: 77; VM.
[46] GA I/5: 170; SL 4: 184.

puts it, the maxim of his behavior would be that of *"unrestricted and lawless dominion over everything outside us."*[47] For such an *Eigenwilliger*, it just *happens to be the case* that he possesses a blind will for independence from external determination.

This stage marks an obvious advance on the previous one, inasmuch as one is no longer acting in accord with the norm of self-interested happiness. On the contrary, our rebel without a cause is willing to sacrifice his own personal happiness to the urgings of his blind and lawless will for self-sufficiency and dominion.[48] Like the truly moral person, such a rebel determines the object of his willing spontaneously from within himself, solely by means of what he considers to be his own "heroic" will (albeit as determined arbitrarily by pure *Willkür*), rather than receiving it from nature. Hence, notes Fichte, "with respect to its form, there is no difference between this and the genuinely moral way of thinking."[49] Nevertheless, he cautions that such a character is "very immoral," for there is a vast difference in terms of content, or *what* is willed in each case.[50]

4. *The Moral Standpoint. Full Material Freedom.* The preceding degrees or levels of material freedom are all incomplete and insufficient in comparison to the kind of material freedom associated with the highest level of reflection. At the second level the agent was indeed aware of his formal freedom to some extent and of his material freedom as well, insofar as he was at least vaguely aware of choosing and willing in accord with the naturally given norm of self-interested happiness. But from the first and second standpoints one fails to recognize that formal freedom must express itself as a drive to the self-sufficiency of reason as such on the part of the individual. Instead, it is associated entirely with *Willkür*, or freedom of choice. In contrast, an individual at the immediately preceding third level of reflection *is* aware of his full capacity for material freedom, that is, of his pure drive for self-sufficiency, but his awareness remains defective and blind, because he fails to understand that this is the drive of *I-hood as such* (or of the "pure I") and not just a contingent feature of his own heroic individual character. This is why he fails to grasp the necessary connection between formal freedom and the moral law – between being an I and acting dutifully.

An agent in possession of full material freedom is responsible not merely for freely choosing a course of action from all of those offered by the natural

---

[47] GA I/5: 172; SL 4: 186.   [48] GA I/5: 175; SL 4: 190.   [49] GA I/5: 173; SL 4: 187.
[50] An additional, special danger associated with such a "rebellious" mode of thinking is that it accustoms us to regarding our materially free actions as especially "heroic" or "meritorious" rather than as moral obligations. See GA I/5: 176; SL 4: 191.

Fichte and the Path from "Formal" to "Material" Freedom 99

drive, he determines this choice on the basis of a norm he himself produces simply by reflecting energetically upon his own formal freedom – or rather, upon the pure drive that ensues from the same.[51] In contrast to the situation at the lower levels of material freedom, where one is responsible for one's *choice* but not for the maxim that guides it, a person at this highest level of material freedom is responsible for imposing a norm (the moral law) as well. As Fichte puts it, "a human being has only to raise to clear consciousness this drive to absolute self-sufficiency – which, when it operates as a blind drive produces a very immoral character – and then, as was shown earlier, *simply by means of that very act of reflection*, this same drive *will transform itself within him* into an absolutely commanding law."[52]

Limitation is specification, determination, and this is the immediate consequence of one's new reflection upon one's own formal freedom, which is now determined as and reveals itself to be a nonnatural, and hence "pure" drive for self-sufficiency. Indeed, this is precisely how one ordinally becomes *clearly and distinctly* aware of one's formal freedom in everyday life (as opposed to transcendental philosophy): namely, through *conscientious awareness of specific, concrete duties*. On Fichte's view, the pure drive (and hence formal freedom) never expresses itself *as such* within ordinary empirical consciousness at all; instead, it is present there only in the form of the mixed "ethical drive," which includes both the pure and natural drives and which "does not manifest itself as a drive that aims at absolute independence, but as one directed toward determinate actions. These actions, however, can be shown to lie in the series [of actions] just described, if this drive is raised to clear consciousness and if the actions that are demanded are more closely examined."[53] To become fully aware of one's formal freedom as an I is thus *the same thing* as to submit oneself entirely to the moral law.

> When you think of yourself as free, you are required to think of your freedom under a law; and when you think of this law, you are required to think of yourself as free, for your freedom is presupposed by this law, which announces itself as the *law of freedom* . . .. Freedom does not follow from the law, no more than the law follows from freedom. These are not two

---

[51] "The moral law is by no means derived from any objective determinacy of the drive, but solely from the form of a drive as such, considered as the drive of an I – that is, the form of absolute self-sufficiency and independence from everything outside the I" (GA I/5: 108; SL 4: 108–109.

[52] GA I/5: 176; SL 4: 191; emphasis added.

[53] GA I/5: 192–93; SL 4: 152. Like formal freedom itself, "the pure drive is something that lies outside of all consciousness; it is nothing but a transcendental explanatory ground of something in consciousness" (GA I/5: 193; SL 4: 152).

thoughts, one of which can be thought to depend upon the other; instead; this is one and the same thought.[54]

When I view myself from this standpoint, "I am *for myself* – i.e., before my own consciousness – only an instrument, a tool of the moral law, and by no means the end of the same."[55] For such a "tool," no potential action is morally neutral, nor does it permit itself any "moral holidays." From this, Fichte does not hesitate to conclude that full material freedom would imply the *abolition* of freedom of choice, inasmuch as "the moral law does not leave any leeway at all for arbitrary choice [*Willkür*]."[56] The maxim (or better, the law) that governs the will of a person at this, highest level of reflection is simply this: "do always and in every case what duty demands, and do so *because duty commands it.*"[57]

This is why freedom of choice, *Willkür* (and hence material freedom itself, insofar as *Willkür* is essential to the same), threatens to disappear at this highest level of reflection. In Fichte's view, "it is absolutely impossible and contradictory that anyone with a clear consciousness of his duty at the moment he acts *should*, in good faith, *resolve not to do his duty*, that he should rebel against the law, refusing to obey it, and taking it as his maxim not to do his duty, *because* it is his duty. Such a maxim," he says, "is diabolical; the concept of the devil is self-contradictory and thus annuls itself."[58] But this does not altogether eliminate any further role for material freedom, for, as he also reminds us, "it is up to our freedom whether such consciousness *continues* or becomes *obscure*" – and the resolve to *retain* one's awareness of duty is just as spontaneous and just as inexplicable as the original attainment of full material freedom.[59]

The irony here is palpable. In freely raising oneself to the level of full material freedom and in choosing to will and to act in accord with the moral law, one renounces any further use of one's power of free choice, which has hitherto been treated as an essential component of willing and hence of material freedom itself: "It is precisely by means of this disappearance and annihilation of one's entire individuality that everyone becomes a pure presentation of the moral law in the world of sense and thus becomes a 'pure I,' in the proper sense of the term; and this occurs by means of free choice and self-determination."[60]

This, anyway, would seem to be the ideal case. In fact, no finite I could ever acquire material freedom in the full Fichtean sense, for in that case it

---

[54] GA I/5: 64–65; SL 4:53; emphasis added.   [55] GA I/5: 230; SL 4:225.
[56] GA I/5: 237; SL 4:264.   [57] GA I/5: 176; SL 4:191.   [58] GA I/5: 176; SL 4: 191.
[59] GA I/5: 177; SL 4: 183; emphasis added).   [60] GA I/5: 230–32; SL 4: 256.

Fichte and the Path from "Formal" to "Material" Freedom   101

would overcome those original limitations that are, according to the *Wissenschaftslehre,* necessary conditions not only for finite individuality but even for I-hood as such. Moreover, as Fichte acknowledges, the *material content* of our willing, even at this stage, has to be provided by the natural drive, and thus it might well seem that nothing is left for us but formal freedom.[61] His solution to this problem is well known. Though I can never actually *achieve* full material freedom, I can nevertheless move closer and closer to it. How? By choosing, among all the courses of action naturally available to me, the one action (and Fichte is supremely confident there is always only one[62]) that lies in that series of actions, which, if continued infinitely, would indeed achieve my necessary goal of full material freedom and independence from nature.[63] Hence, humanity's true *Bestimmung* is not full material freedom after all but an *endless striving* for the same.

5.5 Consciousness of Material Freedom

I posit myself as materially free[64] only when I am *conscious* of undergoing a self-engendered transition from indeterminacy to determinacy, that is, when I am actually engaging in *willing*, because *"an unfree will is an absurdity."*[65] Hence, in order to become aware of my material freedom, I must, first of all, discover myself to be "undetermined." Second, I must be aware not only of my natural drive and the potential objects of the same but also of something else, something that prompts (but does not compel) me to reflect upon my formal freedom. Fichte calls this the "drive to freedom." But even this is not enough. In order to become conscious of my material freedom, I must also *actually engage* in a free act of self-determination. Let us consider these prerequisites more closely:

---

[61] "This, to be sure, does not annul the drive to absolute, material freedom; but it does annul completely any causality of the latter. In all reality, all that remains is formal freedom" (GA I/5: 140; SL 4: 149.).

[62] "At each moment there is something that is suitable for our ethical vocation; this something is at the same time demanded by the natural drive" (GA I/5: 142; SL 4:151). For further discussion on this topic, see Breazeale (2012).

[63] "It is only insofar as I posit such a [pure] drive that I posit myself as an I" (GA I/5: 140; SL 4: 149). Hence, "the sole determining ground of the material of our actions is [or rather ought to be] ridding ourselves of our dependence upon nature, regardless of the fact that the independence that is thereby demanded is never achieved" (GA I/5: 141; SL 4: 149).

[64] "Freedom is not only formal, it is also material. One can be conscious of both sorts of freedom, or conscious only of formal freedom" (GA IV/1: 77; VM).

[65] GA I/5:148; SL 4: 159.

Indeterminacy of the I. Insofar as I have the power or capacity to act, I must find myself to be undetermined, because Fichte understands action as precisely *self-determination*. More specifically, I must discover myself to be "hovering" between possible determinations. This, according to Fichte, is where my actual perception of my material freedom begins: with my awareness of a manifold of possible self-determinations.

The Pure Drive to Freedom. Consciousness of indeterminacy is consciousness of several possible ways of determining oneself, but the natural drive is unable to produce any awareness of oneself as undetermined in this sense. At best, it could produce a blind propensity to allow one's freedom to be determined by one's natural drive, but this is not something of which one could be conscious. Hence, in order to explain the possibility of the I's becoming explicitly conscious of its formal freedom (and thereby acquiring material freedom), *we must posit a drive to do just that* – a drive "directed toward the conditions for the consciousness of this freedom."[66] As we have just observed, this condition involves consciousness of the "indeterminacy" of the I, which cannot be produced by the natural drive. Therefore, concludes Fichte, "there would have to be a drive to determine oneself without any reference to the natural drive and *contrary to it*, a drive to derive the material of one's action not from the natural drive but from oneself."[67] Because this is the drive that is supposed to make it possible for us to become conscious of our freedom, Fichte calls it "*a drive for freedom, simply for freedom's sake.*"[68] Because the I is always already formally free, the kind of freedom aimed at by this pure drive can only be "material freedom"[69] – and that freedom "for the sake of which" such material freedom is pursued is "formal freedom."

This "pure drive" to freedom is immanent within the I itself and posited in opposition to the natural drive. Indeed, the pure drive, the drive for self-sufficiency on the part of the individual I, is just an *expression* of the original

---

[66] GA I/5: 132; SL 4: 139.   [67] GA I/5: 132; SL 4: 139.

[68] GA I/5: 132; SL 4: 139. Elsewhere Fichte refers to this same drive as "the drive for absolute self-sufficiency" (GA I/5: 135; SL 4: 142) or simply "the pure drive" (GA I/5: 134; SL 4: 141). But he is careful to note that this same pure drive "is something that lies outside of all consciousness; it is nothing but a transcendental explanatory ground of something in consciousness" (GA I/5: 102–93; SL 4: 152).

[69] Fichte makes this clear when he refers to the drive in question as the "drive to absolute, material freedom" (GA I/5: 140; SL 4: 149). With the inexplicable upsurge of formal freedom, a "new force" is introduced in addition to the forces of nature, namely, that of the intellect, which, by bringing nature "under the sway of the concept," establishes the formal freedom of the I, even if what it brings about turns out to be the same thing nature would have brought about on its own. In the case of material freedom, however, "not only does a new force come upon the scene but there is a completely new series of actions, with respect to the content of the same. Not only does the intellect engage from now on in efficacious action, but it also accomplishes something completely different from what nature would ever have accomplished" (GA I/5: 132; SL 4: 139; emphasis added).

Fichte and the Path from "Formal" to "Material" Freedom 103

spontaneity and formal freedom of self-posited I-hood. Becoming aware of this pure drive is the same thing as reflecting upon one's own formal freedom, and therefore an I that has become aware of its pure drive *always* finds itself in a state of indeterminacy, hovering between the demands of its pure and natural drives – or, if you prefer, between its formal freedom and its original limitations as a finite individual.

The Resolve to Act. Discovering oneself to be indeterminate is not sufficient to acquaint oneself with one's formal freedom. For this, one must *exercise* one's material freedom to determine oneself, thereby resolving the indeterminacy in question. That is to say, one must engage in *willing*, which means one must make a *free choice*; for, as Fichte again reminds us, "the will is always a power of choosing . . . . There is no *Wille* without *Willkür*. That is to say, one calls the will *Willkür* when one attends to the feature just indicated: namely, that it necessarily chooses among several equally possible actions."[70] When I become conscious of my freedom in this manner, I am both the determining subject and the object determined. Hence, my act of self-determination is in this case accompanied by something that did not accompany it before: an explicit consciousness – indeed a concept – of my own formal freedom as an I. And this is precisely why freedom can never be grasped from a third-person perspective. One must, so to speak, *act* freely in order to become aware *that* one is free.

At the lowest level of material freedom, Fichte emphasized the necessity of "tearing oneself away" from the object of one's desire and positing it for oneself as an object of cognition. At the next level, he spoke about "tearing oneself loose" from immediate determination by natural desire by freely subjecting the same to a naturally given norm (namely, happiness or pleasure). Here, a still higher level of material freedom, one is again admonished to "tear oneself loose" – but this time not from merely hovering between opposing determinations of the natural drive. Instead, one now opposes one's natural drives *in toto* to the demands of the pure drive for freedom itself and then seeks to discover a natural drive or object in harmony with the latter. Thus, it is only by means of the *deed itself* that one becomes aware of one's formal freedom: "that is, by spontaneously tearing oneself loose from the state of wavering – hovering between several possible self-determinations – and by positing for oneself some determinate end, simply because one posits it for oneself, especially if the end in question runs counter to all one's inclinations and is nevertheless chosen for duty's sake."[71]

---

[70] GA I/5: 148–49; SL 4: 159.   [71] GA I/5: 131; SL 4: 137.

5.6 Movement from Lower to Higher Degrees of Material Freedom

Though there is an undeniably teleological flavor to Fichte's account of the stages of material freedom, no necessity governs the move from one stage to another – other than "moral necessity." Fichte freely concedes that there is nothing *stopping* anyone from remaining at one of the lower standpoints (or even regressing from a higher to a lower one). But, at the same time, there is nothing *preventing* anyone from spontaneously elevating himself or herself to a higher standpoint and ultimately to that of morality. Indeed, he claims, this is precisely what everyone *ought* to do, inasmuch as "a determinate consciousness of duty is itself a duty,"[72] and if one fails to acquire such a consciousness, it is no one's fault but his *own*.[73]

So why does one remain at a lower standpoint? Why do some people achieve an approximation of full material freedom and others not? To this question Fichte appears to provide two rather different answers (though perhaps not completely incompatible ones): On the one hand, he simply confesses that this is something that cannot, in principle, ever be explained – whether by the philosopher or anyone else.

> There is something incomprehensible here, and it cannot be otherwise, since we are now standing at the very boundary of all comprehensibility: namely, the doctrine of freedom as it applies to the empirical subject. So long as I do not yet occupy a higher standpoint of reflection, this standpoint does not exist for me, and hence I cannot have a concept of what I am supposed to do before I actually do it. Yet it nevertheless remains the case that this is what I absolutely ought to do. . . .. The situation could not be otherwise, for an act of freedom is purely and simply because it is, and it is what is absolute primary, something that cannot be connected to anything else and cannot be explained on the basis of anything else.[74]

Reflection upon the drive for absolute self-sufficiency occurs, according to Fichte, "through a special act of spontaneity." Despite the baleful influence of society and false philosophies, some individuals really do succeed in accomplishing such an act, however inexplicable this must appear.[75] This is a thesis that appears frequently in Fichte's early work, in

---

[72] GA I/5:178; SL 4: 193.

[73] Of a person who remains at a lower standpoint of material freedom, Fichte writes: "He absolutely ought to have raised himself to a higher level of reflection, and he also could have done this. He is to blame for not doing this" (GA I/5: 168; SL 4: 181).

[74] GA I/5: 168; SL 4: 181–182.

[75] "It also remains true that, in spite of all hinderances, actual individuals do manage to raise themselves above these hinderances. How they do this is inexplicable; i.e., it can be explained only on the basis of freedom. By analogy with an outstanding degree of intellectual capability, one

Fichte and the Path from "Formal" to "Material" Freedom   105

his essay on "Stimulating and Increasing the Pure Interest in Truth," for example, where he declares that "I was a machine and could have remained one. Motivated by myself by means of my own strength, I have made myself into an autonomous being"[76] – and I have done so "not by means of any *transition,* but by means of a *leap.*"[77] Indeed, at one point he goes so far as to claim that one can elevate oneself to material freedom only by means of a *miracle* – one that has to be performed *by, for,* and *upon* oneself.[78]

Many interpreters reject the preceding account as unconvincing and implausible and call attention instead to those passages, in the *System of Ethics* and elsewhere, that appear to provide a very different, more naturalistic account of how we become aware of our freedom and succeed in occupying the moral standpoint – not by our own bootstraps, as it were, but thanks to the upbringing and moral education provided by our parents, our teachers, and the larger society of which we are a part, inasmuch as "morality develops itself freely and by means of purely rational education in the context of social intercourse and solely from the human heart .... It cannot be artificially produced by means of theoretical conviction or anything similar."[79] Accordingly, Fichte devotes a considerable portion of Part III of the *System of Ethics* to discussions of moral education and the role therein of the family and society. "It is," he writes, "through education in the widest sense, that is, through the influence of society in general upon us, that we are first cultivated in a manner that makes it possible for us to employ our freedom. If we do not raise ourselves above it, then the matter rests with that

could call the capacity in question the genius for virtue" (GA I/5: 171; SL 4: 185). See also GA I/3: 33; BEIW 8: 343.

[76] GA I/3: 90; BEIW 8: 352.   [77] GA I/2: 427; GEWL 1: 298. See also GA I/5: 446; AP 5: 230.

[78] "Before he can freely tear himself loose, however, he must first be free. But it is precisely his freedom itself that is fettered; the very force through which he is supposed to help himself is allied against him. No balance is established here; instead, there is [only] the weight of his nature, which is what holds him in check, and there is no counterweight from the side of the moral law. It is indeed true that a human being absolutely ought to step onto the other side of the scale and decide this conflict; and it is also true that he actually possesses within himself the force to give himself as much weight as is necessary, up to infinity, in order to outweigh his own inertia and that he can, at any moment, release this force from himself by putting pressure on himself, through sheer will. But how is he ever supposed to arrive at this act of willing, and how does he first become able to place such pressure on himself? Such a state [of willing] by no means emerges from the state he is in, which instead yields the opposite state, one that holds him in check and fetters him. It is also true that this initial impulse [*Anstoß*] is not supposed to emerge from his present state, nor can it do so, but instead it emerges absolutely from his self-activity. But where in his state is there a place from which he could produce this force? – Absolutely nowhere. Viewed in purely natural terms, it is absolutely impossible that a human being should be able to help himself; he cannot improve at all in this way. Only a miracle could save him – a miracle, moreover, which he himself would have to perform" (GA I/5: 184; SL 4: 201). See also GA I/5: 187–88; SL 4: 204–5.

[79] GA I/5: 304; SL 4: 349.

106   DANIEL BREAZEALE

cultivation we have received from society …. This does not abolish the possibility of obtaining merit on one's own, but such a possibility arises only on a higher level."[80]

Such remarks, however, are almost invariably followed by impassioned exhortations regarding every individual's capacity and sole responsibility for striving for complete material freedom and his capacity to raise himself to the standpoint of morality *spontaneously and purely on his own,* to freely undertake a complete "rebirth."[81] So far as I can determine, Fichte himself was unaware of any tension between these two accounts of how one acquires full material freedom, and perhaps there is no tension here after all. Perhaps this is simply an acknowledgement of the fact that a human being is not born fully human but must first be "cultivated" – or "civilized" – by his parents and society before he has the intellectual skills necessary to engage in the kind of free "reflection" upon his own formal freedom that is, according to Fichte, an indispensable requirement for material freedom. Only thereby can anyone spontaneously enact the requisite "miracle" of free reflection.

5.7   Freedom of Reflection

Let us now turn to an issue that is implicit in Fichte's discussion of how we become aware of our formal freedom but not explicitly thematized: namely, the character of those "reflections" that are supposed to raise us, first, from merely formal to material freedom, and then, from one level of the latter to the next. However vital the role of acculturation and education may be in this process, Fichte is consistent in his character-ization of such reflection as "spontaneous" or free" – *not* in the same sense in which those *unconscious and involuntary* reflections of the I described in the foundational portion of the system are *formally* free from external determination, but rather in the same sense that *materially* free actions are free: namely, voluntary and consciously undertaken. According to Fichte, "it is by means of free activity that we determine ourselves to reflection."[82] A person engaged in such free reflection can say to himself: I could have been determined by inclinations and impressions received from nature, "but this is not what I have *willed.*

---

[80] GA I/5: 170; SL 4: 184.   [81] GA I/5: 446; AP 5: 230.
[82] GA I/5: 131; SL 4: 131. Each act of reflection is "the starting-point of an absolutely new series, and one cannot say where these acts of reflection come from, since they do not come from anywhere at all" (GA I/5: 168; SL 4: 182). Such a reflection can therefore be described as "an act that is itself a new beginning" (GA I/5: 178; SL 4: 193) – or even as a "rebirth" (GA I/5: 446; AP 5: 230).

Fichte and the Path from "Formal" to "Material" Freedom 107

I have torn myself free. On my own, I have directed my inquires in a direction that I decided by myself."[83]

Though Fichte never explicitly identifies the kind of "absolute freedom" that is involved in such reflection, the answer seems obvious. This can only be an exercise of *material* freedom, because it involves a deliberate *choice* to turn one's attention away from objects and to focus it squarely upon oneself, or rather upon what makes one an "I" in the first place. Hence Fichte's somewhat paradoxical conclusion: In order to become conscious of one's material freedom, one must first reflect consciously upon one's formal freedom; but it would appear that such a reflection already *presupposes* material freedom. Maybe this is why he frequently noted that the occurrence of such a reflection is simply *incomprehensible* – both to the natural historian of morals and to the transcendental philosopher.

5.8 Can Material and Formal Freedom Really Be Separated?

As noted, Fichte's account of how we actually become aware of our freedom presents a puzzle: It would appear that we already have to be materially free in order to engage in reflection upon our formal freedom. But consciousness of formal freedom is, in turn, supposed to be a condition for the possibility of material freedom, because only a formally free being has the *capacity* for material freedom. Indeed, one might say that material freedom is nothing but the *realization* of formal freedom.[84] This suggests that any attempt to separate formal and material freedom must fail. Yes, they can certainly be *distinguished*, but neither is actually possible without the other. This would appear to be the point of the previously cited passage from his lectures on morals, in which Fichte observes that "these two reflections" – an unconscious one, associated with formal freedom, and a conscious one, associated with material freedom – "are not separate in nature; on the contrary, they are one and the same action; for this self-reverting activity is precisely what is required [by the *Wissenschaftslehre*]."[85] Despite Fichte's "genetic account" of material freedom as arising from reflection upon formal freedom,[86] it seems to be the case that only a being who is already in some sense materially free can engage in such reflection in the first place.

---

[83] GA I/3: 87; BEIW 8: 349; emphasis added. As Kien-How Goh has observed regarding this move on Fichte's part, "freedom of choice is not abandoned, but recast in terms of the freedom of reflection" (2012, 441.)

[84] "Formal freedom is a capacity – the capacity for material freedom" (Wood [2016a, 70]).

[85] GA IV/1: 58.

[86] For an insightful discussion of Fichte's "genetic model of freedom," see Ch. 2 of Owen Ware's (2020).

It follows that no actual I or human being can be free in a merely formal sense. Everyone, according to Fichte, has some awareness, however dim, of his own agency and even of the moral law itself and hence some consciousness, however obscure, of his own formal freedom, and hence some degree, no matter how small, of material freedom. It also follows that no finite I will ever attain complete material freedom, because that would coincide with the abolition of I-hood itself.

Formal and material freedom should therefore be viewed as two ends of a continuum, every point of which contains both. Indeed, the relationship between formal and material freedom is similar to that between the pure I, or "I as intellectual intuition," with which the *Grundlage* begins, and the I as Idea [*Idee*], with which it concludes, as described by Fichte in the second introduction of 1797. The former, he says, is nothing but the "the form of I-hood, self-reverting acting." Such a pure I posits itself spontaneously and unconditionally, but it is only *formally* free and can be grasped as such only by the philosopher. (Though every actual I must be formally free, no actual I is *merely* such.) The Idea of the I, in contrast, is shared "by every natural, albeit completely cultivated human being." This is the Idea of a rational being that has "completely succeeded in exhibiting within itself universal reason and has actually become rational through and through, and is nothing but rational." This is obviously just another way of describing what we have been calling "full material freedom," which, though it is indeed "the ultimate goal of reason's striving," is also "nothing but an Idea," and hence "only something to which we ought to draw infinitely nearer."[87]

---

[87] See GA I/4: 260; ZwE I: 515–16. I am grateful to Anthony Bruno for calling this parallel to my attention.

CHAPTER 6

Fichte on the Content of Conscience

Dean Moyar

At the center of Fichte's *System of Ethics* is a theory of conscience that threatens to render the account of ethical content in the second half of the book either superfluous or incoherent. Fichte argues that without an absolute *formal* criterion for the agent's conviction that an action is her duty, no moral action at all would be possible. This criterion is the feeling of conscience at the conclusion of practical deliberation, an ultimate form of moral consciousness that can have no higher judge above it.

> *Conscience as Absolute Formal Criterion* (*CAFC*): Each individual must judge on her own the action that in each case is her duty, and the feeling of conscience is an infallible authority of the correctness of her belief in her duty.

After laying out this theory of conscience, Fichte claims for philosophy the ability to provide an account of the actions that conscience *would* approve. This is a theory of the necessary content of conscience (NCC).

> *Necessary Content of Conscience* (*NCC*): There are duties that obligate every agent and thus necessarily inform the judgments of conscience.

Notice that "inform" here is intentionally vague. Figuring out just how that content informs the functioning of conscience is the issue of this chapter. The claims of absolute form and necessary content are not contradictory, but the potential for conflict is clear.[1] This results in the

> *Two Criteria Problem*: The judgment of an individual's conscience may conflict with the necessary content of duty.

If we have a necessary theory of duties, are we then able to override the verdicts of this or that individual's conscience, which may be telling her something

---

[1] Allen Wood writes of "a conspicuous tension between the 'scientific' account of ethics Fichte provides in his system of duties and the situated choice represented by the conscientious conviction of the ordinary agent" (2016a, 244). Bacin (2017, 320) writes of a "Spannungsverhältnis."

109

quite different? Is a judgment of conscience contrary to these duties ruled out a priori? If so, in what sense is conscience really an absolute criterion?

Though the issue is not always framed in these terms, recent discussions of Fichte's ethics do address and attempt to ameliorate the potential conflict between the two criteria. One strategy is to deny that there is a conflict on the grounds that conscience does not itself determine one's duty. If conscience is a subject-directed activity distinct from the object-directed activity of deliberation, then there need be no conflict of conscience's authority and the bindingness of objective content. This is the strategy of the recent deflationary account of conscience by Michelle Kosch. I argue that Kosch is wrong to deny conscience a duty-identifying function. Her account succeeds, however, in calling much-needed attention to the problem of determining just what Fichte's capacity of reflective judgment does in moral deliberation. Fichte could argues that reflective judgment, as the epistemic faculty operative prior to the final verdict of conscience, is bound to the necessary content (NCC). But Fichte makes a striking split between the perspectives of the ordinary agent and the transcendental philosophy that bars the agent from appealing to the transcendental account. I argue that Fichte's position is untenable, and I turn to two further Fichtean strategies for defusing the Two Criteria Problem. One strategy is to argue that the general duties are like prima facie duties for a moderate moral particularist, and that the final judgment of conscience can incorporate them. This view remains vulnerable to Hegelian criticism, leaving to the Fichtean a final defense that stresses the duty of communication as mediating the immediacy of conscience and the general content of duty.

6.1 The Absolute Criterion

Fichte gives two arguments for conscience: one that deduces conscience as a "higher capacity for feeling" that expresses the ethical drive, and the other based on the requirements of moral deliberation. The first account is the result of Fichte's extended deduction of individual rational psychology on the basis of the drive to self-sufficiency. That account concludes with the claim that conscience is "the immediate consciousness of that without which there is no consciousness whatsoever: the consciousness of our higher nature and of our absolute freedom" (GA I/5: 138; SL 4: 147). There is no economical way to assess this first argument, which would require diving deep into Fichte's complex account of the drives.[2]

---

[2] See Owen Ware's account of the drives in his contribution to this volume.

I therefore set it aside here, though I will bring it back into view in Section 6.3 when I discuss Fichte's argument for conscience's content. I focus instead on the second, "deliberative" argument for conscience, which treats conscience primarily as a belief that concludes a process of practical reasoning. Fichte argues for conscience as the "absolute criterion for the correctness of my conviction concerning a duty" (GA I/5: 153; SL 4: 165) by trying to show that without such a formal absolute criterion, duty would be impossible. Why does Fichte argue for conscience as a *formal* criterion? He is drawing inspiration from Kant's argument for the formality of the moral law, from Kant's argument that acting for the sake of duty, of form, and of lawfulness is what gives an action moral worth. In Fichte's case, one acts because one has achieved the certainty of conscience, the subjective unity that in his view is an even purer form than Kantian lawfulness.[3]

Having already established acting on your certain belief as the principle of morality, Fichte asks: How can I know at any given moment that I am not mistaken in my conviction of my duty? Fichte claims that I can only be certain in acting if I believe that it is impossible that I could ever consider my belief to be wrong. His initial solution is to require that I situate my belief about a duty in the system of all my possible beliefs. In other words, he suggests that I can use the "web of belief" to drastically reduce the possibility of radical error in my individual beliefs. Through this move to a kind of coherence condition on one's beliefs as the criterion of correctness, Fichte seems to have solved his problem. What criterion do I need outside of agreement with my other beliefs, and isn't this exercise of establishing consistency with my other beliefs a plausible way to think of what I actually do when I "consult my conscience"?

Fichte's next move is to object that the whole system of my convictions can only be given at the moment of decision through a punctual representation of my belief system. Because at the moment of specific action I need a second-order representation of my belief system, and because at any moment I could mistakenly characterize all my beliefs, I am not much better off with coherence than I was with my original belief. Fichte concludes from the unreliability of such a second-order representation that without an *immediate* absolute criterion, morality would depend on a coincidence. I would either act relying on good luck or I would not act at all, caught in an uncertain wavering about what my duty really is.

---

[3] See, for instance, his statement of the moral law: "do what you can now regard with conviction as a duty, and do it solely because you have convinced yourself that it is a duty" (GA I/5: 152; SL 4: 163).

Fichte is not arguing that we need a special second-order criterion that is a more inclusive belief about duty, for that would also be unreliable and would therefore start a regress to further judgments. Rather, he argues that there must be an immediate criterion to prevent, rather than stop, the regress in judgments that would start with the move to a second-order representation of my beliefs. Conscience is a final arbiter that puts to an end further deliberation and further doubt through a feeling of certainty that attends the right first-order belief about duty.

At this point in the argument Fichte introduces a crucial subsidiary argument: because conscience is not an epistemic faculty it must rely on the theoretical faculty to deliver the material of judgment. The epistemic capacity is reflective judgment, which delivers to the practical faculty a possible action for approval or disapproval. Fichte writes, "But since the ethical law is not a cognitive capacity [*Erkenntnisvermögen*], it cannot according to its essence establish this belief through itself, but rather the ethical law expects this conviction to be found and determined through the cognitive capacity, through reflective judgment; and then the ethical law authorizes the conviction, and makes it into a duty to stand by it" (GA I/5: 154; SL 4: 165). Reflective judgment is the process of forming a purposive concept, a *Zweckbegriff*, that embodies a proposed action. I represent the proposed action in various ways, with multiple permutations of the various relevant factors. Conscience assents when "the drive to knowledge and the knowledge fall together; the original *I* and the actual will now be in harmony" (GA I/5: 155; SL 4: 166–67). When reflective judgment arrives at an action that accords with this condition of consonance, a feeling of harmony arises to signal the concord of the source of all reasons (the original *I*) with this particular belief (i.e., with the particular action).

How exactly does Fichte separate the formal and material (practical and theoretical, nonepistemic and epistemic) elements of deliberation? One clue comes in his argument that the opposing view is one that includes in the ethical law theoretical propositions with immediate practical force. Recall that in the background of this argument is the idea that one must reach conviction, the certainty that Fichte links to subjective unity, through one's own cognitive capacities. He writes,

> The moral law . . . expects [this conviction] to be found and determined by the power of cognition – the power of reflecting judgment – and only then does the moral law authorize this conviction and make it a duty to stick with it. The opposite claim would imply a material duty of belief, i.e., a theory according to which certain theoretical propositions would be immediately contained in the moral law, propositions which one would then have to

consider to be true without any further examination and regardless of whether or not one could convince oneself of them theoretically.... [T]he moral law is purely formal and must receive its content from elsewhere; but *that* something is its content: the ground for this can lie only in the moral law itself. (GA I/5: 154–55; SL 4: 165–66)

Fichte claims that this "would open the door to deception [*Betrügerei*] and to all manner of oppression and subjugation of the conscience" (GA I/5: 155; SL 4: 165–66). There would be certain principles by which I am obligated regardless of my affirmation of them through rational deliberation. Fichte holds that a material duty of belief is wrong because it does not allow the agent to bring his *theoretical* faculties to bear on the principles directly or to know how to adjudicate their competing claims. Such material duties cut short deliberation by supplying conclusions ready-made, as it were.

The question we need to ask is whether or not Fichte's own sets of duties, the necessary content of conscience (NCC), is a set of material duties. They do seem to be obligating, binding on agents, and beyond further interrogation. If this were so, we would get a more severe version of the Two Criteria Problem, namely,

> *Two Sources of Obligation*: The individual is only obligated through her own conscience, yet there are also universal principles that obligate any agent regardless of their belief.

Fichte avoids this problem by giving the individual's conscience the final say over obligation. He writes, "There is therefore absolutely no external ground nor external criterion for the binding force of an ethical command .... A command is binding only on the condition that it is confirmed by our own conscience and only *because* it has been confirmed in this way" (GA I/5: 164; SL 4: 176–77).

In his treatment of conscience, Fichte wants to cordon off the content from conscience so that every proposed action can get a full investigation by the theoretical capacity before the practical capacity of conscience gives its assent. The problem is that it is anything but clear how we are to think of reflective judgment as a theoretical capacity distinct from the practical. A first thought would be to line up the practical–theoretical contrast with moral–nonmoral, so that reflective judgment would consider possible actions in an evaluatively neutral way. Reflective judgment would present various potential actions open to me at this moment, and conscience would add the moral dimension and affirm the action that furthers my overall end of self-sufficiency. For example, I judge that I could right now help my son with his homework or drink beer with friends without evaluating the merits (morality) of the two options. Considering the two options, I now in conscience size them up in a moral light and determine which better fits the overall end of reason's self-sufficiency. But would this way of dividing the theoretical and the practical make sense of what Fichte says about the "material" of duty, and does it hold up as a view of deliberation?

No, on both accounts. What is missing in this picture is the ability to see the world of practical possibility in moral terms. Without bringing to bear evaluative considerations in reflective judgment, it is just not clear that we would be capturing the possibilities of *moral* action at all. I have to know what is morally relevant to even know there is an occasion for action. For example, a senior visiting speaker at dinner is recommending to my junior colleague that she hurry up and have children because her body is telling her to do so. Would I be able to review the different options in a morally neutral way?

In terms of Fichte's way of making the distinction, the exclusion of material from the side of conscience does mean that he is including moral content on the side of reflective judgment. The sheer immediacy of conscience as a final arbiter also makes it unlikely that Fichte would think of conscience as the repository of moral rules. He leaves us instead with a puzzle, namely, how to think of what I call

> *The Material of Reflective Judgment (MRJ)*: the resources available to reflective judgment for proposing possible actions to conscience.

A major question going forward is how to relate NCC to MRJ. One would think the necessary content just is the material for judgment, but Fichte blocks that move (as we shall see in Section 6.3).

Although reflective judgment is fallible, Fichte holds that the ultimate verdict that comes from conscience is not something I can be mistaken about. Fichte formulates this point in terms of a harmony of the actual self or "I" with the original:

> The feeling of certainty, however, is always an immediate harmony of our consciousness with our original I – nor could things be otherwise in a philosophy that begins with the I. This feeling never deceives us, since, as we have seen, it is present whenever there is complete harmony of our empirical I with the pure I, and the latter is our sole true being, all possible being and all possible truth. (GA I/5: 158; SL 4: 169)

The original I and pure I are Fichte's way of talking about the self-sufficiency or freedom at the heart of subjectivity. Only an action that realizes or furthers that freedom will win the assent of conscience. Later in his elaboration of the infallibility claim he invokes conscience as a final power of judgment: "Conscience never errs and cannot err, for it is the immediate consciousness of our pure, original I, over and above which there is no other kind of consciousness. Conscience is itself the judge of all convictions and acknowledges no higher judge above itself. It has final jurisdiction and is subject to no appeal" (GA I/5: 161–2; SL 4: 174). The difficulty with this claim lies in knowing just what such a judgment of conscience consists in. The appeal to harmony with the original I indicates that conscience embodies a criterion of freedom, an adequacy to the basic demand of freedom at the heart of the system. Fichte insists that only through such judgment does any command have binding force over me. It is up to me in the end to confirm content through my conscience. So whatever content Fichte himself might come up with would also seem to be subject to the testing of conscience, and thus not itself a final criterion for action. There can only be one criterion, and that is conscience.

6.2 Deflating the Criterion of Conscience

There is an obvious problem with conscience as the sole criterion for the correctness of a belief in one's duty. This is the oft-leveled charge of arbitrary subjectivism.

> *Subjectivism*: Making an immediate feeling the criterion for identifying duty puts moral judgment beyond rational standards by leaving it up to the individual alone to decide what is right.

Fichte would deny this charge, because conscience is supposed to express reason and freedom. But his very strong claims about infallible conscience have left him exposed to it nonetheless.

Michelle Kosch has recently sought to defend Fichte's ethics from the charge of subjectivism by arguing that conscience is not a criterion for first-order judgment of duty. Emphasizing the difference between reflective judgment as a theoretical capacity and conscience as a second-order judgment, Kosch has argued that Fichte does not hold that conscience is an infallible criterion for first-order judgment. She criticizes "the criterial interpretation" of conscience for saddling Fichte with an implausible subjectivism,[4] and she argues that Fichte's strong criterial language can

---

[4] Kosch (2014, 1) introduces the label "the criterial interpretation." I keep this label for the interpretation that I think Fichte holds, but I do not endorse all the elements that Kosch attributes to that interpretation, for she holds that the criterial view has no role for reflective judgment at all. In my

be deflated by attention to the framing of the account of conscience as "phenomenological."[5] Kosch asks us to distinguish sharply "between (1) a first-order question about what I should do ('Is x really what I should do?') and (2) a second-order question about my *judgment* that x is what I should do ('Am I really *convinced* that x is what I should do?')."[6] Given that Fichte admits that agents do sometimes make mistakes at the level of reflective judgment, the aim of conscience "cannot be to become convinced that I am correct in my first-order judgment. It can only be to become convinced that I am in fact convinced *of* my first-order judgment."[7] Conscience is thus a second-order judgment that is directed toward the subject's own first-order judgment.

Kosch aligns conscience with a duty of due care in formulating the first-order judgment and thinks there is clear evidence that conscience so conceived is not sufficient for correctly identifying one's duty. She writes, "He assumes that any process of practical deliberation is fallible, and that at any point the x hit upon may in fact not be the action objectively required, that any conviction A may be in error. This is true even where the formal condition is met."[8] Her "decisive evidence" for this last claim is Fichte's consideration of a case where two people with sincere convictions disagree. If Fichte is willing to entertain a case of two individuals whose respective consciences reach different conclusions, then he must be thinking that one of those consciences has approved the wrong action, and he must hold that conscience is not infallible about what is objectively one's duty.

To explain Fichte's strong criterial language, Kosch has recourse to the difficulties involved in providing an external standard for the judgment. In considering a passage in which Fichte worries about how we can act if there is a chance our conviction is in error, she writes, "But in fact it is clear that this entire discussion is premised on the possibility of error, and that it concerns only the *finality* of practical deliberation, under circumstances in which the agent can have no independent confirmation of the *veracity* of its result."[9] Conscience brings practical deliberation to a close, and there is no "independent confirmation" of the truth of my conviction, so in such cases it seems that conscience is the only way to secure the truth. Conviction is the best we can do in such cases even though it does not guarantee objective correctness. Kosch denies that the feeling of conscience occurs only when "the judgment that x is the right thing to do is *objectively correct*,"[10] and

---

view the main interpretive task should be to figure out how one can give reflective judgment a major role while maintaining that conscience is an "absolute criterion," as Fichte claims.

[5] Kosch (2018, 135).   [6] Kosch (2014, 9).   [7] Ibid.   [8] Kosch (2018, 132).
[9] Kosch (2018, 133).   [10] Kosch (2018, 135).

thus imputes to "the criterial interpretation" the view that conscience does determine the "objectively correct" judgment. She further argues that Fichte's denial of an external objective standard of conscience must mean that conscience does not adjudicate substantive first-order correctness: "Fichte is careful to point out that the second-order judgment based upon this feeling is no guarantee of the substantive truth of an agent's first-order conviction. 'This criterion of correctness of our conviction is, as we have seen, an inner one. An outer, objective one does not exist' (IV:170)".[11] Her implicit premise in this passage is that the only "substantive truth" of "an agent's first-order conviction" is an "outer, objective one." She holds that because Fichte denies that there is an outer criterion, he must be denying that conscience guarantees substantive truth.

Before I consider some objections to Kosch's deflationary moves, it is worth considering her take on the operation of reflective judgment (the capacity that in her view does all the deliberative work). She reads Fichte as an agent-neutral consequentialist who holds that only the overall end of self-sufficiency is set by practical reason, and that all of our moral deliberation is "technical-practical" reasoning about the best means to achieve that self-sufficiency.[12] This interpretation gives a fairly straightforward meaning to Fichte's assignment of theoretical reasoning to reflective judgment (which operates with what I have called MRJ), for such "calculative" reasoning about means does not seem to be implicated in the end-setting activity of the practical capacity. Emphasizing the agent-neutral character of Fichtean morality could also be seen as making MRJ more clearly a theoretical issue, because we can calculate based on each individual counting the same as other, and we are not to put our own attachments above the claims of others. On this view, the overall obligation is set by the basic moral principle, and we objectively identify duties in reflective judgment by determining in each case which action best promotes that overall end. Conscience has little left to do besides examine whether we have done our best to arrive at the action that best promotes the end. Kosch takes obligation to come as part of a package with the basic awareness of the moral end, so there is no need for conscience to impose obligation in its final judgment at the close of deliberation.[13]

The first main point to make against Kosch's account of conscience is that she imposes a conception of objectivity onto Fichte that is foreign to

---

[11] Kosch (2018, 137).   [12] Kosch (2018, 18).

[13] I infer this view on obligation from the following: "The second reason is that Kant sees agents as capable of failing to incorporate recognized moral obligations into their maxims, whereas Fichte claims that agents always act on the best reasons they are aware of having and therefore . . . always act on their moral duty to the extent that they are aware of it" (Kosch [2018, 130]).

his ethics. She attacks the criterial interpretation of conscience's infallibility because it holds that conscience is infallible about an objective "fact of the matter." But to say that conscience determines duty for the individual is not necessarily to say that conscience determines the objective fact of the matter. The criterial reader could hold that Fichte is indeed a subjectivist, but not the kind of arbitrary subjectivist who holds that feeling does all the work in deliberation. The affirmations of conscience are rational, not arbitrary, in part because they do depend on the theoretical reasoning of reflective judgment. But the final affirmation, which imposes obligation, comes from conscience and identifies the duty for this individual subject in this situation. It aims at correctness, but it still only imposes obligation on this subject.

Consider in this light the passage that Kosch cites to argue that conscience is not about "substantive truth." When Fichte denies that there is an external criterion, he is not denying that conscience concerns substantive truth, but rather affirming that the substantive truth *can only be an inner criterion*, and so must be given by conscience. So, too, the disagreement passage does not seem to me to be decisive evidence for the deflationary view of conscience. About the two agents who have genuine conviction, Fichte does not say, "one of the two is wrong, so his conscientious moral judgment is fallible." Rather, he says, "Whose conviction should be the guide? Neither conviction, so long as they are contradictory; for each should absolutely act according to *his* conviction, and the formal condition of morality consists in that" (GA I/5: 211; SL 4: 233).[14] A judgment is only valid for the subject if she comes to that judgment for herself. It is open to Fichte to say here that if and when one party comes to agree that the other is correct, that erring party should say "what I thought was the judgment of conscience was in fact misguided. That is, I misidentified my conviction as the conviction of conscience." Or, as Fichte himself says of cases of error, persons can admit that they "have already lost the genuine guiding thread of conscience. In such a case we deceive ourselves about what is our duty and we act, as one usually puts it, from an erring conscience" (GA I/5: 179; SL 4: 195). The fact that we mistakenly *call* this a case of an erring conscience just shows that Fichte is out to reform our loose ways of talking by identifying conscience with the correct (subjective) judgment.

Some of the claims that Kosch makes to explain Fichte's subjectivist-sounding language confirm rather than contradict the criterial

---

[14] Cited by Kosch (2018, 132).

Fichte on the Content of Conscience 119

interpretation. She writes that "From my own perspective in the moment of deliberation, my fulfilment of the formal and material conditions cannot come apart."[15] This can happen "[o]nly for an observer."[16] With this statement she seems to admit that first-person judgment is not compatible with error at the time of judgment when the formal condition has been met. She thinks that an observer can say that you are wrong because she thinks there is an objective fact of the matter that defines your obligation. But Fichte denies that obligation can be imposed externally, so the admission that from the first-person point of view there cannot be a separation of the two criteria becomes an admission that the formal and material conditions really are inseparable. A similar point holds about final judgment and the lack of independent grounds for "veracity." Kosch concedes that conscience is the final arbiter in such situations; in my view, because it is always the case for Fichte that only the subject herself can make the final judgment of her obligation, the concession means that conscience really is a criterion for the first-order judgment. The lack of independent grounds is just a statement of the lack of an external objective criterion for my conviction about my duty. The only ultimate criterion is an inner one, and that criterion is infallible because there is no way to get behind it or outside of it and still have the authority to judge it.

The issues with the other side of Kosch's account, her calculative consequentialist reading of deliberation, are too complex to be argued adequately in this chapter. The key thesis is that practical reason only sets the overall end – reason's self-sufficiency – and all the rest of the work in determining duties can be sorted out by the theoretical capacity of reflective judgment as technical-practical reasoning. A full critique of Kosch's position would question how cleanly one can separate a single overall ethical end from all the subsidiary ends that serve the overall purpose. The difficulty of pinning down the activity of reflective judgment and its relation to conscience can be measured by the massive divergence of the interpretations of Kosch and Allen Wood on this point. Wood vehemently rejects the calculative consequentialist picture in favor of what he calls the "recursive projection of our finite ends."[17] He thinks that the overall end of self-sufficiency is not definite enough to be the basis of technical-practical reasoning, and he recommends thinking instead of deliberation as always starting from "our immediate actions and their finite ends"[18] and working from there out to the final end.

---

[15] Kosch (2018, 139).   [16] Kosch (2018, 140).   [17] Wood (2016a, 179).   [18] Ibid.

A final point against the deflationary reading is that Fichte's conscience is not easily assimilated to Kant's reflections on conscience as "due care" in reaching a moral judgment.[19] Aligning conscience with Kantian due care goes together with a deflationary reading because it allows us to think of conscience as simply directed toward the subject's judging procedure rather than determining what one's duty actually is. Kosch (and Wood, who agrees with her on this point) would seem to be on firm textual ground here, for Fichte cites Kant with approval in writing of Kant's "correct and sublime pronouncement" that "conscience is a consciousness that is itself a duty" (GA I/5: 161; SL 4: 173). But we should not so quickly assume that Fichte is reading Kant in a way that deflates conscience. As Stefano Bacin points out, Fichte's praise for Kant is rather misleading, and appears on closer inspection to be more a case of Fichte trying to enlist Kant in his own very different project.[20] Fichte turns Kant's claim in a duty-constituting direction in following his approving statement with the gloss, "Everyone is simply supposed to convince himself of what his duty is . . .. This is, so to speak, the constitutive law of all morals: the law that one give a law to oneself" (GA I/5: 161; SL 4: 173). It is far from clear that Kant would agree with this gloss, which seems to be a claim not so much about the subject's self-examination as it is about the power of conscience to actually identity what one's duty is. While Fichte does go on in the same paragraph to repeat his claim that conscience "does not provide the material," he claims that conscience does give "the evidential certainty [*die Evidenz*]" (GA I/5: 161; SL 4: 173). The difficulty lies in figuring out just what this evidence amounts to in relation to the material of the theoretical capacity (MRJ).

6.3 The Content that Conscience Would Approve

I have argued that Fichte's texts are not compatible with the deflationary readings, but I acknowledge that answering the Two Criteria Problem and Subjectivism on a criterial reading of conscience is very difficult. In this section, I look at Fichte's initial account of the content of conscience, the general picture that he will expand into a full account of NCC. This account is a key part of his overall argument for the rationality of the

---

[19] See Kosch (2018, 136n6 and 136–7n7) and Wood (2014, 164).
[20] As Bacin (2017) points out, Kant actually writes of a consciousness which "is for itself a duty," whereas Fichte quotes Kant as saying the consciousness "is itself a duty" (2017, 314). See also Moyar (2008), where I highlight the ways in which Kant's own conception of conscience is unstable, and that he himself is drawn in a duty-constituting direction in his claims about conscience as "practical apperception."

feeling of conscience, for in it he is trying to determine through reason those actions that conscience *would* approve. In addition to the Two Criteria Problem, the other issue raised by this account of content is where NCC fits into his division of labor model of ethical deliberation, and in particular how NCC and MRJ are related. Taking the content to have the form of a list of duties, we can ask, how do such duties figure into the reflective judgment that precedes the approval of conscience? Fichte is frustratingly unforthcoming on this question. Rather than tell us how the content factors into reflective judgment, Fichte actually seems to foreswear any practical significance for his account of NCC. He holds that NCC is supposed to be simply a matter for science, not for the deliberating agent. But this cuts off the one clear route to linking NCC and MRJ, and it does little to resolve the Two Criteria and Two Sources of Obligation Problems.

Before we get to Fichte's official attempt to defuse the clash of form and content, let us look at his first argument for how ethical content is determined. He introduces the account with a by now familiar claim: "There is no outer, objective criterion, nor can there be one, since it is precisely here, where the I is regarded as a moral being, that it is supposed to be entirely self-sufficient and independent of everything that lies outside it. This, however, does not preclude us from indicating the general type of convictions that will be sanctioned by this criterion" (GA I/5: 158; SL 4: 170). Notice that he is talking about convictions with a "general type" of content that would be approved by conscience. To develop this account of ethical content, Fichte relies on a teleological argument from an early part of the *Sittenlehre* that freedom can serve as a theoretical principle (for the philosopher, not for the deliberating agent) to establish necessary features of the world.[21] Fichte invokes the primacy of the practical in the thesis that "objects are only there for us at all owing to the practical drive" (GA I/5: 158; SL 4: 170). The "objects" at issue are those that can be effected by my action. They are purposes that are originally given through the drives, but that are subject to free reflection, and hence become purposes "for us." Sounding like an egoistic utilitarian, he writes, "I posit, e.g., that the object can be modified in a certain way, and in doing this I determine its purposiveness, *its usefulness for certain freely chosen ends* that one might set for oneself with regard to this object" (GA I/5: 159; SL 4: 170–71). He is careful to say that purposiveness comes from the relationship of an object to freedom in general, not to *my* freedom. Fichte's view is not, in other

---

[21] For a discussion of Fichte's development of this thesis through arguments for natural teleology and a "system of drives," see Rohs (1992, 170–75).

words, a view in which objects "for me" are determined as possible *means* for achieving my purposes. Rather, "a conviction is not sanctioned by conscience until it includes an insight into the final end of the thing, and such cognitions are at the same time those which guide moral conduct. The moral law therefore aims to treat everything in accordance with its final end" (GA I/5: 159–60; SL 4: 171). This argument allows Fichte to link conscience to those other regarding actions – actions toward beings who are ends in themselves – that form the core of Kantian morality.

What follows is one of Fichte's more explicit reflections on the relation of the practical and theoretical, a passage that should give us some insight into how reflective judgment as theoretical and conscience as practical are related.

> [W]e have shown that the ethical drive and theoretical knowledge stand in reciprocal interaction with each other and that all morality is conditioned by this reciprocal interaction. The ethical drive, insofar as it appears within consciousness, demands some concept = X, which is, however, insufficiently determined *for the ethical drive*; and to this extent the ethical drive formally determines the power of cognition: i.e., it drives the reflecting power of judgment to search for the concept in question. The power of cognition is, however, also determined materially with regard to concept X by the ethical drive, insofar as the latter is viewed as what is original; for, as we have just seen, X arises through the complete determination of the object by means of the entire original drive. It follows from this that all cognition, considered objectively as a system, is thoroughly determined in advance and that it is determined by means of the ethical drive. (GA I/5: 160; SL 4: 172)

Putting this together with the claims about final ends, Fichte seems to be saying that the ethical drive sets reflective judgment to work in order to find the concept that captures the final end of objects in the world. Only the concept that takes account of the final end of each thing will be approved by conscience. The second half of the paragraph is Fichte's attempt to say that even this theoretical faculty is determined by the original, ethical drive, for the objects of cognition are themselves only the objects they are as a function of our freedom.

Let me attempt to translate the above into an answer to the question of how this necessary content (NCC) provides the material for moral deliberation (MRJ). The necessary content (NCC) is determined by considering final ends. But those final ends are themselves determined by freedom or self-sufficiency. This means that reflective judgment must come up with a concept of a purpose (a possible action) that accounts for the final purpose of everything within its purview by referring those things to the

Fichte on the Content of Conscience

purpose of self-sufficiency. Fichte's language of objects or things makes it seem that any action will take a discrete object, but of course every action has multiple objects that bear on it. When Fichte sets about determining duties, he determines general types of duties by considering different objects of activity (the body, thinking, other people). Thinking of these types of objects in terms of their end and the overall end of self-sufficiency gives us a way to cognize ethical situations in both specific terms and in the service of the overall purpose of action. We can thus say that reflective judgment tracks the purposiveness of objects in the world (including other agents), and conscience confirms the purpose that unites those discrete elements in the proper way, in the way that best serves (harmonizes with) the overall end of self-sufficiency. If that were the picture, we would have to say that each of the discrete aspects is not finally obligating on its own, and is thus not an equal criterion to that of conscience, and that conscience must rule over those discrete factors as the final authority.

The picture I have sketched does not, however, seem to be Fichte's strategy in his official response to the Two Criteria Problem. Fichte instead emphasizes the difference between the standpoint of life and the standpoint of philosophy. There is nothing more that the ordinary consciousness needs than the feeling of certainty in conscience to know that its judgments are well-grounded. He writes, "This would suffice for actual acting, and nothing more would be required in order to make possible such acting. The educator of the people, for example, can leave it at that and can conclude his instruction in morals at this point" (GA I/5: 190; SL 4: 208).[22] Philosophy can go further in identifying our true duties, but for the ordinary consciousness, or what Fichte calls the standpoint of life, such knowledge would involve a contradiction. In a passage that insists on the need for a sharp division on this point, Fichte writes:

> Feeling decides. This decision on the part of feeling is surely based on some law that is *grounded in reason*, a law that cannot, however, be an object of consciousness so long as one continues to occupy the standpoint of ordinary human understanding. To do so would involve a contradiction, since all that occurs in consciousness is a feeling, which is how this law manifests itself in a specific case. From the transcendental point of view, however, it must certainly be possible to discover this law. Instruction of the purely popular sort remains at the standpoint of ordinary consciousness, and thus nothing that lies within the transcendental standpoint is present for this sort

---

[22] At the very outset of the book, Fichte claims that his deduction will change nothing in the practice of morality, and that its results are merely theoretical, for it is not a doctrine of wisdom but a science (GA I/5: 34–35; SL 4: 15).

of instruction. Instruction becomes philosophical only insofar as it elevates itself to the transcendental standpoint. (GA I/5: 190–91; SL 4: 208)

The goal of Fichte's ethics is to provide a "real applicable science," but a science whose conscious application by agents themselves would disrupt the very capacity Fichte is trying to explain. The split between a theoretical science of ethical content and the practical feeling of formal conscience is what for Fichte eliminates the threat of competing criteria.[23]

This is a strange result, especially given the role that the "theoretical" is supposed to play in ethical deliberation. What material can reflective judgment (MRJ) employ if not the duties that Fichte outlines in the second half of the *System of Ethics*? Fichte is clear that the immediate practical feeling of conscience is not the result of an argument. But the fact that he then goes behind the feeling to identify its basis puts him in an odd position. Peter Rohs captures the issue:

> Yet Fichte's approach is bewildering. He grounds the necessity of conscience with the claim that argumentation that requires proof cannot continue ad infinitum (ibid., 158/169); but then holds nonetheless such proofs to be a priori possible and then says, thirdly, that this possibility is entirely superfluous for actual ethical decision, for "life," and that it is only of interest for "science."[24]

My view is that Fichte's split between the perspectives of life and science is not an actual solution to the problem of competing criteria. The fact is that NCC does give us resources to tell someone who has acted against one of the duties that they have not *in fact* acted on conscience, and yet Fichte is quite clear that only the subject himself or herself is in a position to say what his or her obligation in each case is. Before we say that Fichte's view is simply incoherent, we should look at two further strategies for uniting form and content on the basis of what he actually says about our duties.

6.4 Concrete Ethics and the Particularist Conscience

The most promising way to think of the relation between the criterion of conscience and the duties that are the necessary content of conscience is to think of Fichte as a kind of *moral particularist*. Fichtean conscience affirms

---

[23] Owen Ware (2020) maintains that Fichte can avoid the Two Criteria Problem through his split in perspectives. On this view, my worry about this problem is too external to Fichte's system. I think that if his system cannot answer the problem clearly, that would ground a serious charge of incoherence.

[24] Rohs (1992, 181).

in each case an all-things-considered judgment of a specific action, leading some to describe his view as a "situation ethics."[25] Recent debates in metaethics over particularism versus generalism have brought out different ways to think of contributory moral reasons. Strong particularists (such as Jonathan Dancy) hold that moral reasons can switch their valence from case to case, and thus should not be thought of as generally binding single valence principles.[26] Strong particularism departs too much from principles to capture Fichte's view, but a more moderate position such as the one identified with W. D. Ross might fit. It is open to Fichte to say that the duties that are ethical content are *prima facie duties* that have to be accounted for in an overall judgment. They are obligatory, but not in a conclusive way until an all-things-considered judgment is reached. This dynamic would help make sense of Fichte's claim when turning to content that science identifies the "general type of convictions" that conscience would approve.[27] One question is whether Fichte's duties are of the right form to play the role of prima facie duties. It would be a problem for this particularist view if the Fichtean duties were exceptionless laws, for then there would be little room for conscience in the concrete case to say anything different from the law. The second question, once we have made a case for a particularist reading, is whether that gives conscience too much of a say over the ultimate content, reopening Fichte to a charge of arbitrariness.

Let us look, then, at Fichte's account of ethical content to see if it does indeed fit with the particularist view. We have already seen above that his account of content refers to the drives. His overall strategy is to say that the conditions of freedom, what makes the freedom of the I possible and realizes the end of self-sufficiency, are the basis of the content of conscience (NCC). This grounding of duty in freedom can be taken in two ways that lead in two seemingly different directions. One way leads to strict deontology, as in the following claim about our relation to other agents: "My

---

[25] See Breazeale (2012) and Wood (2016a, 151–52).   [26] Dancy (1993) and (2004).

[27] Bacin (2017) has made a strong case for Fichte's particularism in contrasting Fichte's view of a case of moral action with the view of Kant. He writes, "While for Kant each case is still to be thought as a case under a law, for Fichte each individual case appears de facto independent of relation to a law. A law, or rule, does not play the role in the standpoint of the agent of a ground of justification; conscience operates immediately in that it brings each duty to consciousness" (2017, 320–21). He cites Novalis: "In Fichte's morality one finds the most correct views on morality. Morality says absolutely nothing determinate – it is the conscience – a mere judge without law. It commands immediately, but always singularly [*einzeln*]. It is complete resoluteness. Correct representation from conscience. Laws are completely opposed to morality." (Novalis, cited in Bacin [2017, 321–22])

I-hood, along with my self-sufficiency in general, is conditioned by the freedom of the other. It follows that my *drive to self-sufficiency* absolutely cannot aim at annihilating the *condition of its own possibility*, that is, the freedom of the other" (GA I/5: 201; SL 4: 221). This would not fit so well with the particularist account, for it does not leave any room for the kind of subordination of one duty to another that characterizes an overall judgment in a context of competing prima facie duties. The other way of reading the content is teleological, thinking of the world as so many conditions for the expansion of self-sufficiency. Prima facie duties on this view would be the determinate routes to that expansion, the means as it were to the overall end of the expansion of self-sufficiency. This teleological way of connecting content to self-consciousness does seem like it could fit the particularist view. We could combine this with Kosch's consequentialist reading to say that there are various consequentialist principles that determinate prima facie duties, and that conscience affirms that combination of principles that best promotes the overall end.

Let us look at the first set of duties. I cannot posit myself without positing myself as a natural being, which means that I have duties vis-à-vis my body. In Fichte's typically extreme language, I should seek to make my body the "tool of morality." He deduces a negative, positive, and limitative duty, where the first and third do seem to have deontological strictness and the second is less strict in imposing a general positive duty to cultivate one's capacities. Fichte writes of the limitative duty, "It is absolutely contrary to the moral way of thinking to care for our body if we are not convinced that we are thereby cultivating and preserving it for dutiful acting; i.e., it is absolutely contrary to the moral way of thinking to do this for any reason other than for the sake of conscience and with the latter in mind" (GA I/5: 197; SL 4: 216). On the one hand, such a general duty of care for one's body seems like it could be something like one factor that must be taken into account in action. On the other hand, the language of "absolutely contrary" has a distinct deontological ring to it, and it does not leave much room for subordination to other prima facie duties. What would Fichte say about a case in which I neglect my bodily health because I am too busy caring for my family and doing my job? Would this be absolutely contrary to duty? Or could one still do one's duty in most respects while failing in this one respect? There remains the general problem of the one and the many, for how are we supposed to get from a host of absolute duties to a final verdict?

The worry here is that if the particularist interpretation identifies duties as universally binding, and then says that we have to bring our knowledge

Fichte on the Content of Conscience

of them to bear on the case, it is unclear what the rational grounds would be for deciding how the various duties are combined in a specific case. Fichte would then seem to be subject to Hegel's critique in his *Differenzschrift* that either mere choice among duties determines what one does or we are left with a contingent inexplicable insight. The problem is what happens when the unity of self-consciousness (which Hegel calls in the following passage "the concept") is employed to deduce a plurality of duties. Are those duties absolute or, as the particularist maintains, are they conditioned? Hegel writes:

> Because the duties are equally absolute, selection [*Wahl*] is possible, and because of their collision, selection is necessary; and there is nothing present to do the deciding, except arbitrary choice [*Willkür*]. If arbitrary choice were to be excluded, the duties could not have the same degree of absoluteness. In that case we would have to say that one duty is more absolute than the other. This contradicts the concept, for every duty is, as duty, absolute. Yet where there is such a collision, if one must act, absoluteness has to be given up and one duty preferred to another. So, if self-determination is to be possible, everything depends on finding the way to decide which concept of one's duty is to be preferred to the other, and on choosing among the conditional duties according to one's best insight. If arbitrary choice and contingency of inclinations are excluded from the self-determination of freedom through the highest concept, then self-determination now passes over into the contingency of insight and hence into the unconsciousness of what it is that decides a contingent insight.[28]

The charge is that if Fichte goes the particularist route, he will have to endorse "conditional duties," and because the ethical drive – as "the highest concept" – demands action, one must select from the duties on the basis of one's "best insight." It seems that Hegel is here taking "insight" to cover both reflective judgment and conscience. If we leave it up to the final unifying activity of feeling/insight, then we are left saying that the ultimate judgment is unconscious, not the result of reasoning, and therefore hard to distinguish from a contingent subjectivism.

In response to Hegel's charges, Breazeale has argued that the Fichtean "agent by no means possesses any arbitrary freedom of choice regarding his concrete duties and the content of the same."[29] He thinks that Hegel has missed the idea that for Fichte "conscience depends entirely upon an *involuntary* feeling of duty, one that is *necessarily* produced whenever a determinate concept of a possible act is discovered, via reflective

---

[28] Hegel (1970: 2, 89–90; 1801/1977, 150–51). [29] Breazeale (2018, 126).

judgment, to 'harmonize' with the ends of pure willing or the I's original drive to complete self-sufficiency."[30] Breazeale links the necessity of the feeling of conscience to content through the reference to "the ends of pure willing" and "the *I's* original drive." The problem with Breazeale's appeal to the "involuntary" is that it blocks arbitrary choice only by embracing what Hegel calls "unconsciousness." Breazeale is right to state Fichte's aims in terms of reflective judgment's capacities, but the key problem remains, and is highlighted by the contrast between the *plural* "ends of pure willing" and the *singular* "original drive." The harmony is involuntary, and the necessity is supposed to make it a matter of reason, but the gap between universal duties and specific action remains, and with it the dependence on individual "insight" to close the gap. This is not a mere invention by Hegel, for Fichte clearly endorses this role for insight when he writes, "Everyone ought to do and everyone simply must do whatever his situation, his heart, and his insight order him to do – this, and nothing else; and one simply must not do anything one is prohibited from doing by one's situation, heart, and insight" (GA I/5: 242; SL 4: 270). This leaves Fichte exposed to the charge that he only closes the gap between form and content with an affect (heart) and insight that simply relies on the contingent capacities of the individual subject.

6.5 Communication and Conscience

There remains one untapped resource within Fichte's theory for uniting the criteria of form and content. In his treatment of duties of communication, Fichte appears to have a strong basis for overcoming the arbitrariness of insight and for securing the rational credentials of the feeling of conscience. We have a duty to engage in rational communication with other agents prior to reaching our deliberative conclusions, and we must reexamine our conclusion if we cannot find a single person who agrees with us.[31] It might seem that Fichte is hereby introducing a third criterion for ethical action, but I think it makes more sense to think of this intersubjectivity as an ethical duty to unite the two criteria. This view has considerable merit, but it puts serious pressure on both the absoluteness of the formal criterion and the split between the ordinary and scientific points of view.

In the context of how we are to treat the actions of others on their conscience, Fichte raises the most important question for his conception of moral judgment (and also the most obvious): "which use of freedom

[30] Ibid.   [31] See Wood (2000) and Breazeale (2018).

violates the moral law, and who is able to be universal judge?" (GA I/5: 211; SL 4: 233). If each of us claims to have acted on his best conviction, who is to say which action is the moral one? Neither will be moral in the eyes of the other until we agree, and we cannot – without giving up "all interest in universal ethical life" – simply leave each other alone. The agent is strictly bound to convince the other, and all others, that he is right. This line of thought leads to some of Fichte's most explicit reflection on Kant's Categorical Imperative, including the well-known passage on the merely heuristic nature of the universal law formulation of the categorical imperative.[32] Fichte claims in the following passage that willingness to communicate with others is a necessary element of the certainty of your conviction:

> [E]veryone wants only to convince the other of his opinion, and yet, in the course of this conflict of minds, he is perhaps himself convinced of the other's opinion. Everyone must be ready to engage in this reciprocal interaction. Anyone who flees from such interaction, perhaps in order to avoid any disturbance of his own belief, thereby betrays a lack of conviction on his own part, which simply ought not to be the case. From this it follows that such a person has an even greater duty to seek such engagement in order to acquire conviction for himself. (GA I/5: 213; SL 4: 235–36)

If I cannot defend my conviction, if I shrink from reciprocal interaction with others, then it cannot be the case that I am in fact certain. He says as much even more directly a bit later in the text: "It is therefore by means of communication that I first obtain certainty and security for the cause or matter itself [*die Sache selbst*]" (GA I/5: 222; SL 4: 246). We all share the same reason, so communication with others is the best way to reach rational certainty.

How exactly do these claims about communicating with others fit with the claims of conscience as an absolute criterion and with the claim that life and science are split? The stress on communication supports the idea that the main work in practical deliberation takes place at the level of reflective judgment rather than at the level of conscience itself. It seems that we must think of the communicative activity as part of that process of reflective judgment, considering all the elements of action and reconsidering them in light of the views of others (a dynamic and intersubjectively informed MRJ). Yet Fichte clearly does not give up the absolute criterion of conscience. Fichte does not take back the idea that the final criterion for action is the involuntary immediate feeling of conscience. He also does not further

---

[32] GA I/5: 211–12; SL 4: 233–34.

thematize the split between that feeling as the guide for life, on the one hand, and the development of content from the perspective of science, on the other. There would be a fairly clear path for him to overcome this split in so far as the communicative activity is itself implicitly scientific, leading the ordinary agent to consider the content of duty from the perspective of the philosopher. Again, though, taking this route would create problems for the immediacy of conscience that is supposed to put an end to arguments over reasons that thereby secure the conviction to act.

The question in the end is whether Fichte can maintain his view that there is only an inner criterion of obligation while holding that rational judgments are constituted by communicative activity. Every attempt to make Fichte into a more Hegelian (or Habermasian) theorist of the sociality of reason must confront his very strong claims about the role of conviction and the strict individuality of final judgments of conscience. I am inclined to agree with Breazeale when he argues for keeping apart Fichte and Hegel based on a fundamental difference concerning "the place therein of immediate and allegedly self-evident claims to truth, claims which, on the Fichtean account, play an indispensable 'foundational' role in both life and philosophy."[33] There are certainly grounds for a robust conception of rationality in Fichte's ethics, and I think that further work connecting his account of content and deliberation to recent work on moral particularism should prove fruitful. The sticking point that I have tried to locate and elaborate in this chapter is the relation of scientifically derived content (NCC) to the "theoretical" material of reflective judgment (MRJ). If we can come up with a convincing interpretation of how his actual account of duties provides the material for the purpose-entertaining capacities of judgment, we would be well on our way to sorting out how each of us is both the seat of an absolute criterion and responsible to rational norms.

[33] Breazeale (2018, 128).

CHAPTER 7

Fichte's Theory of Moral Evil

David James

7.1 Introduction

Fichte's ethical theory is said to be not only "both radically individualist and radically collectivist," but also "at its most radical in insisting that individualism and collectivism must not be separated from one another or seen as rival values."[1] The idea that this ethical theory attempts to combine individualist elements with social elements is justified, given some of Fichte's own claims, and his treatment of moral evil is a case in point. There is an individualist element in the shape of each individual's responsibility for being in a state of moral evil and how it is ultimately up to the individual to escape this state. Moreover, this individualist element is connected with the absence or presence of certain feelings and psychological states, of which only the individual concerned can be directly aware. Yet Fichte's theory of moral evil also features a claim that signals the importance and indispensability of intersubjective mediation when it comes to escaping a state of moral evil. This claim concerns the role of society in making the individual aware of his or her freedom and how he or she should exercise it in the appropriate way, though it comes with the caveat that this social influence represents only a first stage, because individuals ought then to raise themselves above the standpoint that they have been led to adopt by their own society:

> [I]t is through education [*Erziehung*] in the widest sense, that is, through the influence of society in general upon us, that we are first cultivated [*gebildet*] in a manner that makes it possible for us to employ our freedom. If we do not raise ourselves above it, then the matter rests with that cultivation [*Bildung*] we have received from society. Were society better, then we would be better as well, though without any merit on our part. This does

[1] Wood (2016a, 101).

131

not abolish the possibility of obtaining merit on one's own, but such a possibility first arises only at a higher point. (GA I/5: 170; SL 4: 174–75)

In what follows, I shall first emphasize the subjective, individuating aspects of Fichte's account of moral evil by showing how it appears to generate a paradox that Fichte himself acknowledges. I shall then argue that the beginnings of a potential solution to this paradox can be identified on the basis of the psychological state of anxiety diagnosed by Søren Kierkegaard, a psychological state which, by its very nature, remains inaccessible to others and thus signifies a purely personal relation to one's freedom. This mood needs to be interpreted, and it is here that we encounter a move toward a form of social influence. This social element cannot, however, explain how an individual can escape the condition of moral evil in a way that accords with the idea that his or her freedom makes him or her responsible for being in this condition: If everything depended on the influence exerted by society on an individual, then this individual would, at best, only reach the level of moral cultivation that his or her own society has attained, and he or she would deserve no moral credit if he or she thereby happened to become morally good. In order to explain the paradox mentioned earlier, I shall begin with Kant's theory of radical evil in which a similar paradox can be detected. This approach is justified by the way in which Fichte claims that his account of moral evil explains Kant's claim that although radical evil is inborn, its ground lies in freedom (GA I/5: 169; SL 4: 173).

7.2 Kant on Radical Evil

Kant identifies the goodness or evilness of human nature with the adoption of a basic maxim that determines an agent's choice of particular action-guiding maxims. The human being would be either naturally good or naturally evil depending on whether or not the higher-order principle to make respect for the moral law the incentive of all relevant actions had been adopted as this basic maxim. Kant accordingly stipulates that by the term "the nature of a human being" he means only "the subjective ground – wherever it may lie – of the exercise of the human being's freedom in general (under objective moral laws) antecedent to every deed that falls within the scope of the senses" (6: 21). With regard to moral evil itself, he states that, "'[t]he human being is *evil*', cannot mean anything else than that he is conscious of the moral law and yet has incorporated into his maxim the (occasional) deviation from it" (6: 32). These deviations from the moral law, and thus lack of respect for it, are to be explained by the human propensity not to obey this law although one recognizes its rational authority. It is not, therefore, a matter of remaining unaware of this law; indeed, Kant stresses that the individual "is conscious of the moral law." The propensity to exempt oneself from the moral law instead involves being determined by self-love to make compliance with its conditional on nonmoral incentives, whereas the moral law is "the supreme condition" of the satisfaction of any incentives that derive from inclinations whose source is self-love, and respect for this law should, therefore, "have been incorporated into the universal maxim of the power of choice [*Willkür*] as the sole incentive" (6: 36). In short, human beings have the propensity to adopt the rule to obey the moral law as the basic maxim that conditions all particular maxims only when it aligns with self-interest.

The existence of such a propensity suggests that human beings *cannot* choose to adopt instead the general maxim to make respect for the moral law as their only incentive and thus come to possess an altogether different moral disposition and character. Yet Kant insists that the fundamental maxim that conditions all particular ones and the actions that they govern must be freely chosen, for otherwise an individual could not be held morally responsible for having adopted it. Thus, it is only contingently true that human beings are evil by nature, for it is, in principle, always possible for an individual to choose to make respect for the moral law his or her fundamental principle of action. Nevertheless, Kant implies that evil is a constant, if ultimately contingent, feature of human nature, when he claims that the propensity to evil has "deep roots . . . in the power of choice, on account of which we must say that it is found in the human being by nature" (6: 35). Kant highlights the propensity to fail to make respect for the moral law the incentive of one's actions, and how each individual is nevertheless responsible for this failure, in the following passage, in which the paradox to which I want to draw attention can already be detected:

> This evil is *radical*, since it corrupts the ground of all maxims; as natural propensity, it is also not to be *extirpated* through human forces, for this could only happen through good maxims – something that cannot take place if the subjective supreme ground of all maxims is presupposed to be corrupted. Yet it must equally be possible to *overcome* this evil, for it is found in the human being as acting freely. (6: 37)

The paradox can be stated as follows. On the one hand, moral evil must be viewed as an ultimately contingent feature of the human will, in that the adoption of the fundamental maxim that allows us to describe a human being's moral disposition and the actions that follow from it as morally good or evil is a matter of free choice. It must therefore be possible for a human being whose disposition is evil to have a morally good disposition instead. On the other hand, it is possible to have a morally good disposition *only if* a human being already possesses one, because it requires that he or she has *already* made the principle always to act from respect for the moral law his or her fundamental principle of action. This is because making the right moral choice, including the choice of the right moral disposition, depends on having the right moral disposition. Yet this disposition itself depends on an agent's having made the right moral choice concerning the fundamental principle of action that is to govern the choice of particular maxims. An individual's original failure to come to have the right kind of disposition by making the right moral choice, or his or her failure to continue to have this disposition, would therefore appear to condemn him or her to a state of moral evil, in that making the right moral choice that would enable him or her to escape this state is no longer possible for him or her because of his or her prior choice of an evil disposition. Indeed, Kant himself concedes that "[h]ow it is possible that a naturally evil human being should make himself into a good human being surpasses every concept of ours" (6: 44).

I intend to show in the next section that Fichte's morally evil human being arguably faces a similar fate and to an even greater extent, because for him or her there cannot be a sufficiently clear consciousness of the rational authority of the moral law and ipso facto no feeling of respect for it that might motivate him or her to change his or her moral disposition. Moreover, an individual who is in a state of moral evil would not even be aware of a choice between good and evil, given that the source of the good, the rational authority of the moral law, is something of which he or she is not sufficiently conscious. This problem extends to the original choice whereby an individual would become either morally good or morally evil, because the act of choosing to adopt the moral law as one's fundamental principle of action is also not an option for a person who lacks consciousness of this law, which, for reasons provided below, is true even of a person in a state of amoral innocence. At the same time, Fichte, like Kant, accepts that each individual is responsible for his or her moral character because it is something that he or she freely chooses and is, therefore, also in the position to change: "If a human being's present character is unworthy, then he is absolutely supposed to form for himself another character; and he is able to do this, for it depends purely upon his own freedom." Immediately afterward, however, Fichte claims that "[t]here is something incomprehensible here, and it cannot be otherwise, since we are now standing at the boundary of all comprehensibility: namely, the doctrine of freedom as it applies to the empirical subject" (GA I/5: 168; SL 4: 172). Let us now turn to Fichte's explanation of the incomprehensibility of moral evil.

7.3 Fichte on Radical Evil

To see how the paradox in question arises in Fichte's account of moral evil, we first need to look at the role that he assigns to conscience in moral deliberation. For Fichte, conscience "is *the immediate consciousness of our determinate duty*" (GA I/5: 161; SL 4: 164). This description of conscience reflects its role in deciding what the moral law demands in a given situation. There is a process whereby the power of judgment considers various possible, but conflicting, actions presented to it by "the free power of imagination" until the thought of one of these actions is accompanied by "a feeling of truth and certainty," which provides the "absolute criterion for the correctness of our conviction concerning duty" (GA I/5: 156; SL 4: 159). Conscience is therefore identified with the demand "*always act in accordance with your best conviction concerning your duty*" (GA I/5: 146; SL 4: 148). Because conscience concerns the application of the concept of morality and the law that expresses this concept, it presupposes consciousness of the rational authority of the moral law, together with the appropriate affective response to it. A state of moral evil, in contrast, arises when consciousness of the authority of the moral law has been "obscured" and the voice of conscience can therefore no longer speak to an individual in the required way. Thus, moral evil primarily involves a state of being rather than an act of choosing evil over good, an act that presupposes awareness of that which ought or ought not to be chosen.

Fichte explains how consciousness of the rational authority of the moral law becomes obscured in terms of the force of inertia characteristic of nature as such or, as he otherwise calls it, the "not-I." This explanation of the possibility of moral evil is thus based on a metaphysical claim rather than on experience. To explain "the efficacy of a free being," it is necessary to think of a temporal series of actions. Each of the actions is finite in that it is limited by obstacles presented by objects that resist the agency exercised upon them by this free being. Resistance of this kind presupposes that these objects possess a certain quantum of force. The force itself, however, is only a passive one possessed by something that seeks to remain what it already is, as opposed to a force that seeks to bring about change (GA I/5: 183; SL 4:

189). In human beings, this passive force assumes the form of an inertia or laziness (*Trägheit*) that consists in pursuing "the direction that nature . . . would have taken had it been left to itself," and thus such particular shapes as "a tendency to remain on the habitual track" (GA I/5: 183; SL 4: 190). This inertia or laziness is "[t]he true, inborn radical evil lying in human nature itself . . . which infinitely reproduces itself through long habit and soon becomes a complete incapacity for what is good" (GA I/5: 185; SL 4: 191). The evil in question is radical, then, in the sense that it is part of the human being's natural condition. Although this explanation of moral evil suggests that Fichte is speaking of a failure to leave this natural condition to attain the higher sphere of a moral being, he claims that it is "quite possible for one to *render obscure* within oneself the clear consciousness of what duty demands" (GA I/5: 177; SL 4: 182). This statement is compatible with the idea of someone who had previously left the natural condition only to relapse into it. Although an individual can be held responsible for such a relapse because, as a result of inattention or carelessness, he or she allowed his or her consciousness of duty to become obscured, Fichte suggests that regaining the moral standpoint becomes increasingly difficult the more the consciousness of duty becomes obscured.

If their natural inertia or laziness generates in human beings a propensity to remain in a natural condition in which they lack a sufficiently clear consciousness of the rational authority of the moral law, then their escape from a state of moral evil presupposes that they have *already* left this condition, given how this escape requires consciousness of the moral law. This would be equally true of a human being who had left the original, natural condition but had subsequently relapsed into it by allowing his or her consciousness of duty to become obscured, for the transition from the natural condition and a state of moral evil to a moral state of being in which the voice of conscience speaks clearly would have to be made anew. A major difference between Kant's and Fichte's explanations of radical evil here emerges. Kant's notion of an original choice of disposition presupposes a sufficiently clear consciousness of the moral law on the part of an agent because freely choosing whether or not to make respect for this law the incentive of one's actions determines what this disposition is. Thus, this choice presupposes that the agent concerned is sufficiently conscious of the possible objects of choice, which include the moral law. Fichte, however, appears to rule out the possibility of any such original choice by suggesting that a natural being would not, and could not, have any consciousness of the rational authority of this law. He characterizes this problem in terms of the difficulty of explaining how an individual can generate within him- or herself the force that would counteract his or her natural inertia, thereby enabling him or her to adopt the standpoint of morality. Fichte's response to this problem appears to be a purely negative one insofar as it seeks to avoid introducing any kind of supernatural intervention:

> But where in his state is there a place from which he could produce this force? – Absolutely nowhere. If one views this matter in purely natural terms, then it is absolutely impossible that a human being should be able to help himself; he cannot improve at all in this way. Only a miracle could save him – a miracle, moreover, which he himself would have to perform. (GA I/ 5: 184; SL 4: 191)

To understand the precise nature of the problem, we need to look at the account of freedom that forms the background to it. I shall argue that this account of freedom provides the basis for an explanation of how the rational authority of the moral law might be thought to announce itself to an individual who is yet to achieve the standpoint of morality or who has achieved this standpoint but then relapsed into the natural condition. This explanation is, however, ultimately provided by Kierkegaard rather than Fichte, though I shall argue that it is consistent with many of the fundamental elements of his theory of moral evil. The limitations of this explanation will nevertheless require another step. This step involves a different kind of external influence to the improbable miracle mentioned in the passage quoted above. The influence is a human one that marks the transition from the subjective realm of the psychology of moral evil to a realm in which individuals stand in moral relations with other individuals as members of the same society.

7.4 Moral Evil and Freedom

Fichte's account of moral evil appears difficult to reconcile with his account of freedom. On the one hand, he states that we must be conscious of the moral law if we are to be conscious of ourselves as free. On the other hand, the way in which he explains moral evil in terms of how the consciousness of duty becomes obscured implies the absence of any such consciousness of this law. An individual in a state of moral evil could not, therefore, be conscious of him- or herself as free, whereas the consciousness of him- or herself as free is a necessary condition of being a moral agent at all, making it difficult to see how a human being could be responsible for the state of moral evil that he or she is in. A fundamental difference

138   DAVID JAMES

between Kant's account of moral evil and Fichte's account of it is therefore said to concern how the latter explains moral evil in terms of the natural force of inertia, and thereby denies that it is the result of an act of freedom, whereas the former does locate it in act of freedom.[2] We shall shortly see that the contrast between Kant's position and Fichte's one is here drawn too sharply because Fichte provides reasons for thinking that human beings would never be in a purely natural condition governed by the force of inertia once society had reached a certain level of development. Nevertheless, the difficulty of reconciling Fichte's account of moral evil with the notion of moral responsibility is suggested by the following claim that he makes in connection with the idea that the thought of freedom requires the thought of the moral law and the thought of the moral law conversely requires the thought of freedom:

> Neither of these is thought without the other, and insofar as one of them is thought, then so is the other. When you think of yourself as free, you are required to think your freedom under a law; and when you think of this law, you are required to think of yourself as free, for your freedom is presupposed by this law, which announces itself as the law of freedom. (GA I/5: 64; SL 4: 55)

The relation between freedom and the moral law here is one of mutual implication to the extent that the thought of freedom and the thought of the moral law are, in effect, aspects of one and the same thought: "Freedom does not follow from the law, no more than the law follows from freedom. These are not two thoughts, one of which can be thought to depend upon the other; rather this is one and the same thought" (GA I/5: 64–65; SL 4: 55). This identity is required by the fundamental problem to which Fichte's ethical theory is attempting to provide the solution.

The problem is to explain the "absolute" identity of the subjective and objective aspects of the I. Although this identity must be presupposed, it cannot itself form a direct object of knowledge, because the finite I suffers the limitation that it must always think of an object that stands opposed to itself. This is even true of the I insofar as it attempts to think itself, because the attempt to think its own identity inescapably produces the distinction between the I as subject of consciousness and the I as object of consciousness (GA I/5: 24, 56; SL 4: 11, 45). The concept of morality explains this identity at the same time as it incorporates the distinction between the I as subject and the I as object because the I's

---

[2] See Piché (2000).

"self-sufficiency" (*Selbständigkeit*), understood as the capacity or power (*Vermögen*) to act as a cause that is undetermined by anything other than itself, finds its objective correlate in the "law" or "norm" of "self-sufficiency" that demands that the I exercise the capacity or power to act as an entirely free cause (GA I/5: 63; SL 4: 53–54). An agent that was not conscious of the rational authority of the moral law, and cannot become so, would therefore not be conscious of itself as a free *moral* agent, and it is precisely where the self-legislation of moral autonomy is absent that "immorality begins" (GA I/5: 67; SL 4: 58). Freedom understood more generally, however, is not coextensive with this moral autonomy. Rather, Fichte identifies different stages of freedom that the human being can attain, of which moral autonomy is the highest stage.

One stage of freedom consists in consciousness of the possibility of exercising choice when it comes to the satisfaction of natural drives (GA I/5: 151; SL 4: 153). The agent is here confronted with various given desires but is at the same time conscious of the capacity to act in accordance with one desire rather than another one. The desire upon which the agent chooses to act is not necessarily the strongest one at the time. The agent may instead choose to act upon a weaker existing desire that accords more with what this agent believes will eventually, if not at the present moment, produce the most happiness for him or her. Thus, some kind of second-order desire is at work.

This consciousness of the capacity to exercise choice, as opposed to being immediately determined by whatever happens to be the strongest desire at any given moment, presupposes an element of reflection and independence of that which Fichte calls the natural drive. This independence points to a higher level of freedom, of which an individual becomes conscious by reflecting on his or her consciousness of the capacity to exercise choice. It even becomes possible, by reflecting on this act of reflection, to achieve awareness of how this second act of reflection "contains nothing but the pure, absolute activity that occurred in the first act of reflection; and this pure activity alone is the proper and true I" (GA I/5: 133; SL 4: 133–34). This act of reflection reveals to the subject that engages in it the capacity to perform acts of self-determination free of any purely given ends. In the absence of any purely given ends, the agent becomes responsive to the demand to engage in self-activity for its own sake, as expressed in "the completely formal concept of an absolute ought," which, given how it is completely undetermined by anything external to itself, and is in this regard self-generated, renders a moral agent "absolutely self-sufficient" (*absolut selbständig*) (GA I/5: 145; SL 4: 147). This moral self-sufficiency manifests itself in acts of judgment whose ultimate source of validation is the voice of conscience.

Although the human being whose consciousness of duty has become obscured to such an extent that he or she has, in effect, returned to the natural condition governed by the force of inertia cannot be thought to achieve this self-sufficiency, he or she could still achieve consciousness of his or her "formal" freedom. Fichte claims, in fact, that this requires only gaining some experience, and that it can explain the postponement of natural satisfaction demanded by such nonmoral phenomena as prudence and the long-term pursuit of happiness, which can themselves be explained in terms of self-interest (GA I/5: 151–52; SL 4: 153–54). This type of consciousness of freedom is likely to be achieved by anyone in a society that educates its members in ways required to maintain public order and guarantee the effective functioning of the society. For example, a society whose members were at the mercy of their given desires and unable to act with a view to the long-term consequences of their actions would arguably be one that could not maintain itself because its members would consistently fail to act in accordance with laws and norms that are conditions of social order and stability. Nor would they be able to cooperate effectively with one another, although cooperation is required by any complex form of social organization. The society in question need not be viewed as a morally good one, however, because it is built upon self-interest and need not encourage individuals to transcend the standpoint of self-interest to attain a genuinely moral standpoint. Moreover, the force of inertia could here come into play in such a way that it assumes a distinctively human form, for individuals may then, as a matter of habit and self-interest, lead lives that externally conform to the demands of duty at the same time as they themselves lack any consciousness of the rational authority of the moral law, which is itself a condition of consciousness of the absolute self-sufficiency that characterizes moral autonomy.

We are therefore still confronted with the question of how to explain the transition to the highest level of reflection and agency demanded by the idea of moral autonomy, given the natural *human* tendency to seek to remain in an existing state of being.[3] Clearly, the idea of the influence of

---

[3] Even if the earlier stages of freedom, and the fact that it is not necessary that a human being remain at any of them prior to the stage of moral self-sufficiency, are enough to justify the claim that we should not confuse the inertia to which human beings are subject with the inertia to which purely natural entities are subject (see Ware [2015]), this would not by itself solve the problem that I have in mind. For Fichte does not directly identify moral evil with a conscious choice of good over evil, but instead identifies it primarily with a state of being in which individuals are not even aware of the moral law

Fichte's Theory of Moral Evil

society is not sufficient to explain this transition. Indeed, Fichte suggests that this influence can present a potential obstacle to achieving it: "If . . . a human being is left to himself and is fettered neither by the example of his age nor by a ruinous philosophy, it is then to be expected that he will become conscious of that drive to absolute self-sufficiency that is always enduring and active within him" (GA I/5: 170; SL 4: 175). Despite this rather optimistic claim about what individuals who are not subject to detrimental external influences, including social ones, might achieve, Fichte not surprisingly describes the idea that individuals can raise themselves to the level of genuine moral reflection as "inexplicable" (*unerklärlich*) (GA I/5: 171; SL 4: 175). As implicitly free, in the sense of possessing the capacity for moral autonomy, if not self-consciously free, human beings are nevertheless able to attain the moral standpoint by becoming conscious of themselves as morally autonomous beings, which requires that they achieve clear consciousness of the rational authority of the moral law. Fichte describes the paradox that this situation generates in the following way:

> Since he is, in accordance with his original being, free and independent of nature, even if he is not free in actuality, he always ought to tear himself loose from this state [of inertia]; and if one considers him to be absolutely free, then he is also *able* to do this. Before he can freely tear himself loose, however, he must first be free. But it is precisely his freedom itself that is fettered; the very force through which he is supposed to help himself is allied against him. No balance is established here; instead, there is [only] the weight of his nature, which is what holds him in check, and there is no counterweight from the side of the moral law. (GA I/5: 184; SL 4: 190–91)

As with Kant's theory of radical evil, we are confronted with the question of how to explain that which is presupposed by the idea of a transition from a state of moral evil, or, as here, a state in which the choice between moral good and moral evil cannot even be made, to a state of moral goodness, namely, the possibility of choosing that which is morally good instead of that which is morally evil. In Fichte's case, the paradox can be expressed in the form of the following question: How can the individual who has never left the pre-moral natural condition, or transcended the standpoint of his or her own society with its functional requirements, or whose conscious-ness of duty has become so obscured that it is as if he or she had never

---

that determines what is good and what is evil. Toward the end of this chapter, I shall suggest that Fichte appears to commit himself to a version of the doctrine of original sin which reintroduces the problem of how individuals can be held responsible for moral evil.

become conscious of the rational authority of the moral law escape the state of moral evil which he or she is in?

Although the idea that the consciousness of duty is obscured rather than obliterated altogether might be thought to suggest a solution, in that individuals who had once attained this consciousness could retain a dim awareness of the rational authority of the moral law, we would then also need to explain why this consciousness of duty cannot become so obscured that it in effect disappears. For the idea of letting oneself be governed by the natural force of inertia opens the way for a gradual obscuring of the consciousness of duty to the point at which it disappears altogether.[4] Fichte acknowledges such a possibility when he claims that this inertia "infinitely reproduces itself through long habit and soon becomes a complete incapacity for what is good" (GA I/5: 185; SL 4: 191). I shall now argue that a dim awareness of the authority of the moral law might nevertheless then take the form of a psychological state, namely, the state of anxiety diagnosed by Kierkegaard, and that this psychological state must be interpreted, allowing a social element to be introduced into Fichte's theory of moral evil.

7.5 The Psychology of Moral Evil: Fichte and Kierkegaard

Kierkegaard discusses the concept of anxiety in connection with the state of innocence. Fichte, in contrast, implies that the state of innocence has already been lost when he speaks of the consciousness of duty becoming obscure and how individuals are responsible for the inattention and lack of resolve that explain this. If the obscuring of the consciousness of duty goes far enough, however, the individual who allows this to happen will, like someone in an amoral state of innocence, lack any explicit awareness of the

---

[4] The examples of moral evil that Fichte provides imply that a sufficiently clear consciousness of duty is retained, for in each case the individual concerned exempts him- or herself from the moral law, by fixing upon a duty other than the one demanded by the situation, by recognizing that something is a duty but failing to recognize that it is a duty at this particular time, by allowing obedience to it to be deferred, or by viewing that which is demanded by duty as if it were a piece of advice that it is at one's discretion to obey or disobey, allowing one to do one's duty only when it suits one to do it (GA I/5: 179–81; SL 4: 185–87). A consciousness of duty that becomes so obscure that there is, in effect, no longer any consciousness of the rational authority of the moral law is nevertheless possible on the basis of Fichte's explanation of moral evil and it therefore needs to be considered. This form of moral evil cannot be reduced to a case of willful self-deception or perversity in the sense of an attempt to deny or escape one's moral nature, as has been argued (see Ware [2015], Wood [2016a, 168–69], and Wood [2016b, 193–94]), because it entails a lack of any awareness of this moral nature, of which the individual could become aware only if he or she had left the kind of state of moral evil that he or she had entered as a result of the complete obscuring of the consciousness of duty.

rational authority of the moral law and thus knowledge of good and evil. This allows us to draw one parallel between Fichte's account of moral evil and a central feature of Kierkegaard's account of the concept of anxiety, namely, how the source of anxiety is not located in any determinate object or state of affairs but is instead essentially "nothing," in the sense of the absence of something. This something which is absent is nevertheless a possibility for the individual concerned, for the "nothing" of which Kierkegaard speaks is the unactualized possibility of a form of knowledge: "the whole actuality of knowledge projects itself in anxiety as the enormous nothing of ignorance."[5] Thus, on the one hand, anxiety involves a dim awareness of something that *could* be, and, on the other hand, it lacks any explicit awareness of what this something is. As we shall see, this broadly corresponds to how an individual in a state of moral evil could be aware of the possibility of the transition from this state to a moral condition and the corresponding form of freedom, despite how his or her consciousness of duty has become completely obscured.

The "nothing of ignorance" that explains the mood of anxiety that overcomes the individual concerns the absence of knowledge of good and evil. The possibility that also explains this mood cannot, therefore, be directly equated with the possibility of choosing what is evil over what is good, for this possibility presupposes prior knowledge of what is good and what is evil, or at least knowledge of the means of finding out what they are, whereas the individual in a state of innocence lacks such knowledge. For this individual, it is simply a matter of "the anxious possibility of *being able*."[6] There is here an awareness of possibility that at the same time lacks any determinate object or end. Nevertheless, there must be some intimation of the distinction between good and evil and the possibility of sin understood as the choice of evil in opposition to the good. Otherwise, there would be no reason to think that the awareness of mere possibility could not manifest itself in entirely different ways, such as in a jubilant or frivolous sense of freedom from constraint. But how can this intimation of knowledge of good and evil, and thus the possibility of sin, be explained prior to any explicit consciousness of the moral distinction between good and evil? One possible explanation is that although the awareness of freedom is reduced to an awareness of being able to choose that does not also involve awareness of the moral choices facing one, there is some anticipation of the knowledge of these choices, and thus of the possibility of making the wrong choice, because this knowledge and this possibility

---

[5] Kierkegaard (1980, 44).   [6] Kierkegaard (1980, 44).

are rooted in the same freedom. This would help to explain Kierkegaard's claim that anxiety is not something that individuals can escape. Rather, anxiety is an integral part of their own selves as free beings.

Kierkegaard's account of anxiety is here compatible with Fichte's theory of moral evil insofar as it also contains the idea of a possibility rooted in freedom that has yet to be actualized. In the case of this theory, however, the possibility concerns the achievement of the level of reflection that consists in direct consciousness of the rational authority of the moral law and corresponds to the "absolute" self-sufficiency of that which Fichte terms "autonomy" and "self-legislation." Yet, for the individual who has allowed his or her consciousness of duty to become completely obscured, or who has not even achieved this consciousness, this possibility will remain a mere possibility, in which case this individual may be aware of his or her freedom to choose but not his or her freedom to make essentially moral choices. This aligns with Fichte's account of the various stages of reflection and corresponding forms of freedom prior to the final, distinctively moral one. Given that this individual is already aware of the freedom to choose, we can nevertheless say that he or she is on the way to achieving the higher level of reflection accompanied by explicit consciousness of the rational authority of the moral law and thus freedom understood as moral autonomy. There is, however, no necessity that dictates that the individual will actually accomplish this transition, which therefore remains a mere possibility that announces itself in a state of anxiety. Because the individual would become morally autonomous only once this transition had been made, freedom itself also remains a possibility which announces itself in a state of anxiety. This would correspond to that which Kierkegaard says about Adam before the Fall: "[H]is anxiety is not anxiety about sin, for as yet the distinction between good and evil is not, because this distinction first comes about with the actuality of freedom."[7]

I have so far shown only that something like a mood of anxiety would be a way in which the human being's moral nature announces itself, however obscurely, despite the way in which the possibility of escaping a state of moral evil appears difficult to comprehend, given how Fichte explains moral evil in terms of the human tendency to succumb to the natural force of inertia in such a way that the consciousness of duty is progressively obscured or never achieved in the first place. An individual may nevertheless be thought to possess some awareness that things are not quite right, that there is something of which he or she ought to be aware, that there is

---

[7] Kierkegaard (1980, 52).

a mystery that cannot be solved as long as he or she remains in his or her present condition. Anxiety is discomforting, moreover, and it is therefore precisely the kind of mood that one would expect to encounter in such circumstances. This discomfort might then motivate the individual who experiences it to seek to escape his or her present condition, despite the natural force of inertia to which he or she is subject, even if he or she lacks any clear idea of what is required to escape this condition. Finally, the affective element that a state of anxiety introduces into Fichte's account of moral evil is of the right kind, despite how the way in which it inexplicably overcomes an individual may appear incompatible with the freedom which it announces. It is of the right kind because only a being capable of both the relevant moral knowledge and acting contrary to the good could experience it. Anxiety is, in short, produced by the individual's own moral nature, as opposed to having a purely external source. This accords with Kierkegaard's statement that "[i]f a human being were a beast or an angel, he could not be in anxiety," and his claim that the individual produces the anxiety which he or she suffers.[8] Anxiety would in this regard be on a par with the affective elements that are integral to Fichte's account of conscience, which include not only a feeling of truth and certainty, but also "concern" (*Besorglichkeit*), given the seriousness of the act of determining correctly that which duty demands of oneself in a particular situation (GA I/5: 156; SL 4: 159).

Although a mood of anxiety may help explain how there could be some presentiment of the possibility of attaining the moral standpoint but then failing to choose good instead of evil, it does not by itself explain how an individual could transcend the mood that has overcome him or her by actually attaining the moral standpoint and choosing good instead of evil, because there is still no clear consciousness of duty, which itself presupposes consciousness of the rational authority of the moral law. Indeed, if there were a clear consciousness of duty, the individual would have already transcended a condition in which he or she experiences anxiety because the awareness of possibility is not accompanied by knowledge of that which is possible. This brings me to the need for intersubjective mediation.

Toward the end of his discussion of moral evil, Fichte claims that the difficulty of explaining how an individual could raise him- or herself to the moral standpoint can be removed only if we assume the existence of exemplars who "elevate" the individual and "provide him with an image of how he ought to be, who infuse him with respect, along with a desire to

---

[8] Kierkegaard (1980, 155).

become worthy of respect himself" (GA I/5: 187; SL 4: 194). How might this seemingly ad hoc solution relate to the role that I have assigned to a mood of anxiety? One way in which it might be thought to do so is as follows. These exemplars not only provide models of moral integrity capable of bringing about a dispositional change in others, but also act as educators in that they develop teachings that provide the key to discovering the correct interpretation of the mood of anxiety that inexplicably overcomes an individual whose consciousness of duty has become obscured or who is yet to achieve this form of consciousness, that is to say, teachings that lead this individual to comprehend that the source of this mood lies within his or her own moral nature, which this mood announces to him or her. This would be compatible with how Fichte proceeds to speak of a positive religion that consists of "institutions arranged by excellent human beings for the purpose of influencing others to develop their moral sense," though not with the aim of fostering blind obedience (GA I/5: 187; SL 4: 194). These institutions are useful because their authority is employed to direct an individual's attention to his or her moral nature by means of certain teachings, from which, however, the individual must draw his or her own conclusions. Thus, the miracle required to solve the paradox identified earlier is not a supernatural one but one facilitated by other human beings. Yet this explanation generates problems of its own.

To begin with, the existence of these moral exemplars and teachers itself needs to be explained, for one must assume either that they naturally possess a clear consciousness of duty that cannot be obscured or the existence of a miracle by means of which they came to possess it, despite the natural force of inertia to which they are subject. Otherwise, we would be faced with an infinite regress, with the existence of one moral educator having to be explained in terms of an earlier one, whose own existence needs to be explained, and so on.[9] Another problem concerns a religious teaching closely related to the notion of moral evil, namely, the concept of sin. The relation of Kierkegaard's account of anxiety to the concept of sin can be used to show how Fichte's theory of moral evil in fact entails that human beings could never have been in a condition of genuine innocence. It then looks as if Fichte is committed to some version of the doctrine of original sin, whereas he himself clearly rejects this doctrine when he states

---

[9] Fichte clearly recognizes this problem and he eventually sought to solve it by means of the idea of a *Zwingherr,* who, if necessary, coerces individuals in such a way that they become moral beings. Once they have become such beings, these individuals will achieve insight into the moral grounds of this coercion. See James (2016).

that "[h]uman nature is originally neither good nor evil. Only through freedom does it become either of these" (GA I/5: 174; SL 4: 179).

Kierkegaard's account of the concept of anxiety is bound up with the concept of sin because he explains anxiety in terms of the possibility of knowing the distinction between good and evil and then choosing evil instead of good, thereby making oneself guilty. As we have seen, innocence is ignorance of this moral distinction but anxiety announces the possibility of knowledge of it and thus the possibility of knowingly choosing evil instead of good. The transition from possibility to actuality comes about through "a qualitative leap" whereby an individual "posits" sin by making such a choice.[10] It is only with this leap, moreover, that the distinction between good and evil becomes explicit. Knowledge of this distinction is therefore necessarily accompanied by awareness that one has sinned by making the fateful choice of evil instead of good. Thus, anxiety is described as "the dizziness of freedom" that an individual, like someone staring into an abyss, experiences immediately before that moment in which "everything is changed, and freedom, when it again rises, sees that it is guilty."[11] Although these claims invite the question as to why an individual could not instead have happened to choose good rather than evil when it was possible for him or her to do so, I take it that this is precisely the point that Kierkegaard wants to make. Just as Christian dogmatics presupposes sin, the concept of anxiety presupposes it, because it cannot itself explain that which it anticipates while lacking actual knowledge of it: "Anxiety is the psychological state that precedes sin. It approaches sin as closely as possible, as anxiously as possible, but without explaining sin, which breaks forth only in the qualitative leap."[12]

Fichte, in contrast, needs to explain the possibility of sin in such a way that it is not shown to be presupposed, for there would then appear to be some kind of inexplicable original tendency to choose what is morally evil instead of what is morally good. His explanation is that sin arises when individuals fail to act in accordance with that which their own conscience would have told them is morally demanded of them if they had not allowed the consciousness of duty to become obscured, or if they had originally overcome the natural force of inertia to which they are subject to achieve the consciousness of duty. Human beings have a strong tendency toward moral evil, however, precisely because they are subject to this force of inertia, to which they themselves nevertheless ought not to succumb because they have the power to resist it: "If ... one acts without being

---

[10] Kierkegaard (1980, 54).   [11] Kierkegaard (1980, 61).   [12] Kierkegaard (1980, 92).

certain of the pronouncement of one's conscience, then one acts unconscionably; one's guilt is clear, and one cannot pin this guilt on anything outside oneself. There is no excuse for any sin; it *is* a sin, and it remains a sin" (GA I/5: 162; SL 4: 165–66). Yet are the various claims that Fichte makes in this connection compatible with the idea that sin is not something that must be presupposed?

The question of whether or not an individual acts without being certain of the moral truth of the pronouncements of his or her own conscience is meaningful only if it is assumed that this individual already has a clear consciousness of duty in accordance with which he or she may or may not choose to act, whereas in the case of an individual whose consciousness of duty has become completely obscured, it would make no sense to talk about acting in accordance with such pronouncements simply because there would be no such pronouncements insofar as this individual's own conscience is concerned. Rather, their existence presupposes the transition from something like a state of anxiety, which is to be explained in terms of possibilities of which an individual is aware without knowing what they are, to the moral standpoint, where individuals are conscious of their moral autonomy, which entails that they are also conscious of the rational authority of the moral law. Yet, as we have seen, Fichte claims that this transition requires the influence of others and is therefore not something that individuals are capable of bringing about by themselves.

Once the transition to the moral standpoint has been made with the help of others, it looks as if those individuals who were previously in a state of moral evil will then recognize that they were *already* guilty of the violation of a specific moral duty to which Fichte appears committed, given his description of Kant's statement that "conscience is a consciousness that is itself a duty" as "a correct and sublime pronouncement" (GA I/5: 161; SL 4: 164). This is the duty to have a consciousness of duty and it is violated either by failing to make the transition to the moral standpoint in the first place or by allowing the consciousness of duty to become completely obscured. In short, once individuals have made the transition to the moral standpoint, they must retrospectively comprehend that they had been in a state of moral evil even if they could not at the time have been conscious of this fact, and that they would not have been in this state if they had not allowed themselves to succumb to the natural force of inertia. In this respect, it is not the anxiety of innocence that is most relevant but another form of anxiety that Kierkegaard identifies. Although the transition from possibility to actuality might appear to abolish anxiety, given how anxiety is explained in terms of an indeterminate possibility, sin involves the production of "an unwarranted actuality," which is a determinate something (i.e., a specific sin that the individual has committed), the awareness of which presupposes knowledge of the distinction between good and evil. This in turn produces anxiety with regard to the future, because an individual now fears either committing the same sin or the consequences of the original sin.[13] Fichte's moral agent is likewise someone who has already committed a sin with which he or she is now confronted, making it difficult to see how this agent could have ever been free of sin.

---

[13] Kierkegaard (1980, 111–12).

CHAPTER 8

Embodiment and Freedom
Fichte "On the Material of the Ethical Law"

Angelica Nuzzo

Fichte's ethical theory or "doctrine of ethics" conceived as a "special" and "real" philosophical science is formulated for the first time in the *System of Ethics* (1798). In the development of Fichte's thought, the *System of Ethics* fulfills the crucial *systematic* task of placing the discipline of ethics in relation to the foundational part of philosophy conceived as Doctrine of Science or *Wissenschaftslehre*.[1] The fundamental revision of the Doctrine of Science occupies Fichte at the time of the *System of Ethics*. Furthermore, in connection with this systematic task, the *System of Ethics* is charged with addressing the *methodological* problems of obtaining the highest principle of ethics from the foundational principles of the *Wissenschaftslehre*, and of accounting for the intersection between the genetic-transcendental method of philosophical thinking (the *theory* of ethics) and the ordinary standpoint proper of moral conscience and common ethical practice as such. Accordingly, the highest principle of ethics is obtained in relation to the transcendental structure of I (*Ichheit*), while the natural human impulse to act is investigated by bringing to light the transcendental origin of our moral concepts. Finally, in developing the structure of the *System of Ethics*, Fichte takes on the *historical* task – a delicate balancing act – of advancing Kant's ethics beyond what are generally perceived as its short-comings while at the same time maintaining what are taken to be its unrenounceable gains. In fact, while Kant's moral theory stands firm at the center of the contemporary discussion, there are other important influences and figures that should be kept in mind in order to understand the peculiarity of Fichte's ethics in relation to and after Kant. Significantly, in its engagement with Kant, Fichte's ethics points forward toward Hegel's distinctively non-Kantian (and nontranscendental) practical philosophy but is also, at once, projected back to crucial moments of the early modern

---

[1] See Breazeale (2015).

150

tradition of Spinoza and Leibniz. In short, while Fichte does not renounce but rather corrects Kant's ethical formalism by addressing the crucial problem of the "application," the "reality," and the "materiality" of the moral principle, he sets out to mend the Kantian split within the human acting subject by reconciling the sensible and the intelligible in a theory of practical drives that ultimately converges with the enactment of reason's ethical law in the phenomenal world. Thus, because the actual deduction of the contents of "ethics proper" (or, more narrowly, the "doctrine of duties in the proper sense": GA I/5: 229; SL 4: 254ff.) is the program that Fichte's *System of Ethics* undertakes at the intersection of the above-mentioned systematic, methodological, and historical tasks, the reconstruction of the third part of the 1798 work should keep this larger picture firmly in view.

This is the aim of the present chapter, which is concerned, specifically and more narrowly, with the argument developed in §18 of the second part of the third main division of Fichte's *System of Ethics*. At the center herein is the "material of the ethical law (*das Materiale des Sittengesetzes*),"[2] the presentation of which constitutes the second step in the "systematic application" and indeed realization of the ethical principle.

A preliminary look at the overall structure of the *System of Ethics* can help us approach the problem tackled in the third, more extensive part of the work. For, its very articulation already hints at the general issues mentioned above. While the first main division is concerned with the "Deduction of the Principle of *Sittlichkeit*" and contains a new presentation of the foundational part of the system or *Wissenschaftslehre*; and while the second division is concerned with the "Deduction of the Reality and Applicability of this Principle," the third division brings the "*Sittenlehre* in the narrower sense" to the center and does so by addressing the problem of the "systematic application" of the previously deduced principle. Integrating more than countering the necessary formality of Kant's foundational moral principle, Fichte's ethics aims at being a "concrete" ethics in which the highest principle is deduced both in its formality and in its materiality, both in its rational ideality and possibility, and in its "reality" and "applicability" but also actual "application" within human life and the broader, social world of human practice. To be sure, while Fichte underscores the importance of an ethics that is "concrete" (in the sense of material in addition to formal, and both applicable and *de facto* applied),

---

[2] In this chapter, I will focus on the methodological and historical issues more than on the systematic one, which is truly at the center in the first two main parts of the *Sittenlehre*.

he rejects the casuistic concreteness that informs the Aristotelian tradition of eighteenth-century ethics and remains significantly important for Kant.[3] In fact, the *material contents* that progressively realize Fichte's ethical principle are derived or deduced *systematically* from the *formal* conditions of the morality of the action itself and from the *formal* conditions of the acting subjectivity (*Ichheit*).[4] Moreover, in contrast to Kant, Fichte presents the theory in which the deduction of the ethical principle is complemented by (and, for common moral conscience, is one with) its application to human nature and action as a *system of ethics* (*Sittenlehre*), not as a *metaphysics of morals* (*Metaphysik der Sitten*).[5] Ultimately, this shift signals both the need for the moral principle to be material and not only formal, and the need to rethink the acting subject as the integrated connection of practical reason and natural drives. Indeed, Fichte maintains, "[i]f one considers only the higher power of desire, then one obtains a mere *metaphysics of morals* (*Metaphysik der Sitten*), which is formal and empty. The only way to obtain *ethics* (*Sittenlehre*) – which must be real – is through the synthetic unification of the higher and lower faculty of desire" (GA I/5: 126; SL 4: 131).

This constellation already suggests that for Fichte the issue of application concerns two distinct and interconnected issues. On the one hand, it concerns the relation between the formal conditions of the morality of human action and the material content of the moral law (or our particular and determinate duties); and on the other hand, it concerns the relation between the general formal principle of ethics and the world of actual practice within which that principle ought to be implemented and realized.[6] The *System of Ethics* is the theory that brings these threads together. Now, despite his many references to Kant, on this point Fichte's formulation of the problem is much closer to Hegel's theory of *Sittlichkeit* (in its systematic distinction from *Moralität*) than one may suspect.[7] Indeed, as we shall see in what follows, the relation between the

---

[3] See De Pascale (1995, 120 ff.)

[4] See, respectively, the title of the first section of the third main division (GA I/5: 147; SL 4: 157) and the title of §18 (GA I/5: 194; SL 4: 212).

[5] Although, as we shall see, the metaphysical background is highly relevant to his theory. For the relation to Kant's "metaphysics" of morals, see Nuzzo (2011).

[6] While the former relation hints at a peculiarly Kantian problem, the latter already anticipates a Hegelian issue.

[7] The terminological distinction between *Sittlichkeit* – ethical life or ethics – and *Moralität* – morality – becomes significant only with Hegel. Consequently, in reference to Fichte, I use the terms morality and ethics without technical distinctions and qualifications. When I do choose one term over the other, my choice is generally guided by a distinction that comes close to Hegel and reflects the claim concerning the proximity Fichte–Hegel presented in this chapter.

problem of application, the issue of the material of the ethical law, and the role of the living body in connecting them – or what I call Fichte's idea of the necessary embodiment of freedom – brings to light Fichte's crucial proximity to Hegel. It is precisely in this framework that the role of the ethical principle, which Fichte formulates as the rational drive (or the command) of "*absolute Selbständigkeit*" and "*Unabhängigkeit*" (self-sufficiency, independence, autarchy as successors of Kantian autonomy) in §18 of the *Sittenlehre*, will henceforth be examined. While Fichte's formulation has recently received attention in the literature, a truly satisfactory explanation is still lacking. Hegel – but also Spinoza – will help us shed some new light on this principle and its implications.[8]

In sum, here is the claim that I set out to establish in this chapter. Once the issue of the realization or actualization of freedom in the world – the "sensible world" of nature and human natural drives as well as the "rational world" of other rational moral beings and their social bonds – is recognized as constitutive and foundational for the concept of freedom and for the moral principle as such, Kant's opposition of formal and material ethics (an opposition that regards the nature or indeed the very form of the moral principle independently of anthropological conditions and independently of its contents and concrete enactment)[9] is *ipso facto* overcome. What obtains is an ethics that – the insistence on the continuity with Kant notwithstanding – unavoidably develops in a fundamentally different direction than Kant's. The end result of this development is Hegel's idea of *Sittlichkeit* and its relation to *Moralität*. But the crucial moment in this process and its real turning point is Fichte's *Sittenlehre*. Unlike Hegel, Fichte thinks of the actualization of the ethical principle – and of freedom – as "*Anwendung*." Application (of the ethical principle to human nature as well as to concrete human action) is realization in the sensible world. But application is realization because it is, first and foremost, embodiment. It is the incorporation of the principle in the human body and in the materiality of the world. In a first step of my argument, I examine the idea of "application" and its relation to the "material" of the moral law that occupies the third main division of the *Sittenlehre*. I then move on to

---

[8] I will not extensively elaborate on Hegel's *Moralität-Sittlichkeit* transition. The reference, however, becomes clear at different points of my reconstruction of Fichte's argument. For Hegel's critique of Kant in this connection, and his proximity to Fichte, see Nuzzo (2013) and Nuzzo (2016). Fichte's idea of self-sufficiency is at the center of Michelle Kosch's interpretation (Kosch [2015]; more recently, Kosch [2018, ch. 3–4]). In short, she reads Fichte as a utilitarian, an idea against which Allen Wood reacts (e.g., Wood [2016a, 174ff.]). It should be clear from what follows that I think this debate misses the metaphysical framework in which Fichte places his correction of Kant's position.

[9] See for this Nuzzo (2015).

a closer analysis of §18, and to establish the claim of the centrality of the living body in the progressive and open-ended actualization of the ethical principle of absolute self-sufficiency and independence, that is, the idea of freedom's necessary embodiment. Application as realization is embodiment. Embodiment is the material process of progressive and expansive incorporation of the law into the world and, reciprocally and just as necessarily, of the world into the ethical law. By incorporating the world (and thereby first positing it as a human world) the acting subject progressively appropriates it, thereby approximating its own independence – the independence not (abstractly) *from*, but (concretely) *within* the complex and multifaceted nexus that is the world.

8.1 "Applicability" and "Application" of the Principle of Ethics

Quite generally, Fichte's ethics in the strict sense is concerned with the problem of applying morality to human nature. It deals with the specific predicament and constitutive limitation of the human being viewed as a finite temporal being (a *Zeitwesen*: GA I/5: 155; SL 4: 166) endowed with reason as well as with a set of natural drives, a rational-sensible being that is itself part of nature and whose action unfolds in time within nature. Ethics regards the way in which the highest moral principle and the drive to freedom are actually and materially implemented in the larger natural and human world. Thus, unlike Kant, Fichte recognizes the fundamental anthropological dimension of ethics from the outset and sees the issue of application as belonging to the theory of ethics as a constitutive moment, not as a successive step following its accomplished foundation (as in Kant's case).[10]

Citing and commenting on Kant's definition of freedom as spontaneity or as "the power to begin a state (a being and a subsistence) absolutely," Fichte observes that this "is an excellent *nominal* explanation, but does not seem to have done much to improve our general insight" (GA I/5: 52; SL 4: 37, my emphasis),[11] because it has remained nominal and empty. For, Kant's definition does not answer the crucial, indeed in Fichte's view the "still higher question": "*how* can a state begin absolutely?" And properly, how can the so-begun process endure and unfold phenomenally in the temporal dimension that constitutes the life and activity of the finite agent (who is in charge of actually beginning

---

[10] See Nuzzo (2011, 201).
[11] See KrV A445/B473 and B561/A533: Fichte, however, does not address the distinction between transcendental and practical freedom drawn by Kant in the latter passage. See Fonnesu (1999, 2010).

Embodiment and Freedom

such a state)? In order to answer *this* more fundamental (and genuinely practical) question, Fichte suggests a change in method, or better, a correction of the transcendental strategy. He maintains that transcendental philosophy must *generate* its own concepts thereby moving from a nominal to a *real* (because genetic) definition of freedom, in this way becoming truly practical.[12] The issue of application is already contained herein: Kant's merely "nominal" definition should be replaced by the "genetic concept of freedom," which, most properly, is freedom's direct enactment in time and in the sensible world. It is the latter, not the former, that answers the question of "how" an absolute beginning (a being or an event) can be put into existence, that is, can be practically produced. On Fichte's view, despite Kant's reassurance to the contrary, his (transcendental) concept of freedom, remaining purely formal (and noumenal), has no practical validity,[13] that is, it is not truly "real" and, in this sense, is also "inapplicable." The point is that while nominally it is true that freedom is the power to begin a state absolutely, this is not how freedom actually (i.e., practically) works. For, "it is not the case that the state that is begun absolutely is simply connected to nothing at all, for a finite rational being necessarily thinks only by means of mediation and connections. The connection in question, however, is not a connection to another being but to a thinking." This latter point requires the inquiry to be set on the transcendental "path of the *Wissenschaftslehre*" (GA I/5: 52; SL 4: 37) and to move from "being" and the fact of freedom's absolute beginning to the conditions of its enactment in the manifold nexus that hints at both the development of human action and its connection to the (natural and social) world. This is the shift from one's being originally free to one's positing and making oneself free (GA I/5: 52 f.; SL 4: 38). "In the case of a free action, it can be asked *how* this action must come about in order to be a free action, as well as *what* it is that must come about; i.e., one can inquire about the *form* of freedom and also about its *matter* or content" (GA I/5: 144; SL 4: 153; my emphasis). Moreover, in order to be moral, the subject must know, each and every time, "*what* it is that must come about." Indeed, Fichte's inquiry sets out to go beyond Kant's merely nominal definition of freedom and his purely formal moral law in a twofold respect – that

---

[12] "In order to answer this question one would have to generate this concept before our eyes" (GA I/5: 52; SL 4: 37).

[13] In Kant's view, of course, things are exactly the opposite: the moral law (and the concept of freedom as autonomy) has practical (i.e., strictly moral) validity precisely to the extent that it remains purely formal.

is, both with regard to the modes of freedom's implementation ("how" a free action must come about) and to its determinate matter or contents ("what" it is that must come about). The idea of application and the issue of the material of the moral principle address the same twofold systematic problem. Being placed within the world of appearances and endorsed by a particular human subject moral action is always and necessarily determined action – determined, first, by its material content and objective matter; second, by the sensible-rational will that endorses it; and finally, by the particular living body through which the natural drive to action exercises causality in the world, thereby executing the moral command. It is this manifold complex that constitutes the issue of application tackled in the third part of the *System of Ethics*.

Fichte's methodological approach ultimately leads to a far-reaching transformation of Kant's idea of (transcendental) freedom as absolute spontaneity – a definition that is indeed nominally true but does not lead to real freedom, hence is not truly practical. First, for Fichte, freedom is a formal process that is always already materially and temporally determined. Because of my finite nature, Fichte maintains, "I must always have a material (*Stoff*) of my activity," which means that "I cannot create out of nothing that which duty requires of me" (GA I/5: 75; SL 4: 66). Free action is always action within a temporal, phenomenal nexus. Freedom's spontaneity is not creation out of nothing but appropriation, incorporation, and transformation of the material conditions that keep the subject's action rooted to the sensible world. It is only within such a nexus that "independency" and "self-sufficiency" as final moral ends can be conceived. Second, in the process that is human action in its development (*after* the absolute *Anfangspunkt*: GA I/5: 155; SL 4: 166), freedom is manifested not in the beginning or in the "first state" but in each moment of my choice and further (self-)determination in connection with other rational beings. It is precisely through all these successive moments (and choices) that "I become *materialiter* who I am" (GA I/5: 202; SL 4: 222). In this respect as well, it is only within the interconnection that constitutes free action in its ongoing development and constitutes freedom in relation to other rational beings that "independency" and "self-sufficiency" as final moral ends can be conceived.

Fichte's deduction of the principle of morality in the first part of the *System of Ethics* is the genetic explanation of the practical reality of the principle as enacted by the human subject within the world. The reality of the principle is directly connected to its applicability and application. Reality and applicability guarantee the practical efficacy of the ethical principle. "To say that a concept possesses reality and applicability means that our world – i.e., ... the world for our consciousness – is in some respect determined by this concept." This means that a concept has reality when it displays causality not only on the will (as Kant maintains) but also on the phenomenal world. Thus, "[t]o seek the reality of a concept means to investigate how and in what way it determines an object" (GA I/5: 73; SL 4: 63). Fichte clarifies this statement (a statement Kant could very well endorse at least in this general formulation) by discussing the concepts of causality and right. The concept of causality has reality because it generates for me the world of a manifold of objects set in different connections; the concept of right has reality because it generates for me the intersubjective world of free beings (GA I/5: 73; SL 4: 64). On this basis, however, Fichte proceeds to differentiate the two concepts with regard to their applicability.[14] While I cannot (choose to) act against the principle "all event has a cause," that is, I cannot decide not to apply it ("it can never occur to me to deprive an effect of its cause, this is something I can neither think nor will or accomplish": GA I/5: 74; SL 4: 64); I can very well act against the principle "all human beings have rights," that is, I can decide not to apply the concept (hence to withheld reality from it). In the case of practical concepts, applicability and application have a more fundamental relation to the reality of the concept than in the case of merely theoretical ones. For, the reality of practical concepts directly depends on the subject for its implementation, that is, for the concept's capacity of actually (and materially) determining our world. Application is realization. Through application *I* am the one who decides whether or not to give reality to the concept, that is, to make it real in the objective world or to determine the world according to it. In the case of theoretical concepts, on the contrary, their deduction is also, at the same time, the proof of their applicability and *de facto* application. This position differs significantly from Kant's, for whom the reality and validity of moral concepts (as *Vernunftbegriffe* or ideas) is utterly independent of their (contingent and empirical) implementation by the will of finite agents in the phenomenal world. Although Fichte maintains Kant's view of the ideality of the practical realm as well as his insistence on the open-ended endeavor characterizing the ethical goal (*Sollen*), he posits the reality of the moral principles within the sensible world, thereby making their validity as principles dependent on their applicability by finite sensible-rational agents. The reality of the ethical

---

[14] And thereby differentiating the issue of practical applicability from the Kantian problem of "deduction" as presented in the first *Critique*, see Nuzzo (2011).

law must be displayed not only within consciousness but in the objective and intersubjective sensible world as well. Indeed, the former cannot be understood (and experienced) without the latter. This is precisely the issue of the applicability of the principle of morality. Applicability regards the "object" or "the idea of *what* ought to be done" as well as the *subject* who ought to perform the moral action in the outside world (GA I/5: 75; SL 4: 65 f.). On this basis, one must proceed beyond the mere formality of the ethical law to its material, concrete determination and application.

8.2 The Embodiment of Freedom: *System of Ethics* §18

Transcendentally, the "application" of the ethical principle requires, first, an account of "the formal conditions of the morality of our action" (GA I/5: 147; SL 4: 157, title), which includes, echoing Kant, an account of the will (of the "good will": *ibidem*; §14) and of the "absolute criterion" concerning the validity of our conviction of the morality of our actions, which is the formal immediate conscience or *Gewissen* of the law (§15); and it requires, second, an account of the "material of the ethical law," which constitutes the "systematic" account of our duties (GA I/5: 186; SL 4: 206, title; §§17–18). Only on this basis can the "doctrine of duties in the proper sense" (*die eigentliche Pflichtenlehre*) be developed. If we keep in mind the preceding discussion concerning the way in which Fichte frames the problem of application as integral to ethics, it becomes clear that the division of the third part of the *System of Ethics* comes close to articulating the *Moralität/Sittlichkeit* distinction in Hegel's 1821 *Philosophy of Right*, to which, importantly, the idea of "right" should be added (and this expansion is relevant both for Fichte and for Hegel). Indeed, in a broad sense, at this juncture of their respective books Fichte and Hegel voice the same systematic intention of moving beyond Kant's critical-transcendental foundation of morality opening up the ideas of freedom and ethical law to their necessary realization (or indeed "application") within the intersubjective and institutional world of human action. Or, to put the point differently, Fichte and Hegel – respectively with the issue of the "material of the ethical law" and with the transition from "morality" to "ethical life" – bring to the fore the necessary connection between the immediate formal consciousness or "conscience" of duty and the larger context of the objective world in which moral duty is always already mediated and always materially and synthetically determined. For, as Fichte maintains, consciousness does not itself give the material of the law (see GA I/5: 161; SL 4: 173). Both for Fichte and for Hegel, it is this expanded context that

Embodiment and Freedom 159

constitutes the proper realm of the "doctrine of duties." This is a context that is materially determined, fundamentally social, and socially and institutionally shaped. Such context, for Hegel, is the sphere of *Sittlichkeit* within which the true "ethical doctrine of duties (*ethische Pflichtenlehre*)" must be developed in its "objectivity" beyond "the empty principle of moral subjectivity."[15] The formal, and for Hegel still "abstract," conditions of morality found in (Kantian) conscience and subjectivity, by contrast, constitute the sphere of *Moralität* – a sphere that receives its true and concrete meaning only when reframed and, properly, enacted within the more advanced standpoint of ethical life.[16] In a systematically similar way, this is, I contend, the framework in which Fichte develops the argument of *System of Ethics*, §18. This argument outlines the sphere of a "doctrine of duties in the proper sense" as the sphere in which the "material" of the ethical law is obtained beyond the formal dimension of moral conscience (as the ultimate criterion of the validity of our actions) by mobilizing the embodied worldly context in which action is executed and freedom is progressively and expansively realized.[17]

The question of the "matter" or "material" of the law is formulated in §17 of the *System of Ethics* as follows: "Which are . . ., with regard to their matter, those actions that lie in the series of approximation to absolute self-sufficiency?" (GA I/5: 192; SL 4: 210). At stake herein is no longer an issue of mere "applicability" or possibility, which regards the merely theoretical judgment of the morality of our actions and concerns conscience and the will alone (GA I/5: 191; SL 4: 209). At stake is rather the question of the actual "application," that is, of the practical execution and actualization of the law that commands absolute independence and self-sufficiency. This connection between the material of the law and its application-realization is relevant in the development of Fichte's argument in §18 on at least two grounds. For one thing, because the human finite agent can only execute the end prescribed by the law in an ever-approximating progression, the problem of ascertaining *which* are the materially determinate successive

---

[15] Hegel (1821/1970, §148 Remark).
[16] Analogously, "Abstract Right" (the first division of the *Philosophy of Right*) receives its true meaning only when enacted within the sphere of ethical life.
[17] Significantly, albeit still on a merely superficial level, *System of Ethics*, §§14–16 develop much of the same topics as Hegel's *Moralität* section of the *Philosophy of Right*. It is not my aim to develop this point in the space of this chapter. The aim of the Hegelian reference is to highlight the nature of the systematic context in which Fichte's argument in *System of Ethics*, §18 develops, a context that cannot be entirely appreciated when the only reference is Kant. For further discussion, see Chapter 9 by Luca Fonnesu in this volume.

actions within the series is distinct from the act of embracing the final end as commanded by the ethical law. Because the series is never complete as a totality (a claim with which Fichte, unlike Hegel, upholds the validity of Kant's *Sollen*), the end is actualized only distributively (hence always imperfectly) in the succession of actions within the series (which is to say, absolute independence as an "idea" cannot be fully actualized in the sensible world). Now while the absolute end as a whole (or as idea) is *formally* contained in the law in its completeness, the dutiful actions within the series can only be *materially* determined in their succession, which remains always incomplete. These actions are determined as the progressive "limitation" of the drive to independence, a limitation that must be material and yet not empirical and contingent but necessary and original (GA I/5: 193; SL 4: 211). On the other hand, Fichte insists that the "final end of the ethical law is absolute independence and self-sufficiency not merely with respect to our will, for the latter is always independent, but also *with respect to our whole being* (*in Absicht unseres ganzen Seins*)" (GA I/5: 191; SL 4: 209, my emphasis). And our "whole being" is a being that, comprised of its natural drives (which I must embrace in their "totality": GA I/5: 192; SL 4: 210), is necessarily embodied, finds itself within a world, acts only within the connection of this world, but also, at the same time, in its action first institutes the manifold connection that is its own world. To the extent that absolute independence and self-sufficiency are referred "to our whole being" and to the "totality" of our original drive, the actualization of this final end is precisely the ongoing progression whereby we ought to constitute ourselves – or our "whole being" – as the totality of the world in which our action is placed, or, to put the point with Fichte in a formulation that we shall amply discuss later on, we ought to constitute the world as our own body, that is, we ought to make the world our own just as our body is (made) our own (GA I/5: 208; SL 4: 229). Independence is an ongoing act of incorporation. The end of self-sufficiency is the end of attaining a body so capacious (and so physically as well as morally capable) as to extend to all possible interconnections. It follows that the final end to make myself into an "independent I" converges with the end in light of which all things in the world ought to be considered, namely, the end of instituting and sustaining such independence (GA I/5: 193, 208; SL 4: 212, 229). If I am to be independent as the totality of the world – the world which is (made into) *my world*, the world which is *me* just as my body is me – then the world's "end" is the same independence that is my independence.

This framework accounts, first, for the general procedure whereby "the material content of the ethical law" is to be obtained "by synthetically

Embodiment and Freedom 161

uniting the concept of *Ichheit* and the concept of absolute self-sufficiency" (GA I/5: 193; SL 4: 211).[18] And it accounts, second, for the centrality that the living body plays in the entire derivation of the material content of the ethical law in §18 of the *System of Ethics* – and not only in its first step, which concerns, specifically and more narrowly, the duties toward the body. For, the body is both "condition of *Ichheit*" (GA I/5: 196; SL 4: 215) as well as its point of contact with the world, and immanent material part of the world. Indeed, the general trajectory of Fichte's argument goes from my living body as condition of the causality of the I, through the material duties regarding intelligence which are construed in parallel to those toward the body, to the material duties toward others which open up to the incorporation of the world into the law and the law into the world as condition of the I's approximation to the end of independence and self-sufficiency. This is the larger interconnected and intersubjective "body-politic," as it were, in which a novel kind of self-sufficiency and freedom is ultimately attained.

8.2.1 The Living Body and the Material of the Ethical Law

The deduction of the material of the ethical law, which Fichte's "theory of ethics" stages as the scientific derivation of the determinate duties instantiating the progressive action toward the end of self-sufficiency, when considered from the side of the I, is a phenomenological process of material or real self-appropriation that starts in the living material body and ends in the intersubjective social and political world – the "enlarged" body of free (increasingly) independent subjectivity. Self-sufficiency requires – and properly *is* itself a process of – self-appropriation. This is also, at the same time, the process of freedom's actualization. Although methodologically quite different, Fichte's and Hegel's ethical programs do converge on this latter point. To put this point with Hegel, the extended, that is, intersubjective, body of free independent subjectivity is the sphere of *Sittlichkeit* in which alone a content-determined theory of duties and virtue can have its place.[19] To be sure, Spinoza can be appealed to here as well. This time on a metaphysical level, freedom is the extension of the *ordo et connectio,* which the embodied self (or mind) is progressively

---

[18] See Wood (2016a, 185 f.), which draws attention to Fichte's modeling of the synthesis on Kant's categories of relation.
[19] Hegel (1821/1970, §148 Remark).

able to master in her activity (instead of passively suffering from it) therein actualizing herself.

The "drive to absolute independence" enjoins the I the obligation "to be an independent I." At the outset of §18, this obligation yields the beginning of the phenomenological process[20] whereby the I "finds itself," thereby starting the movement of the I's self-appropriation. "The (reflecting) I must find itself as I" (GA I/5: 194; SL 4: 212). This is indeed the very first condition of independence. For, to "find" oneself practically is an act of free self-constitution: What is merely given and found in its givenness is made into one's own and thereby fundamentally transformed. Importantly, it is transformed materially, not only formally. The process of self-finding is a process of self-appropriation but also liberation. Practically, what is merely found and given as "alien" and external to me (hence as conditioning me) is turned into "my own" by an act of freedom and thereby becomes the objective, material embodiment of freedom (GA I/5: 194; SL 4: 212 f.). What is given and found is truly (and retroactively) *posited as given and found* by an act of freedom.[21]

In the first step of this self-finding process, the I "finds itself" as "given," hence as having no independence. By the progressive appropriation of what is given, the I expands the sphere of its independence. The I is posited "as natural drive," or rather as a complex nexus of natural drives. However, the act of finding in myself natural drives, forces, desires, and longings (that I may or may not decide to satisfy) is a theoretical (or "ideal") act that leads to self-appropriation only when it is complemented by the practical free decision to actually ("*realiter*") fulfill those drives and desires (GA I/5: 194; SL 4: 213). This is the act whereby found or given natural drives are made my own so as to freely – and materially – constitute me as who I am. An important reversal takes place in this movement. While the *Naturtrieb* – which is indeed the *Urtrieb* – found in me (as a given) is the mere "*Treiben der Natur*" in me, by positing the natural drive as "mine" (i.e., by deciding to actually satisfy it), I truly "put an end" to nature's agency and replace it with my own. More properly, I recognize that nature's causality "is grounded in my own *Treiben*" as "free being." This reversal is an act of "self-determination" and a first way of gaining independence from nature (GA I/5: 195; SL 4: 213 f.).

The next step in this process of self-appropriation, the step in which nature's drive is more fully replaced by (or posited as) an expression of my

---

[20] GA I/5: 195; SL 4: 213: "*im gemeinen Leben.*"
[21] For a parallel to this Fichtean claim in Hegel's Psychology, see Nuzzo (2012, ch. 2).

own agency, implies the intervention of my living body. This step is predicated on a crucial Spinozistic-sounding metaphysical premise that further elaborates on Fichte's appropriation of the framework of Kant's third *Critique*.[22] On this premise, Fichte now introduces the organic material body (*Leib*) and articulates the relation between nature and freedom. Because I am part of the whole of nature, my force and efficacy within nature is truly "nothing other than the efficacious action of nature (in me) upon herself (nature outside of myself)" (GA I/5: 195; SL 4: 214). "My nature, however, stands under the sway of freedom," and nothing can ensue through my nature (my nature as the representative of the whole of nature in me) unless it is determined through freedom. My free self-determination is the principle (the "prime mover," suggests Fichte) through which my nature is completed, thereby becoming efficacious and properly actual. Now, the entire "system of our natural drives" is posited by reflection as a necessarily material and spatial whole. Thereby the "system of natural drives becomes a material living body." In the material living body, nature's own *Treiben* is concentrated. This body as the "embodiment" (*Verkörperung*: GA I/5: 196; SL 4: 215) of nature's drive has no causality (originally, of its own) but obtains the power of causality "*immediately* following our will," just as nature has no efficacy through me unless my free self-determination is mobilized. Reciprocally, just as the body becomes cause "*immediately* following our will," the will becomes cause "*immediately* in our body" (GA I/5: 196; SL 4: 214, my emphasis): "we only need to will, and what we have willed ensues in our body" (*ibidem*). Significantly, herein the body is not viewed as the *means* through which the will gains its efficacy in the world; the body is rather itself the *immediate* material manifestation of the will's choice. The body is the will in the material (or the real) *ordo et connectio* of Spinozistic ascendency: The will becomes cause *immediately* in the body; the body has causality *immediately* following the will.[23] The living material body is introduced as the point of intersection of nature and freedom, as the interface between nature in me and nature outside of me (nature as a whole).

Importantly, while the body has already been thematized in the deduction of the reality and applicability of the ethical principle in the second division of the *System of Ethics* (GA I/5: 122–124; SL 4: 127–129), at the

---

[22] For the latter point, see Nuzzo (2015).

[23] Interestingly, while the two statements – the body becomes cause immediately following the will, the will becomes cause immediately in the body – are construed as parallel, the claim that the body has no causality without the will is not paralleled by the claim that the will has no causality without the body.

present juncture (§18, Section I) it functions as the crucial channel through which the material content of a theory of duties is brought to light and the ethical principle is actually applied. In order to be efficacious within nature and through my nature, freedom becomes materially embodied in my *Leib* and thereby inserted within the order of nature. My body is the point of connection between the whole of nature in which my agency is always already inscribed and from which I am dependent in my found givenness, and my freedom – the freedom that posits the natural drive as my own, thereby beginning to make me independent and self-determining; the freedom that in my acting body ultimately lends causality to nature itself. As the dynamic point "from which all causality issues" (GA I/5: 196; SL 4: 214 f.), the body is the point of convergence of natural necessity and free causality; it is both the will's causality (its necessary and immediate embodiment) and an immanent part of nature. This predicament betrays the peculiar place that my living body occupies in the material world. Unlike everything else outside of ourselves, "our body is [always already] in our power without first having to be brought under it." Uniquely, in the case of the living body, no antecedent act of appropriation is needed to make it *mine*. Freedom begins immediately in it. "It alone nature has already placed under our power without any free assistance from us" (GA I/5: 196; SL 4: 215). My body is the point from which the appropriation of the world and its ethical transformation expansively issues because my body is already (in its very givenness) the first material instance of such a transformation.

It should be noted that the body is presented in this way insofar as it is both crucial "condition of *Ichheit*" and crucial condition of self-sufficiency. Or rather, "*such a body (ein solcher Leib)*, a body determined in this way, is a condition of *Ichheit*" (GA I/5: 196; SL 4: 215, my emphasis) because *such* a body (i.e., not any body) follows directly from the "reflection upon itself" through which the I becomes an I. As reflected, the body is no longer something contingently found and given but the necessary "condition of *Ichheit*" and the first embodiment of freedom. It is material but not empirical (because it follows from the "reflection upon itself," which constitutes at once the I and its body). On this basis, the body gains its place in the scientific deduction of the material of the ethical law, that is, in the synthesis of "the concept of *Ichheit* and the concept of absolute self-sufficiency" (GA I/5: 193; SL 4: 211). Indeed the body is the first concrete instantiation of such a synthesis.

Fichte underlines that with regard to the "matter" or material content, all possible acting is a demand of the *Naturtrieb* because all our acting takes place within nature, that is, is possible and becomes actual only within nature as the response to and satisfaction of the natural drive. Because the natural drive "addresses itself to me only through my body, and this drive is realized in the world outside me only through the causality of my body," the body becomes the pivotal point around which the scientific derivation of the material of the ethical law revolves. The body is both the necessary condition for the address of the natural drive to me and the necessary condition for my actual causality in the world. The body is "*Instrument*" – theoretically, of our perception and through perception of all our cognition of the world, and practically, of our causality in it. But it is also itself "*Zweck*" of our nature. For, the natural drive, just as Spinoza's *conatus*, "aims at preservation, cultivation, and well-being – in short, at the perfection of our body" (GA I/5: 196; SL 4: 215). Indeed, as our nature "is contained and enclosed in our body," our body becomes our final end (in our body nature is end in and for itself). Thus, the cultivation and the ongoing action of perfecting our body is our first and necessary moral duty. It is the condition of *Ichheit* as such, as well as the condition of our moral agency in the world. Now, because our highest moral drive is the drive to absolute self-sufficiency, the perfection and moral cultivation of the body becomes the first material duty in the process of gaining independence and self-sufficiency. To *morally* perfect our body is to make ourselves increasingly independent and self-sufficient within the order of nature. Again, the body to which our duty is directed is not the empirically and contingently given natural body but the reflected, morally shaped body in which freedom is actualized or incorporated in the world and as our world. Such a body is not "product of nature" but "the product of the exercise of freedom" (GA I/5: 124; SL 4: 129).

Because all action is possible only "through my body," the "satisfaction" of the moral drive, hence ultimately "all morality (*alle Moralität*), is conditioned by the preservation and highest possible perfection (*Vervollkommung*) of the body." The physical and material preservation of the body along with the ongoing action of morally perfecting it is the first material condition of "all morality." However, at the same time, Fichte underlines that because self-sufficiency is the objective to which all conscious action should be directed, the material duty toward the body must be subordinated to it: "I must preserve and cultivate my body purely as an instrument of moral acting (*Werkzeug des sittlichen Handelns*), not as an end in itself." Thereby, while the living body is turned into an instrument of moral action, the end of morality shapes the body in its ethical transfiguration. The body for which I ought to care and which I ought to preserve and cultivate is not the natural, merely given body but the moral (and morally constructed) body, that is, the first embodiment of my freedom in the world. Indeed, it is my duty "to transform the body into a suitable instrument of morality (*Werkzeug der Moralität*)" (GA I/5: 197; SL 4: 216). On this basis, the first three material duties of ethics are derived. These are duties that have the body as their content or matter (or object) but are also duties that are implemented by the embodied human subject, that is, by the body itself as acting subject. The first is a negative duty, which commands, "absolutely," never to consider the body as a final end: the body ought never to "become an object of enjoyment for enjoyment's sake." The second is a positive duty, which imposes, "to the extent that is possible," the cultivation of the body "in a manner that will make it suitable for all possible ends of freedom." The third is a limitative duty, whereby all pleasure and enjoyment not connected to the ends of freedom are "impermissible and contrary to the law" (GA I/5: 197; SL 4: 216).

But what does it mean for the body to be "instrument of morality" and for its "*Artikulation*" to be "instrument of freedom (*Werkzeug der Freiheit*)" (GA I/5: 197, 124; SL 4: 216, 129); and in what sense ought it to be cultivated so as to be suitable for and such as promoting the ends of freedom? In order to appreciate the broader metaphysical framework of Fichte's position in presenting the duties toward the body in connection with the highest moral end of absolute self-sufficiency, it is helpful to consider his argument against the background of Spinoza's view of the body in relation to the mind in *Ethica* V. To be sure, Fichte's position entails a response to Kant's much criticized split of the acting subject into two unreconcilable parts, that is, the sensible and the intelligible, that plays itself out not only on the strictly ethical level but on the broader metaphysical level as well. The appeal to Spinoza allows us to highlight this point, and to connect the view of the body as an instrument of freedom to the ethical principle of absolute self-sufficiency.[24]

Far from claiming that the body ought to be left behind in the mind's highest quest for eternity, Spinoza makes the eternity of the mind's "greatest part" dependent on the perfection of the activity of the body and on its multifaceted capacity for action (*corpus ad plurima aptum*).[25] Indeed, the mind's eternity and blessed freedom consist in the knowledge of its body's essence *sub specie aeternitatis*[26]). In Part V, Proposition 39 of the *Ethica* Spinoza states: "He whose body is capable of the greatest

---

[24] Significantly, for Fichte, these duties are not simply another version of duties toward oneself.
[25] *Ethica* V, P39; Spinoza (1677/2002, 380).   [26] See P23S, P29, P31 in *Ethica* V.

amount of activity has a mind whose greatest part is eternal."[27] This is no longer a body that suffers and is affected by passions or other external bodies. In fact, this is the most active body, a body that extending its efficacy to the widest connections of the world (ultimately, to the whole of nature of which the body is part) is ethically transformed quite in Fichte's sense of being a body "instrument" of morality and freedom. At the beginning of *Ethica* V, Spinoza claims that in order to rein in the passive emotions we must shape the order and the connection of bodily affections according to the order of the mind.[28] This constitutes the mind's power with regard to the affections. At the height of *Ethica* V,[29] Spinoza shows that once the mind conceives the essence of its body under the form of eternity, hence discovers and indeed affectively "feels and experiences,"[30] its eternal part as constituted by the second and third kind of knowledge, then the body displays its own power on the mind in allowing it to increase its eternal share, that is, the activity of the intellect. At this point, the body's power in extending the range of its actual connections, its greatest complexity, activity, and flexibility, its capacity to actively and perfectly fit within the whole of nature and be part of the greatest number of connections corresponds to and even fosters the mind's capacity to increase its activity – to be conscious of itself and of God and of all things with the second and third of knowledge.[31] This constitutes the mind's *increasing* eternity and freedom – an eternity and freedom that can be increased to the extent that the mind is *embodied* in the most active or most perfect body.[32] At this point, the fully active body is the body of a subject who has the *potestas* (power) "to arrange and associate the affections of the body according to the intellectual order *(secundum ordine ad intellectum)*."[33] This body, far from being a source of suffering and passivity and hence an obstacle to the mind's conquest of freedom and blessedness is the basis of its intellectual cognition and practical empowerment: It is the body of the sage. In this regard, the sage can be said, with Fichte, independent and self-sufficient to the extent that her power extends to the order of nature and is properly one with it instead of suffering from and being dependent on it. In an analogous sense, in Fichte's ethical theory the body ought to become "*Werkzeug der Moralität*" or "*Werkzeug der Freiheit*" to the extent that its active power and causality within the interconnected whole of the sensible world is progressively increased and extended.

[27] Spinoza (1677/2002, 380).   [28] *Ethica* V, P1; Spinoza (1677/2002, 365).
[29] *Ethica* V, P35; Spinoza (1677/2002, 378),   [30] *Ethica* V, P23S; Spinoza (1677/2002, 374).
[31] *Ethica* V, P39S; Spinoza (1677/2002, 380).   [32] *Ethica* V, P40; Spinoza (1677/2002, 380 f.).
[33] *Ethica* V, P39dem; Spinoza (1677/2002, 380).

In the argument of §18 of the *System of Ethics,* the material duties toward our body are paralleled by those toward our "intellect (*Intelligenz*)." Indeed, the phenomenological self-finding of the I, the first stage of which is the I's self-finding as living body, leads us to acknowledge our active engagement in the "ideal activity" of the "intellect." Just as the *Naturtrieb* "addresses me only through my body," the "ethical law addresses itself to the intellect as such" (GA I/5: 198; SL 4: 217). The movement from the natural drive to the moral law is a continuum of reflective self-determination. Thus, the material duties toward our intellectual nature are construed in parallel to the duties toward the body. The first is a negative duty to disinterested knowledge, to "absolute freedom" of inquiry unrestricted by external motives and conditions; the second is a positive duty to cultivate our cognitive powers; the latter is the limitative duty whereby all our knowledge should be ultimately referred, *formaliter,* to our highest moral end (GA I/5: 198; SL 4: 218). Ultimately, both the material duties toward the body and the material duties toward the intellect promote the highest goal of independence, which is thereby viewed not as isolationist autarchy but as the appropriation of the world through the realization of freedom and the progressive application of the law. Indeed, the appeal to Spinoza's *Ethica* V illuminates the connection between the ethical principle of absolute self-sufficiency and the process of self-discovery and self-appropriation that starts with the material duties toward the body and the intellect and culminates in the claim: "The world must become for me what my body is" (GA I/5: 208; SL 4: 229). While for Kant independence of external (heteronomous) determination is the negative definition of freedom as autonomy, for Fichte the final end of independence is the positive act of extension of the moral law to the manifold interconnections of the sensible world, which is both the progressive incorporation of the world into the subject and the action whereby the subject becomes progressively embedded within the world.

8.2.2 The Intersubjective Body and the Material of Ethical Life: "Make the World as Your Own Body"

While the material duties toward the body and the intellect define the first stages of the subject's self-finding "as individual," the third stage of the movement opens up the "consciousness of individuality" (GA I/5: 199; SL 4: 218) to a world that is not just the world of nature but is a fundamentally intersubjective world – a world where the ethical law is concretely embodied in material duties toward other free agents. It is at this juncture of Fichte's argument that we can place the movement corresponding to the "transition" from *Moralität* to *Sittlichkeit* in Hegel's *Philosophy of Right*. Very generally, the common point is that the moral law (of Kantian ascendency) has actual validity only in an intersubjective and ultimately institutional context, and freedom is actualized freedom, that is, true freedom, only in such a context. Moreover, the common idea is that the embodiment of freedom in intersubjective relations is, most properly, the necessary condition – transcendental for Fichte, and dialectical for Hegel – of individual freedom. To be sure, this point is clear to Hegel as early as the reflection on the dialectical relation of "dependence" and "independence" of self-consciousness in the *Phenomenology of Spirit* (1807).

The I, which in its body has found itself as natural drive and as part of nature, must now ascribe the natural drive to itself. The I must become "object of reflection," hence "limited." Because the I is free activity, it is precisely this free activity that must be limited. Now this happens as my free activity is opposed by another free activity. Self-appropriation in one's free activity is possible only by positing and confronting another free activity not belonging to the I, that is, a free activity materially embodied in other actual beings in the world outside of me. Fichte's crucial point is that merely *possible*, "ideal activity" does not determine me as an actual individual. Rather, "I must *find myself as free*, I must be given to myself as free," that is, I must find and be given to myself, reflectively, as an actual object endowed with freedom. While "to be given to myself as free" seems to be a contradictory predicament – or as Fichte remarks, seems indeed "strange" at first sight (GA I/5: 200; SL 4: 219) – the formulation entails Fichte's crucial insistence that the consciousness of freedom must proceed from the position of real actuality (not from mere ideal possibility). What does it mean then to find myself as "*freitätiges*"? As it turns out, there is, in fact, a contradiction here. Its solution leads Fichte to the notion of *Aufforderung* – the concept already mobilized in a similar connection in the *Natural Right*. "I cannot find as a given the properly real self-determination through spontaneity; rather, I must give it to myself." Indeed, to *find* real self-determination *as a given* would be an "utter contradiction." When at stake is the type of reality and ultimately materiality proper to the act of self-determination (i.e., to Kantian freedom as autonomy and spontaneity, this time, however, in its real and material significance as embedded in the sensible world), the "givenness" of such a reality is of a peculiar kind. For, it is not just given to me without my intervention but (i) I must *find* it as given and (ii) "I must give it to myself." Now these conditions are satisfied when I find my free self-determination as given by or as the result of an *Aufforderung* or summons to determine myself in this way (GA I/5: 200; SL 4: 220). The summons is that through which I am given to myself as free and I make myself free. To the extent that I understand this summons (i) I think of my self-determination as given in this summons (without my intervention), and (ii) I act on it by ascribing to myself a determinate sphere for my freedom. The understanding of the summons is my consciousness of freedom. But I cannot understand the summons without ascribing it "to an actual being outside of myself" – to an actual, not a merely possible being, a being, in addition, who wants to communicate a concept to me (the concept of a free action), hence is able to grasp and to produce such a concept. Thus, I posit myself as individual (which is "condition of *Ichheit*") only in relation to another rational free being, that is, only insofar I posit another rational being in relation to myself. This is, Fichte announces, the strictly a priori proof that a free rational being cannot exist in isolation because there is at least one other individual whose summons elevates this being to freedom. From this deduction follows, first, a fundamental "limitation of the drive toward independence," and second, a more precise "material determination of morality."[34] Both are implications of the fact that "my drive toward independence" cannot negate the "condition of its own possibility": I cannot destroy the freedom of the other because my own free action necessarily depends on it. From this, three material duties toward others are derived. The first is a negative duty: It is the absolute prohibition to disturb and interfere in the freedom of the other. The second is a positive duty: It is the absolute command to consider the other as self-sufficient, and never as a means to my ends. The third is a limitative duty: by positing one other free rational being outside of me, some of all possible actions become impossible, namely, those actions that are condition of the other individual's freedom (GA I/5: 201; SL 4: 221).

The action that unfolds in the real process determined by the material duties derived so far – duties toward the body, intelligence, and other free beings – determine who I am: again, who I am materially, as embodied *Zeitwesen* in the sensible world (and not merely ideally and noumenally); who I am determinately in my body, my intelligence, and in relation to (at least) another free rational being who in turn is materially determined in

---

[34] We are still operating in terms of the synthesis of "the concept of *Ichheit* and the concept of absolute self-sufficiency" (GA I/5: 193; SL 4: 211).

Embodiment and Freedom

body, intelligence, and in reciprocal relation to me. This ongoing action is both the process of freedom's actualization in the sensible world and the process toward the I's absolute independence.

While the *Aufforderung* allows Fichte to establish with a priori necessity the *actuality* of one other rational free being outside of myself and in relation to myself (GA I/5: 201; SL 4: 221) as well as to think of the *possibility* of many other rational beings (GA I/5: 203; SL 4: 223), their actuality, while compatible with my freedom and its necessary limitation, is the object of an argument that draws on Kant's *Critique of Judgment* and on its concept of *Kunstprodukt* (in contrast to the *Naturprodukt*: GA I/5: 203 f.; SL 4: 223ff.) as the result of embodied rational free agency. In line with the argument we have been following so far, the point is that the efficacy of a free rational being in and on nature (i.e., the actuality of its action as the realization of freedom) is the same as the efficacy that is embodied and actualized in the "product of art." Ethical freedom just as the freedom of *poiesis* or art production is embodied freedom, that is, freedom actualized in a material sensible body and recognizable objectively as an effect in the sensible world. The artifact and nature transformed by rational free action are structurally the same. They are ways of freedom's embodiment. As Fichte has made clear at the beginning of §18, my living body is the first instance of such a process; other rational beings' bodies follow by implication. They are no mere "natural product[s]" but "product[s] of the exercise of freedom" (GA I/5: 124; SL 4: 129).

Fichte's critique of Kant's (merely) nominal definition of freedom as spontaneity is now clear in its full-fledged implications. From the deduction of other free beings through the summons, it follows that "the first state, the root of my individuality is not determined through my freedom" (GA I/5: 202; SL 4: 222 f.) but rather by the connection with another rational being. All the actions following that first summons are determined by my freedom. Thereby, Fichte overturns Kant's position. In Kant's definition, freedom as spontaneity is the absolute, noumenal beginning of an action outside of the temporal connection of the sensible world.[35] The actualization of the action, by contrast, taking place within the time–space continuum, is subject to the determinism of natural phenomena. On Fichte's view, by contrast, freedom is not an absolute atemporal and purely noumenal beginning but the ongoing, immanent, and engaged continuous application or implementation of the moral law in the natural and intersubjective world – an

---

[35] See GA I/5: 52; SL 4: 37, discussed earlier.

application or actualization that follows from and is conditioned by but also constantly and freely renews the original summons. Freedom is not production "out of nothing." My free action is instead always materially conditioned. It is materially conditioned by the content of the ethical principle; by my embodied nature through which the natural drive addresses me and through which I establish the first material point of contact with the world and with other embodied rational beings; is conditioned (or indeed, "pre-determined" or "*prädestiniert*" says Fichte, echoing an early modern debate: GA I/5: 207; SL 4: 228) by the material given to me in which my action is necessarily inscribed; and finally is conditioned, "*materialiter*," by the limitation that goes back to other rational beings and their efficacy on my body and my sensible world, a limitation that does not necessarily belong to the structure of *Ichheit* (GA I/5: 205; SL 4: 226). While the summons mark the beginning of my free action, the actuality of other rational beings in my sensible world sets a limit to my freedom, that is, generates a *Nichtsollen* for me (GA I/5: 205; SL 4: 226). Given that, from the outset, that is, from the standpoint of my living body, freedom's actualization is the process whereby I appropriate the sensible world for myself by extending my active participation in and connection with it, the limit that others posit to this process consists in the fact that "I cannot be nor become everything; nor am I permitted to do so, because there are several others who are free as well" (GA I/5: 205; SL 4: 226). This predicament orients the ethical end of absolute independence in a fundamentally intersubjective way. Again, at stake cannot be a sort of individualistic and isolationist autarchy. Independence is, rather, the harmonious interconnection of reciprocal actions of rational beings[36] – actions that are both predetermined in their necessary interconnection and free in the renewed individual choices that propel them forward in time.

Summing up the process of derivation of material duties, which has extended from my living body and intelligence to the summons and the reciprocal action with others, Fichte proclaims: the ultimate goal of self-sufficiency consists in this: "that everything depends on me and that I do not depend on anything; that everything that I want to occur in my entire sensible world occurs absolutely and only because I will for it to occur." Fichte clarifies that this must be understood in the same sense (*gleichwie*) in which things occur "in my body" as the "starting point of my absolute

---

[36] I use the Leibnizian-sounding term 'harmony' on purpose: GA I/5: 207; SL 4: 228, in which Fichte "reconciles" predetermination (and predestination) and freedom sounds remarkably Leibnizian.

Embodiment and Freedom

causality" (GA I/5: 208; SL 4: 229). In other words, the ultimate goal of self-sufficiency must be construed, Fichte argues, on the model of the moral transformation of my body, the first step of the self-finding of the I. This, I suggested earlier, is best understood by appealing to the complex meta-physical context of Spinoza's *Ethica* V (EVP39). To make everything dependent on one's embodied self (mind) and to make the embodied self independent of everything is to increase the body's activity and its mani-fold participation in the interconnection of the whole of nature. Ultimately, Fichte presents the highest ethical goal in the following terms: "The world must become for me what my body is." This aim, Fichte acknowledges, is unattainable in its full actuality. And yet, although it remains a moral *Sollen*, it is not devoid of reality. For, the infinite process of freedom's actualization must be the "finite end" of all my activity. This is the finite end of "fashioning (*bearbeiten*)" and transforming the world so as to make it instrumental to the realization of freedom and morality (GA I/5: 208; SL 4: 229), just as my body ought to be increasingly made *Werkzeug* of freedom and morality (GA I/5: 124, 197; SL 4: 129, 216).

Set in this framework, however, the command of absolute independence and the moral demand arising from other rational beings collide with one another. For, at this point, the moral law seems to be caught in a contradiction with itself (GA I/5: 209; SL 4: 230). While the material conditions that make my free action embodied action within the world of nature triggered by the summons do not infringe on my freedom (they are rather conditions of its actualization), the prohibition to modify the world the way I want if this impedes the freedom of another rational being seems to involve a contradiction in the "drive for self-sufficiency" and hence in the "moral law with itself" (GA I/5: 209; SL 4: 230). For, a conflict arises between the demand (i) that I subjugate everything in the sensible world to my "absolute final end," and (ii) that with regard to some beings in the sensible world I do not subjugate them to my end (I ought to let them be in their freedom). In other words, the end of absolute independence, namely, the end of making the sensible world like my body, contradicts itself because of the presence (necessary for my own freedom) of other rational beings: significantly, *it is them that I cannot make like by body*.[37] In order to solve this contradiction, Fichte explicitly shapes the world in which the moral law is applied and freedom actualized as a social-political and institutional world, thereby showing that there is really no conflict between

---

[37] This is the point that Wood does not seem to recognize in analyzing the issue of the contradiction of the moral law with itself (Wood 2016a, 178).

174 ANGELICA NUZZO

the end of (individual) self-sufficiency and (the respect of) the freedom of others. Accordingly, the action of rendering the world just like my body will turn out to be a *collective* action. Ultimately, the ethically transfigured body, which is the ongoing result of freedom's actualization, is a *collective body* – a society or body politics. It is here that Fichte's ethical law shapes a world that comes close to Hegel's concept of *Sittlichkeit*.[38] The world, which is itself the actualization of freedom, is not just the natural world but the *Vernunftwelt* of society (GA I/5: 212 f.; SL 4: 235).

Within Fichte's argument, then, the next material duty to be deduced is the duty to live in society (GA I/5: 212; SL 4: 234 f.). The key to this deduction consists in specifying the addressee of the idea of absolute independence as "reason in general." At stake in the highest moral end, Fichte declares, is "the absolute self-sufficiency of reason in general," not of contingent individuals A, B, and C (GA I/5: 209; SL 4: 231). Fichte argues that the contradiction in the moral law would be solved by the single presupposition that "all free beings necessarily share the same end" (GA I/5: 209; SL 4: 230). For, this convergence would eliminate the conflict among individual processes of appropriation of the world for the sake of (individual) self-sufficiency. In this case, the "liberation (*Befreiung*)" of one would be the liberation of all. However, while *formally* all rational beings do have the same end, which is given by the moral law, the question remains whether they also have the same end *materially*. On the answer to this question depends, Fichte maintains, "the distinctive character of the presentation (*Darstellung*) of the *Sittenlehre*" (GA I/5: 209; SL 4: 231). The "drive for self-sufficiency" is the drive of the *Ichheit*. The *Ichheit* is individuality, but "individuality as such or in general (*Individuum überhaupt*)." At stake in the moral end is not contingent individuality but the "self-sufficiency of reason in general (*Vernunft überhaupt*)." It is this latter that must be the collective aim. The contingent individual is that through which the ethical drive has causality or is embodied. While at the beginning of the deduction my individual living body was the site (and indeed the "instrument") of my moral causality on the sensible world and thereby the first instance of freedom's embodiment and actualization, at the present stage the context of ethics' validity has broadened. Now it is the "entire sensible and empirically determined human being" that becomes the embodiment

---

[38] On this general methodological point, however, the proximity of Fichte and Hegel ends. Herein I shall also end my reconstruction of the overall argument of §18. Once Fichte has guided us to the derivation of the duties to society, church, and the state, the remainder of §18 offers a brief outline of some major points of Fichte's political philosophy (social contract, state, right of rebellion).

and the "instrument and vehicle of the moral law (*Werkzeug und Vehicul des Sittengesetzes*)" (GA I/5: 210; SL 4: 231). If the drive to self-sufficiency concerns reason in general, and if the self-sufficiency of reason in general is progressively achieved in and through individuals A, B, and C, then it is quite indifferent to me whether I represent A, B, or C. For, ultimately, there is "no (material) self-sufficiency except by means of the formal freedom of all individuals" (GA I/5: 210; SL 4: 232). However, while my moral goal is achieved when the other acts morally, the problem arises when the other acts against the moral law. Ought I not, in this case, abolish the effect of the other's freedom? It is at this point that the duty to live in community or society arises (GA I/5: 212; SL 4: 234). This is the duty to engage in a process of progressive harmonization of our moral judgments, a harmony that, starting with one's agreement with oneself, is necessary if the "interest in universal morality and the rule of reason" in its fundamental unity is to be maintained. Because universal "reason is one," Fichte reassures us, we must eventually come to one common agreement or "result." This is the ultimate *Sollen* of Fichte's theory of ethics. Until then, it is a duty of each individual "to preserve the external freedom of the other" (GA I/5: 211; SL 4: 233). The duty to live in society is accompanied by the duty to participate in a church or an "ethical commonwealth (*ethisches Gemeinwesen*)" as the communal space of reciprocal interaction in which agreement is further pursued and the shared ethical goal is fostered (GA I/5: 212; SL 4: 234). The "absolute duty of conscience to unite with others in a state" through the "state contract" follows (GA I/5: 215; SL 4: 238). At stake in these last three duties is the constitution of a community in which alone the intersubjective condition of moral action can be established.

Relevant to the point made earlier that aimed at framing Fichte's argument in *System of Ethics,* §18 in terms generally analogous to Hegel's *Moralität-Sittlichkeit* transition (at least as far as the criticism of Kant's theory is concerned) is the shift that moves the moral law from the individual to "universal reason" as locus of the collective good. Just before introducing the duty to society, Fichte appropriates but also fundamentally corrects Kant's categorical imperative, which he reads as a confirmation of the demand of "the self-sufficiency of reason in general, hence of the morality of all rational beings," that is, the claim that "we all ought to act in the same way": "Act in such a way that you could think of the maxim of your will as principle of a universal legislation" (GA I/5: 211; SL 4: 233 f.). Fichte implicitly takes Kant's proposition as a demand of "agreement" among agents – and he fully subscribes to this formulation. Thus, Fichte translates Kant's imperative into an intersubjective context: reason in general and its law are embodied in intersubjective activity. Unlike Kant, however, who "only talks about the *idea* of an agreement and by no means about any actual agreement," Fichte insists on "the *real use* of this idea," that is, on the actualization of the end in the world (GA I/5: 212; SL 4: 234: my emphasis). Ultimately, it is universal reason that, for both Fichte and Hegel, is the subject of freedom's actualization in the ethical world. And yet, it is relevant that Fichte still upholds the Kantian *Sollen* – a position that sanctions a deferral or infinite postponement of freedom's embodiment in the world. This clearly points to the opening of the theory of ethics to the philosophy of history. To be sure, this holds true for Fichte as well as for Hegel. In fact, despite his longstanding protestations against Kant's *Sollen*, Hegel acknowledges the opening of a chasm as "international right" leads on to the idea of "world history" (Hegel 1970b, §330).

8.3 Conclusion

In conclusion, I want to sum up the guiding thread of my reconstruction of the overall development of §18. I have argued that Fichte's concern about the centrality of the law's "application" in the theory of ethics amounts to a fundamental correction and critique of Kant's position. The application of the law is its actualization in the sensible world – a world that is both the world of nature and the intersubjective, institutional world of human practices and collective activity. Herein Fichte's project comes close to Hegel's articulation of freedom's realization in the spheres of *Moralität* and *Sittlichkeit*. Actualization is the embodiment of the law in the world and, reciprocally, the embeddedness of the world in the law. This process is the practical reality of freedom. Such a reality is no longer merely noumenal, ideal, and formal but is, instead, phenomenal, real, and material. Accordingly, §18 outlines the process of progressive embodiment of the ethical law or of freedom that starts with the individual living body and ends with the expansion to the intersubjective and collective "body" of society and the state. Throughout this process, and tied to this process of freedom's embodiment, the highest end prescribed by the moral law, namely, the end of absolute self-sufficiency and independence, comes better into focus. What ought to be pursued is not some kind of individualistic and isolationist closing off of the I's sphere of freedom, pursued by mastering

Embodiment and Freedom 177

all things in the world in the name of a utilitarian goal. I suggested that the model on which Fichte's moral end is to be understood is rather Spinoza's sage, who pursues the highest freedom and blessedness by expansively – and bodily – inhabiting and appropriating the world with her increasingly active life.

CHAPTER 9

Ethics as Theory of Society
Morality and Ethical Life in Fichte's System of Ethics

Luca Fonnesu

9.1 Introduction

In a frequently mentioned passage from the essay on *The Scientific Ways of Treating Natural Law*, Hegel offers the first explicit distinction between *Moralität* and *Sittlichkeit*, morality and, in current translations, "ethical life":

> We notice here also an allusion of the language, which, otherwise repudiated, is fully justified by what has been said; that it is of the nature of absolute ethical life to be a universal or *ethos* (*Sitten*); that therefore the Greek word which designates the ethical life (*Sittlichkeit*), like the German one (*Sitte*), expresses its own nature admirably; but that the newer systems of ethics, in making a being for itself and the individuality into a principle, cannot fail to expose the relation with these words, and this inner allusion proves so powerful that these systems, to define *their* subject-matter (*Sache*), could not misuse that word but adopted the word morality (*Moralität*), which indeed originally meant the same thing, but, because it is rather just an invented word, does not quite as directly conflict with its inferior meaning.[1]

Through the two words – *Moralität* and *Sittlichkeit*, which in fact, as Hegel writes, "originally meant the same thing" – Hegel wants to oppose the Greek world of the absolute ethical life to the modern, private, individualistic attitude of morality. The opposition will be developed by the philosopher later, in the different versions of the *Encyclopedia*, in the

---

[1] "Wir bemerken hier auch eine Andeutung der Sprache, die, sonst verworfen, aus dem vorherigen vollkommen gerechtfertigt wird, daß es nämlich in der Natur der absoluten Sittlichkeit ist, ein Allgemeines oder Sitten zu sein, daß also das griechische Wort, welches Sittlichkeit bezeichnet, und das deutsche diese ihre Natur vortrefflich ausdrücken, daß aber die neueren Systeme der Sittlichkeit, da sie ein Fürsichsein und die Einzelheit zum Prinzip machen, nicht ermangeln können, an diesen Worten ihre Beziehung auszustellen, und diese innere Andeutung sich so mächtig erweist, daß jene Systeme, um *ihre* Sache zu bezeichnen, jene Worte nicht dazu mißbrauchen konnten, sondern das Wort Moralität annahmen, was zwar nach seinem Ursprung gleichfalls dahin deutet, aber weil es mehr ein erst gemachtes Wort ist, nicht so unmittelbar seiner schlechteren Bedeutung widersträubt" (Hegel 1802/1970, 504/112). In this and other occasions, the English translation will be modified.

178

lectures and in his masterwork on practical philosophy, the *Outlines of the Philosophy of Right* (1820), probably the last *philosophia practica universalis* of Western thought. The polemical target – from Heidelberg to Berlin – will still be the privatistic spirit of modernity and Hegel's positive model will still be, against the latter, the ethical life. But modernity will be considered not only as privatistic; on the contrary, the modern constellation of institutions reconciles itself with modern individualism, the "principle of subjective particularity," born with Christianity and developed through the privatistic spheres of Roman Law, of modern morality, of modern family and of civil, that is bourgeois, society. After the ancient, undifferentiated and compact form of ethical life, a new modern form of it proves its own reality of *Sittlichkeit*. As Hegel writes at the end of the *Outlines*: "the true reconciliation . . . has become objective."[2] The modern reality of ethical life, with the conciliation between individuality and objectivity, emerges also in the structure of the *Philosophy of Right*, through the development of different stages of freedom. *Abstract* (i.e. more or less, *private*) *Right* and *Morality* (*Moralität*), the first two parts of the book (and of the objective spirit of the *Encyclopedia*), are forms of the modern right of particularity and prove in a certain measure the integration in Hegel's project of Kant's and Fichte's distinction between right and morality. But they do find a true realization only in the institutions of *Ethical life*: family, civil society and the state.

The distinction between *morality* and *ethical life* is for us one of the most important contributions of Hegel's thought to philosophy. One can prove this thesis with the help of both contemporary *Hegel-Forschung*[3] and thinkers who today recall explicitly Hegel's philosophical attitude, such as Jürgen Habermas and, more recently, Axel Honneth.[4] It sounds odd today to remember and recall – as Claudio Cesa did some years ago – that Hegel's contemporaries did not notice the distinction, with few exceptions, such as Paulus, that remarked that it was an *etymologically peculiar distinction*. In other words, the distinction did not have at Hegel's time the importance that we think it should have had. Even many years later, at the end of the nineteenth century, Johann Caspar Bluntschli noticed that Hegel's terminology was in contradiction with the most usual one.[5]

The history of the terms *Moralität* and *Sittlichkeit* would need an analysis which I cannot offer here. Just a few notes. Generally speaking, they do have

---

[2] Cf. Hegel (1821/1970, § 360).   [3] Cf. Siep (2010), Cesa (2013).
[4] Cf. for example Habermas (1988) and, more recently, Honneth (2011).
[5] Cesa (2013, 10 and footnote 2).

180   LUCA FONNESU

throughout the eighteenth century – the century of the formation of a German philosophical language and, at its end, of a proper "German philosophy" – more or less the same meaning, and something similar may be said for their linguistic constellation (e.g. the *Sittengesetz*, moral law, or the *Metaphysik der Sitten*, metaphysics of morals).

In volume 37 (1743) of the *Zedlers Universallexicon*, *Sittlichkeit der Handlungen* is a very short entry, but a reference is made to the much longer entry *Moralität*, already published in volume 21 (1739).[6] The latter refers to the *Philosophisches Lexicon* of Johann Georg Walch published in 1726,[7] which was not the first philosophical lexicon in Germany but the first one in German. In Walch's work, the entry *Sittlichkeit* does not occur at all in any edition between 1726 and 1775, while it of course contains several entries concerning morality or ethics. There is a long entry *Moralität* and then: *Moral* (called "a Latin word", whereas *Ethic* was labelled "a Greek word"). A very short entry is devoted to the German word for *ethica*, that is *Sittenlehre*. The entry *Sitten* refers generally to custom. Walch is fully aware of the ambiguity of moral words, and presents the different options, or at least the multiplicity of meanings of each term. *Sittlichkeit* as an autonomous entry does not occur at all and does not play a significant role.

To sum up, in the wide field of moral terminology, *Sittlichkeit* seems to be in eighteenth-century Germany either a minor term or a synonym of morality, *Moralität*. Even the entry *Sittlichkeit* in the dictionary of the brothers Grimm – at the beginning of the twentieth century (1905) – gives first of all the Latin term *moralitas*. The entry does in fact mention some philosophers, such as Kant, Herder, Schiller, Goethe, Hamann, but not Hegel.[8]

In the above quoted passage from the text on natural right, Hegel speaks of *Moralität* as an *erst gemachtes Wort*, a "just created word," but, to tell the truth, throughout the eighteenth century, *Moralität* was the leading word in German philosophical language, and the new word was *Sittlichkeit*. Hegel does probably mean, with his curious remark, that the new character of the word "morality" consists exactly in a new use, referring to individual morality, to a merely "moral" point of view juxtaposed to the "ethical" one.

With regard to Fichte's *System of Ethics*, it is important to recall that Hegel certainly read this book, because he discussed it critically in *Glauben und Wissen*. In fact, several questions of Fichte's work of 1798 are probably

---

[6] Zedler (1731–1754, Bd. 37, col. 1867; Bd. 21, cols. 1482–1485).   [7] Walch (1726).
[8] Grimm (1905, col. 1271).

Ethics as Theory of Society   181

the source of Hegel's thought, or, to say the least, the way in which Fichte deals with that question does influence Hegel's views. Just a few examples: the loss of relevance of the (Kantian) law as a *nomos* and, consequently, the terminological transfiguration of Kant's *Autonomie* in *Selbständigkeit*; the interpretation of freedom as a process in which it assumes several shapes or figures; the very idea of a history of consciousness illustrated by Fichte not so much in the 1794 *Wissenschaftslehre*, but rather in § 16 of the *System of Ethics*; the theory of drives with the outcome of a theory of action as a real expression of freedom. It may be that also with regard to *ethical life* Fichte played a role. This is the thesis of this chapter.[9] Fichte's *System of Ethics* does propose a distinction between *Moralität* and *Sittlichkeit* and a theory of the latter. This happens with hesitation and ambiguity from the strictly linguistic point of view, but in a deeper, perhaps still more interesting way from the conceptual one. In the framework of the *System of Ethics*, Fichte's *Foundations of Natural Right*, his most important work on natural law, can be seen in a new light.

9.2   The Language of *Sittlichkeit*: Morality

In the last decade of the eighteenth century, many true or alleged "Kantians" attempt to offer themselves to the philosophical public the part of Kant's system of philosophy which the philosopher had long since announced but never published. After the foundational works, the proper *system* of practical philosophy as a doctrine of duties is in fact still missing. This is a partial explanation of the great number of texts of "Kantian" practical philosophy which appear in these years.

The publication in 1797 of Kant's book on the subject, the *Metaphysics of Morals*, was a surprise for many supporters and followers of Kant's thought. Among many others, a brilliant, young follower of Fichte does present – he too – a practical philosophy in the form of a "new" deduction of natural law. Schelling is in fact the author of the *Neue Deduktion des Naturrechts*, published in 1796.

Schelling's book is worth mentioning here because he proposes a suggestion which has to do with our problem, that is with the internal articulation of the wide, general space of morality. Schelling writes that there is "a passage from the domain of morals (*Moral*) in that of ethics (*Ethik*). Morals gives generally a command to an individual . . . ethics gives a command, which presupposes a realm of moral beings."[10] Schelling

---

[9] On the common ground of Fichte and Hegel, see Siep (1992).
[10] Schelling (1856-, 1:252, § 31).

speaks here of a possible distinction between forms or aspects of morality as a general term, referring, on the one hand, to individual morality and, on the other hand, to an intersubjective ethics. Later in this chapter, this terminology occurs again, but the question is neither here nor elsewhere deepened by Schelling. It would be unfair to recall that Schelling will later observe that to speak of a human "morality" would mean to accept the recent *Aufklärerei*,[11] but practical philosophy will not be the main subject of his intellectual development.

In the very same year of the publication of Schelling's *Neue Deduktion des Naturrechts* – 1796 – Fichte gives in the *Sommersemester* lectures on moral theory. It is the *Collegium über die Moral*, a text published in 1977 in the *Gesamtausgabe*, which is the first version of the *System of Ethics*.

Exactly as in the book of 1798, Fichte's titles of the different parts of the *Collegium* refer to the term *Sittlichkeit*. Of it should be here deduced the *principle* (first part); the *reality and applicability* (second part), and the *systematic application*, or ethics proper (*Sittenlehre im engeren Sinne*; third part). On many occasions, Fichte uses in lectures also the term *Moralität*, but it does not seem that he distinguishes the term from *Sittlichkeit*.

With the last lines of the second part, Fichte's aim is to introduce the systematic application of the principle or the ethics proper. In the third part, Fichte will in fact develop his own *system*, the *Sittenlehre* in the strict sense. *Sittenlehre* or ethics is for Fichte something different from a (mere) metaphysics of morals: Fichte declares explicitly that the latter, that is obviously Kant's ethics, does not consider the lower faculty of desire and is therefore *formal and void*. A proper ethics has to be, on the contrary, *wirklich*, real.[12]

The last lines of the deduction of the applicability of the principle introduce in the 1796 lectures, as the later book, the distinction between *form* and *material*, or better, between formal and material conditions of morality, moving from individual conviction as a criterion of duty:

> Always act in accordance with the best conviction or in accordance with the conscience. This is the formal condition for morality [*Moralität*] (in the first section). In the 2nd of the material conditions of it.[13]

---

[11] Cf. Cesa (2013, 62).

[12] GA I/5: 126; SL 4: 131. For further discussion, see Chapter 4 by Owen Ware in this volume.

[13] My translation: "handle stets nach d[er]. besten Ueberzeugung, oder d[em]. Gewißen. <1>Dieses ist die formale Bedingung der Moralität, (im ersten Absch[nitt].). im 2ten von d[en]. materialen Bedingung[en] derselben" (GA IV/1: 74).

Ethics as Theory of Society

Presenting the distinction between form and content, Fichte mentions in 1796 only *Moralität* as a general term for morality and speaks of moral conscience as its formal condition, different from its material conditions. There is here no new terminology. The first significant, although uncertain, distinction between *Moralität* and *Sittlichkeit* occurs only in the 1798 version, in the published *System of Ethics*, in the very same introductory passage:

> [A]*lways act in accordance with your best conviction concerning your duty*, or, *Act according to your conscience*. This is the formal condition for the morality [*Moralität*] of our actions, and it is what has been preferably called their morality [*Moralität*]. We will discuss these formal conditions of morality [*Sittlichkeit*] in greater detail in the first section of our ethics proper, and then, in the second section, we will present the material conditions for the morality [*Moralität*] of our actions, or the doctrine of their *legality* [*Legalität*].[14]

Fichte's formulation is not so clear, and it is not difficult to understand why some translations[15] do not differentiate even here between *Moralität* and *Sittlichkeit*, translating both with *morality*. Nevertheless, Fichte speaks explicitly of a meaning of *Moralität* in a strict, proper sense, that is, as denoting only *one* part of morality, which is "*preferably* called" just *Moralität* and has to do with the *form*, with the *formal* condition of morality. In fact, something is going to happen – here – in Fichte's philosophical horizon, and if the language does not express with full clarity the distinction between *Moralität* and *Sittlichkeit*, Fichte's argument developed in the third part – the ethics proper or ethics in a strict sense – does go in the very same direction, presenting a theory of *Sittlichkeit* as ethical life with traits which have something in common with Hegel's later construction and answering the same questions, but in a different, original way.

The introductory passage presents in fact the inner articulation of the ethics proper. The first section will deal with the form or formal condition of morality in the wider sense, presenting the theory of individual conscience, while the second section will deal with the content or with the material conditions of the same morality (where "material" is of course

---

[14] "*Handle stets nach bester Überzeugung von deiner Pflicht;* oder: *handle nach deinem Gewissen.* Dies ist die formale Bedingung der Moralität unserer Handlungen, die man auch vorzugsweise *die Moralität* derselben genannt hat. Wir werden über diese formalen Bedingungen der Sittlichkeit im ersten Abschnitte unserer eigentlichen Sittenlehre ausführlicher reden: und dann in einem zweiten Abschnitte, die materialen Bedingungen der Moralität unserer Handlungen, oder die Lehre von der *Legalität* derselben, aufstellen" (GA I/5: 146; SL 4: 157).

[15] For example, the English translation edited by Breazeale and Zöller (2005).

opposed, in a Kantian way, to "form"), a content which Fichte calls *legality*. The third section of the ethics proper – the doctrine of duties – is not even mentioned here.

With the form or formal condition Fichte deals in fact in the immediately following section of the *System of Ethics*, where we do find the analysis of conviction and consequently of moral conscience.[16] In a digression concerning the concept of will, it is possible to find a further explicit reference to a strict meaning of *Moralität* as the only formal part of morality, with at the same time an echo of the well-known passage at the beginning of Kant's *Groundwork for the Metaphysics of Morals*.

I could turn immediately to a synthetic–systematic statement of the formal conditions for the *Moralität* of our actions. But because the formal morality (*formale Moralität*), or the preferably so-called *Moralität*, is also called *good will*, and because I myself intend to characterize it in this way, I first have to provide an account of my concept of the will (GA I/5: 147; SL 4: 157).[17]

Moralität in the strict sense concerns therefore only the form of morality, the individual conviction of an individual conscience as "good will." We could even say that *Moralität* does represent – using a Hegelian terminology – *the standpoint of morality as Moralität*[18] with its own certainty, which, as we will see, will find its proper realization in another domain, the domain of ethical life. The perspective of the moral, individual, formal standpoint is in other words limited for Fichte too, although he does not have towards it the strong critical attitude of Hegel.

After the discussion of conscience as the "form," the second section of ethics proper does concern the further, fundamental aspect of morality in a general sense, its *content* or *material*, what Fichte calls the material conditions of morality or, as he writes, the doctrine of their "legality." This curious terminology has to be discussed, but first of all it is now

---

[16] The concept of "conviction" (*Ueberzeugung*) does play a significant role in Kant's thought. Nevertheless, Fichte's sources for the use of this concept are to be found not only and not so much in Kant's philosophy but in the "pre-Kantian" Fichte and in his confrontation with the German Enlightenment, as shown by Preul (1969). On Fichte's conception of moral conscience, cf. Chapter 6 by Dean Moyar in this volume and Bacin (2017).

[17] Cf. 4: 393: "It is impossible to think of anything at all in the world, or indeed even beyond it, that could be considered good without limitation except a *good will*."

[18] Cf. Hegel (1821/1970, § 105): "The standpoint of morality is the standpoint of the will which is infinite not merely in itself but *for itself* (see § 104). This reflection of the will into itself and its identity for itself, in contrast to its being-in-itself and immediacy and the determinate characteristics developed therein, makes the person into the subject." Cf. Peperzak (2001, 297): The first peculiarity that strikes the reader is Hegel's "presentation of 'morality' as a 'standpoint'."

Ethics as Theory of Society 185

necessary to explain a crucial point of Fichte's *System of Ethics* which opens the door to his theory of ethical life.

9.3 The Shift from the Individual to Society: Towards Ethical Life

The ethics proper of the *System of Ethics* moves from the deduction of body,[19] intelligence and intersubjectivity as constitutive elements of individuality. For our problem, the main role is played by intersubjectivity. It is not necessary to deepen here this very difficult question of Fichte's thought, which the philosopher already dealt with at the beginning of his *Natural Right*.[20] The result of this second "deduction" of intersubjectivity is that the latter is a constitutive element of individuality. This means (among other things) that Fichte is the first thinker who gives a philosophical foundation of a "necessary" sociality of man, a *topos* of philosophical and political discussions in the eighteenth century.

The intersubjective and social nature of human beings offers Fichte the opportunity to develop a theory of ethical life with a radical shift or reorientation of his proceeding. It has to be remarked that this is not the first shift in the *System of Ethics*. The first one occurs in the second part of the book, in a further crucial point where Fichte is looking for the *applicability* of the principle of ethics as a synthesis of drives (the pure and the natural one): the unification of rationality and nature is here shifted from the synchronic to the diachronic dimension, producing in this way the central idea of *series* of actions (later resumed by Hegel in the *Rechtsphilosophie*)[21] as the "vocation" of man (*Bestimmung des Menschen*), *topos* of the German *Aufklärung* and central idea of Fichte's moral anthropology.[22]

The second shift or reorientation, which is of major interest here, is once more the necessity of a solution for a contradiction or, better, for a potential conflict between the imperative which prescribes to human beings to dominate everything with the final end of the absolute self-sufficiency (*Selbständigkeit*) of reason and the necessary limitation of this activity in front of the activity and consequently of the ends of other

---

[19] Cf. Chapter 8 by Angelica Nuzzo in this volume.

[20] Cf. GA I/3: 340ff.; GNR 3: 30ff. On intersubjectivity, see Lauth (1962), Düsing (1986), and Cesa (1992).

[21] GA I/5: 140–41; SL 4: 149–50. Cf. Hegel (1821/1970, § 124): "What the subject *is*, is *the series of his actions*." Fichte's and Hegel's insistence on the importance of the concrete *action* is a further sign of their polemical attitude towards Kant and his (true or alleged) ethics of the *Gesinnung* (character).

[22] Cf. Fonnesu (1993). For a detailed history of the expression *Bestimmung des Menschen*, see Macor (2013).

186   LUCA FONNESU

rational beings (GA I/5: 209; SL 4: 230). Apart from the strong "baconist" attitude of this position, in which the central aim of reason seems to be the control of nature, the question is that actions of different individuals, that is their ends, can in fact conflict, and this danger can be faced in an appropriate way in Fichte's opinion only if all rational, free beings have ultimately the very same end.[23] Fichte's solution is the extension of the notion of reason towards a meta-individual dimension. In fact, writes Fichte, "our ultimate goal is the self-sufficiency of all reason as such and thus not the self-sufficiency of one rational being" (GA I/5: 209; SL 4: 231). This is a radical reorientation of Fichte's argument.

The true subject of the project of reason is not the individual, but rationality *as such*, which presents or expresses itself (*darstellt*) in the sensible world through the whole of rational beings as human society. Individuals are just members of the – though indispensable – inner articulation of human society as presentation of reason in the sensible world, and their role, as individuals, is now to become an adequate function of the whole. The shift from the individual to society implies a new perspective – one could call it a new, *ethical* point of view – and makes of society the subject of the process, making at the same time of the relationship between individual and society a central ethical question. In other words, we are now in the new scene of ethical life.

The true subject of the teleological path of reason towards its self-sufficiency is not the individual – we have just discovered – but human society as a *Darstellung der Vernunft* which finds its concrete expression through different individuals. The derived and instrumental character of individuals reverses in fact the Kantian doctrine of the rational being as an end in itself. It is perhaps for the awareness of this very significant reversal that Fichte, paradoxically, feels obligated to declare the full compatibility of his view with the Kantian one:

> Kant has asserted that every *human being is himself an end*, and this assertion has received universal assent. This Kantian proposition is compatible with mine .... Everyone is an end, in the sense that everyone is a *means* for realizing reason .... It is precisely by means of this disappearance and annihilation of one's entire individuality that everyone becomes a pure presentation of the moral law in the world of sense and thus becomes

---

[23] "The only way to resolve this contradiction and to establish the agreement of the moral law with itself would be to presuppose that all free beings necessarily share the same end, which would mean that the purposive conduct of one person would at the same time be purposive for all others and that the liberation of one would at the same time be the liberation of all the others" (GA I/5: 209; SL 4: 230–31).

Ethics as Theory of Society

a "pure I," in the proper sense of the term; and this occurs by means of free choice and self-determination. (GA I/5: 230; SL 4: 255–56)

The presentation of reason as human society does not find expression only in the many individuals, or in an undifferentiated sociality. After Fichte's shift from the individual to society or, if one wills, from morality to ethical life, this is only the starting point of the theory of ethical life. The new subject is certainly the human society as a presentation of reason expressed through its individual members, but society is organized through institutions that permit its functioning and promote its progress and development.

9.4   The Language of *Sittlichkeit*: Legality

A step backwards. We have seen that Fichte distinguishes *Moralität* as the formal condition of morality in the broad sense, and *Legalität* as concerning its material conditions. The material conditions are the conditions of a content of morality, that is of duty.

The terms "legality" and "legal" occur in fact several times in the *System of Ethics*,[24] but apart from the quoted introductory passage which refers to legality as concerning the material conditions of *Sittlichkeit*, "legality" seems to have in all the other occurrences a negative or at least limiting meaning in opposition to "morality" (*Moralität*). Without deepening here the appropriateness of Fichte's interpretation of Kant's distinction, all those occurrences recall the question of motivation in a sense at least similar to Kant's opening of the chapter on the incentives in the *Critique of Practical Reason*.[25]

The question is that Fichte's argument in the second section goes far beyond mere external behaviour as opposed to, or at least distinguished from, a moral disposition. If the discussion of the material conditions of morality is, as Fichte writes, the discussion of "legality," then this term does indicate something much richer and more complex than a mere individual attitude.[26]

---

[24] Cf. GA I/5: 146, 216, 246, 253, 261, 286; SL 4: 156, 239–40, 275, 284, 294, 326.
[25] "If the determination of the will takes place conformably with the moral law but only by means of a feeling, of whatever kind, that has to be presupposed in order for the law to become a sufficient determining ground of the will, so that the action is not done *for the sake of the law*, then the action will contain *legality* indeed but not *morality*" (5: 71).
[26] It is easy to observe how much Fichte's presentation of the third part in the introductory passage at the end of the second is if not misleading certainly very partial if compared with the actual content of

The very idea of a teleological path towards self-sufficiency has – as already said – a strong baconist character, in the sense that what seems most important is the transformation of nature for reason's sake. This character is not at all refused by Fichte with the shift from individual to society, although once gained the new perspective of society and of ethical life there is a new task to accomplish. This new task is the organization of society through "legal" institutions, that is institutions that make possible a peaceful coexistence (the state) and its progress and development (church and learned public). The characterization of the second section of ethics proper as "legality" can be so understood as marking the passage from the baconist, poietic, economic task of reason – which of course does not disappear but is here no more the primary one – to its necessity of organizing itself in several indispensable institutional forms – of juridical, political and social nature – being in fact the very central task, that of reciprocal communication and education. This view is grounded upon the ethical meaning of labour, an original interpretation of the relationship between law and morality and the decisive role of communication. The deepening of the latter question will imply the analysis of the very *dynamic* of ethical life as a dialectic of its members and institutions. Let us consider the mentioned three aspects in turn.

The ethical meaning of labour. The first aspect of the causality of freedom in the world – a central starting point of Fichte's view and his own way to interpret Kant's most important legacy – does consist in the insistence on the *reality* of action, contrasting Kant's insistence on the mere determination of the will and the *Gesinnung* or character. This aspect is the main expression of the practical necessity of control and rationalization of nature with the goal of self-sufficiency of reason – the baconist side. Exactly this goal justifies and explains the ethical meaning of labour in Fichte's view. Causality of freedom towards absolute self-sufficiency of reason – not the individual reason, as we know – implies that the task of transformation and modification of nature, rational activity in the world for the sake of reason's ends, has to be in some way organized, and this further trait explains the necessity and the ethical significance of the division of labour between different individuals and estates (*Stände*).

---

the ethics proper. And this both for the formal and material conditions. The first section, dedicated to the form, does in fact deal in the central part with the moral conscience (§ 15), but Fichte discusses before (§14) the concept of will, and afterwards (§16), with a misleading title concerning evil, presents a kind of "history of consciousness" as a phenomenology of conscience. The question becomes still more complicated with the second section, while the third section dedicated to the proper doctrine of duties is not even mentioned, in Fichte's introductory passage.

Ethics as Theory of Society

To the question of the division of labour Fichte paid great attention in the well-known cyclus of 1794 *de officiis eruditorum* or on the vocation of the scholar. One lecture is entirely devoted to the question.[27] The very same problem plays a salient role in the *System of Ethics*, influencing in a remarkable way even the doctrine of duties.[28] The division of labour – against Schiller's perplexities expressed in the *Letters on the Aesthetical Education of Man* – is the result of the necessity of internal organization and articulation of the whole of reason in different individuals and *Stände* or offices that have to play different roles in the general task of reason.

Law and morality. Fichte's conception of the relationship between law and morality[29] is a very original one, distinguishing itself at the same time from Kant's and Hegel's views. The separation between the two domains is for Fichte very radical in the sense that the domain of law has to be grounded without reference to morality. This is clear in the criticism of Fichte's *Natural Right* towards "those who attempt to derive the doctrine of right from the moral law" (GA I/3: 320; GNR 3: 10). The assertion sounds like a critical remark against Kant's thought, but not only that. Fichte's position means that the whole construction of natural right, that is the domain of law, is grounded upon a mere hypothesis:

> [I]f one asks, in accordance with what principles could a community among free beings as such be established if someone wanted to establish one, the answer would have to be: in accordance with the concept of right. But this answer by no means asserts that such a community ought to be established. (GA I/3: 320; GNR, 3: 10)

From the juridical point of view, morality has no role to play in the justification of law. But right cannot ground itself, so that the ethical point of view is different, as Fichte already remarked in the *Natural Right*. The domain of the law of right (*Rechtsgesetz*) receives in fact from the moral law "a new sanction for conscience" (GA I/3: 320; GNR 3: 10),[30] although the whole juridical and political construction has to be exposed and presented *also* independently from ethical assumptions. In other words, the deepest justification, or the deduction of the (practical, i.e. ethical) necessity of social life, of the duty to live in a peaceful – that is lawful – society and even of the duty to ground a state can be given only in the moral or, better,

---

[27] *Über die Verschiedenheit der Stände in der Gesellschaft*, GA I/3: 42–50; BdG 6: 312–23.
[28] See GA I/5: 232; SL 4: 258. The last pages of the doctrine of duties in the *System of Ethics* are in fact devoted to the *duties of human beings within a particular profession (Beruf: §§ 28–33)*.
[29] Cf. Verweyen (1975), De Pascale (2003), and James (2011).
[30] It is noteworthy Fichte's assertion that "Ethics (*Sittenlehre*) lies higher than any other particular philosophical science (hence, it also lies higher than the doctrine of right)" (GA I/5: 199; SL 4: 218).

ethical domain.[31] In this way, in the framework of ethical life, the very separation between morality and law is overcome, and the realm of law and the state is included in an ethical perspective. This trait becomes all the more important because all the forms of sociality and all the institutions receive in the framework of the ethical life a "sanction" that is an ethical justification and the explanation of their role in an ethical perspective or from an ethical point of view, as we will see in the dynamic of ethical life.

Communication. The mentioned element of Fichte's theory of society – the lawful organization of external activities and actions of individuals, including the *Herrschaft der Natur* as economic activity – makes possible in Fichte's eyes a peaceful, just and well-ordered society, where rational beings not only can, but also ought to communicate. This salient problem of Kant's thought[32] is made by Fichte the core of his theory of ethical life.[33] What we require from other rational beings in the intersubjective space is in fact not just legality, but morality too. True morality needs the conviction of conscience and there is morality only when a legal or right external behaviour is done on the basis of the conviction of conscience that this is actually the proper duty. All this is possible for Fichte through the development of communicative processes which takes place in the framework of different institutions.

The different institutions, church, the state and *Gelehrtenrepublik* or learned republic, are all functions of the intersubjective communications and through this communication of the progress of society. There are in Fichte's ethical life dialectical relations between different components which should all contribute to the general progress and to what he calls the goal of an *allgemeine Sittlichkeit* or universal morality (GA I/5: 211; SL 4: 233). This dialectic is the principle of the internal dynamic of ethical life.

9.5   Dynamic of Ethical Life

The core of Fichte's theory of ethical life does emerge in the final part of the second section of the ethics proper (§ 18, V; GA I/5: 209 ff.; SL 4: 230 ff.). One has to consider that the three different sections of ethics proper do not consist of three different parts which proceed each to answer its own question. Fichte's aim is to illustrate a process of *determination* of the whole of ethical life, starting with the individual conviction of the moral

---

[31] Cf. GA I/5: 212, 215; SL 4: 234, 238.   [32] See Fonnesu (2019).

[33] The literature on Fichte pays little attention to the question. As far as I know, the only contribution is Naulin (1969).

conscience, going through the constitution of individuality and the inter-subjective communication with its institutions and, finally, the doctrine of duties. In other words, every passage does presuppose and include the preceding stages with the aim of the realization of the whole of ethical life with all its determinations.

In a few pages of the final part of § 18, Fichte develops a dynamic of ethical life as a theory of communication and of the several institutions that make communication possible, promoting its development and conse-quently the progress of human society. As we have seen, while the baconist, poietic economic aspect played a prominent role earlier, now Fichte pays major attention to the whole of reason as human society not for its causality on nature, but for the relationships among its different components. This is the scene of intersubjective communication, that is no more the scene of the confrontation of reason with nature, but of the intersubjective con-frontation between rational beings.

The starting point is now individual conviction and the possibility of disagreement: Every individual has to act following his or her own conviction and never against it, but what if different convictions are in conflict? How is it possible to find an agreement? If somebody thinks himself in the right and his conviction contradicts the conviction of somebody else, how can this dis-agreement be solved?[34] The only possible solution in Fichte's eyes is intersub-jective communication, with the aim of finding out who's right and who's wrong and, consequently, with the aim of intersubjective agreement about the way to act in the world: Directly or indirectly, in fact, the disagreement has to concern action in the world or, in other words, causality of freedom, and that's why agreement is so important. A legal, that is externally correct, causality of freedom by other human beings has to be supported, promoted and helped, but if we disagree with their way of acting and we are convinced of that, while they too are convinced, the risk is the continuous possibility of disagreement and, consequently, of intersubjective conflict.

Fichte here takes the opportunity to criticize once more Kant and his formulation of the categorical imperative, because "Kant's proposition only talks about the *idea* of an agreement and by no means about any *actual* [*wirklich*] agreement" (GA I/5: 211–12; SL 4: 234). What emerges here is not only – a few lines later – the reproach for the mere heuristic and not constitutive role of Kant's formula,[35] but Fichte's transfiguration of

---

[34] "Ultimately, of course, they must arrive at one and the same result, since reason is simply one" (GA I/5: SL 4: 233).

[35] Here again, something similar can be found few years later in Hegel's article on natural law, when he is ironic about Kant's well-known example of the "deposit": Hegel (1802/1970, 462/77–78).

192   LUCA FONNESU

Kant's thought experiment in the test of universalization. Intersubjective agreement has to be in Fichte's eyes a real and concrete one, the result of communication and dialogue. The actual conviction of the individuals has to be confronted in the scene of intersubjective communication with the aim to arrive at one and the same conviction as a *common* conviction about what has to be done and realized in the world.

The opposition between private and common conviction does in fact play a leading role in these pages of the *System of Ethics*.[36] Reason is a common quality which permits communication among rational beings, and even the goal of reason is a common task. The conviction too of individuals has therefore to be – or should become – a common one: "The necessary goal (*Ziel*) of all virtuous people is therefore unanimous agreement concerning the same practical conviction and concerning the uniformity of acting that ensues therefrom" (GA I/5: 213; SL 4: 236).

Human beings have the freedom to act on their own body in the way that they freely choose (although they have the duty to form it as a valid instrument of reason). The problem arises when the activity does concern not only our own body, but also the sensible world outside of my body as a *Gemeingut*, a common good: "What lies outside my body, and hence the entire sensible world, is a common good or possession, and the cultivation of the same in accordance with the laws of reason is not mandated *of me alone* but rather *of all rational beings*" (GA I/5: 214; SL 4: 237). Actions in the world cannot take place following a mere *private* conviction, because every action does have in fact an influence upon others. It is in this context that Fichte declares as a *duty* not only to live in society, but also to find an agreement – one could say a first, fundamental agreement – concerning external actions, that is causality of freedom on the external, sensible world – through a contract. This is the *ethical* justification of the state as an instrument, but as an indispensable instrument. The world of law and the state do have – as we know – an independent justification grounded upon the mere hypothesis of social life, without ethical presuppositions, but here the state itself receives its ethical and in a certain way *absolute* sanction:

> It therefore follows, by virtue of an absolute command of the moral law, that such universal agreement simply must be achieved. Agreement concerning how human beings are permitted to influence one another – i.e., agreement concerning their *communal rights* in the sensible world – is called the *state*

---

[36] It would be interesting to consider analogies and differences between this opposition and the opposition "private/public" which is so significant in Kant's philosophy. I cannot deepen this question here.

Ethics as Theory of Society

contract (*Staatsvertrag*); and the community that has achieved such agreement is the state. It is an absolute duty of conscience to unite with others in a state. (GA I/5: 215; SL 4: 237 f.)

Nevertheless, the political institution, the state, has not for Fichte any intrinsic value. On the contrary, it is another instrument for the goal of reason which consists – ultimately – in a society without a state. In Fichte's eyes there is no doubt about the priority of society over the state: The former is the true subject of morality, the presentation of reason in the sensible world, while the latter is just an instrument.

Before Marx, Fichte is an advocate of the extinction of the state. Even the rational state, the *Vernunftstaat*, has to tend to its own extinction,[37] but in the actual conditions of human society, the state is a necessary instrument not only in the best possible form described by Fichte himself in the *Natural Right*, as a *Vernunftstaat*, a rational state, but also in the imperfect form of the existing state, what Fichte calls a *makeshift state* (*Notstaat*: GA I/5: 215; SL 4: 238). The tension between the imperfection of the actual states and the rational state, between reality and ideal, between the opportunity to obey to the former and the moral duty to work for the latter can be solved with the full awareness of the imperfection of the existing state and the consideration of it as a mere means towards the state of reason. The consideration of the present state without thinking of its progressive perfection is not acceptable from the ethical point of view. The grounding principle of this position is, following Kant, Fichte's critical attitude towards every form of conservatism, stressing on the contrary the moral obligation to believe in the unlimited *perfectibility* of humanity.[38]

---

[37] The life in the state – writes Fichte already in 1794 in the *Lectures on the Vocation of the Scholar* – is not a part of the absolute purpose of human life. The state is only "a means towards the foundation of a perfect society. Like all human institutions, which are merely means to an end, the state constantly tends towards its own destruction; the ultimate aim of all government is to make government superfluous" (GA I/3: 37; BdG 6: 306). Cf. Fonnesu (1996).

[38] "I must not take any measures that would allow things to remain forever as they are now, but I should instead act in such a way that things have to become better. This is purely and simply a duty . . .. First of all, the question is not whether one has to decide on the basis of purely theoretical rational grounds for or against the perfectibility of humanity. This is a question we can totally ignore. The moral law, which extends to infinity, absolutely commands us to treat human beings *as if* they were forever capable of becoming perfected and remaining so, and this same law absolutely prohibits us from treating human beings in the opposite manner. One cannot obey such a command without believing in perfectibility. Consequently, the latter constitutes the first article of faith, something one cannot doubt without surrendering one's entire moral nature" (GA I/5: 217; SL 4: 239–40). "Perfectibility" was a neologism introduced by Rousseau in a critical way in the framework of his criticism of modernity in the second *Discourse*. Fichte discusses Rousseau's position in the fifth lecture on the vocation of the scholar, of course reversing Rousseau's critical evaluation of modernity and stressing the positive meaning of perfectibility (GA I/3: 59–67; BdG 6: 335–46). On the concept of perfectibility, see Hornig (1980).

The provisional character of actually existing, positive institutions emerges also in the case of the further institution considered by Fichte, the *church*, which is not so much an instrument in the sense in which the state is, but rather the proper *means* to the end of intersubjective agreement, the place of communication *par excellence*, of the *Streit der Geister*.

> This reciprocal interaction of everyone with everyone for the purpose of producing communally shared practical convictions is possible only insofar as everyone starts from the same shared principles; and it is necessary that there be such principles, to which their additional convictions must be connected. Such a reciprocal interaction, in which everyone is obliged to engage, is called a *church*, an ethical commonwealth (*ethisches Gemeinwesen*). (GA I/5: 213; SL 4: 236)

Of course, the meaning of the church does not consist for Fichte in the positive, actual, ecclesiastic institution, but in a point of view on human society which considers its members as ethical beings that do participate in the communicative community, as subjects of a *reciprocal* communication and education. The church is the proper ethical institution, and the state, in its ethical meaning, is the institution which does make possible an external pacific coexistence where individuals can develop this positive interaction as moral subjects. If, and only if, citizens and government are sensible to the ethical requirements which come from the church, that is from society, the state itself does promote the perfection of the actually existing juridical and political conditions with the aim of moral perfection through intersubjective communication.

To characterize the main *positive* institution of moral communication and education, that is the church, Fichte does speak of a *symbol* as something which does represent the ethical community and in which everybody can believe and recognize himself or herself:

> [T]hat upon which everyone agrees is its [of the church] *symbol or creed*. Everyone is supposed to be a member of the church. If, however, the church community is not to be entirely fruitless, the symbol in question must be constantly changed, because as these different minds continue to engage in reciprocal interaction the area upon which they all agree will gradually expand. (GA I/5: 213; SL 4: 236)

The communicative community does ground upon common conviction and upon common sensible representations of these convictions: This is the role of symbols of the positive church as a common terrain where people can communicate and, through these common symbols, go beyond them. Symbols too are just instruments, and in this sense the symbol of the church is a *Notsymbol,* a *makeshift symbol* (GA I/5: 218; SL 4: 242). The symbol has and ought to have two main characters: It has to be *sensible*, so that everybody can understand it, and it should at the same time have the highest possible degree of *generality*,[39] because exactly, thanks to this generality, it can be accessible to a great number of individuals and become a genuine means of communication. The symbol is the external sign of a community with its specific, contingent traits – for example of a certain positive religion – but what does matter is just the assertion that *there is something supersensible* (GA I/5: 219; SL 4: 243).

In Fichte's eyes, positivity of law and positivity of an actual church (i.e. of a positive religion) do have the same ethical meaning. To play the role of a means which has to be overcome over time, thanks to the process of perfecting the relative institutions, both juridico-political and ethical commonwealth (in both cases: *Gemeinwesen* or *gemeines Wesen,* the German expression for *res publica*). Actual, really existing institutions have to be considered not only as means but as imperfect means, conditioned by historical, contingent factors, means produced by a situation of necessity, *Not. Notstaat and Notsymbol – the makeshift state and makeshift symbol –* are just results of the necessity to have a peaceful coexistence of rational beings and some starting point for communication.

The analogy between the state and church[40] as mere means is stressed explicitly by Fichte himself in a very clear way, both for its positive and negative aspects:

> Insofar as I actually and sincerely regard the symbol in question only as a means to elevate the others gradually to my conviction, my teachings are surely totally in accord with my conviction – just as my acting in the makeshift state had to be viewed as a means for bringing about the rational state . . . . It is unconscionable to make it one's end, in violation of one's own conviction, to get others to retain a certain belief; indeed, this constitutes true and genuine priestcraft (*Pfaffentum*) – just as the striving to keep human beings in a makeshift state constitutes true and genuine despotism. The symbol is [only] the starting point. (GA I/5: 220; SL 4: 244)

And Fichte takes the opportunity to illustrate his own interpretation of Protestantism as the true religion of progress.[41] Its character does consist exactly in this relationship between positive religion and the necessity to go beyond it:

---

[39] GA I/5: 218; SL 4: 242.
[40] An interesting analysis concerning both Fichte and Hegel in Siep (2009).
[41] Significant similarities (and differences) with Hegel's view cannot be examined here.

> This further progression, this process of raising the symbol to a higher level is precisely the spirit of Protestantism, if this word is supposed to have any meaning at all. Sticking with the old, bringing universal reason to a standstill: this is the spirit of papism. The Protestant starts with the symbol and then proceeds into infinity; the papist proceeds toward the symbol as his final goal. Anyone who behaves in the latter fashion is a papist, in both form and spirit, even though the propositions that he does not want to allow humanity to rise above may be, with respect to their matter or content, genuinely Lutheran or Calvinist or something similar. (GA I/5: 220;SL 4: 245)

Although provisional, positive common institutions as the makeshift state and the church grounded upon a makeshift symbol are in Fichte's view supposed as expressing a certain degree of common conviction, that is the common conviction which is in fact possible in a historical contingent situation. One could say that they give the possibility to have a certain *order*. But what about the individual who has another conviction, different from the current one and therefore would have the duty to communicate and verify it discussing with the other members both of the state and church? This duty would conflict on the one hand with the duty to communicate through the positive institution and its symbol and, on the other hand, with the duty not to undermine the state's authority (GA I/5: 222; SL 4: 247). In fact, Fichte's idea is that there has to be a dynamic principle which should promote perfection, but the constant risk is the private validity of a private conviction used against principles of order such as the community of church and the state: Although provisional, these institutions have for Fichte some kind of validity at least as a means for their perfection and as supposed expression of a common conviction. The risk is the overriding of private convictions and the end of every kind of order.

Fichte's solution of the problem leads to the third fundamental institution of his theory of ethical life, the learned public or the learned republic (*gelehrtes Publikum, gelehrte Republik*) (GA I/5: 223 ff.; SL 4: 248 ff.): "Everyone who has elevated himself to absolute non-belief in the authority of the communal conviction of his age has a duty of conscience to establish a learned public" (GA I/5: 223; SL 4: 248). The scholar does represent in two different senses a new reorientation or shift of the argument. Firstly, the rank of the scholars which derives from the division of labour does represent a kind of intersection between universal and particular traits and, consequently, universal and particular duty. The task or duty of every rational, human being, that is the duty to communicate, does find in the scholar its best and most significant expression. In the case of the scholar, the ideal best condition of expression and communication, a condition

Ethics as Theory of Society

without limits, completely free, without symbols and without any kind of authority apart from the authority of reason, is in fact realized and can really work with complete, full freedom for the perfection of humankind. That's why the learned republic "is an absolute democracy, or, to put it even more precisely, the only law (*Recht*) that applies within this republic is the law of the stronger mind" (GA I/5: 225; SL 4: 251). This democracy limited to the space of the learned public shows the second aspect of Fichte's reorientation in the context of the discussion of learned public: the radical limitation of the initial image of society as the venue of intersubjective communication. In fact, communication does have only one direction, that is from the top-down.

Actual communication is not so much a reciprocal education but rather a process of education of people and of lower classes (*untere Volksklassen*) by scholars, who in their different ways have to play the role of the direction of society and the state. This position emerges clearly in the last pages of the *System of Ethics*. Here, after the discussion of the duties of different kinds of scholars, the question is that of the duties of the lower classes, that is the duty to "honor" (*ehren*) the higher classes (GA I/5: 315; SL 4: 363) and to receive a proper education, with strong paternalist traits.[42] It is one of the points of connection of Fichte's thought with eighteenth-century Germany and its paternalistic institutions. Even scholars as such cannot in fact have a *political* role, but only influence the ruling class. A *direct* political action of scholars has to be excluded, and every attempt in this direction has in Fichte's eyes to be punished:

> The state and the church have the right to prohibit the scholar from realizing his convictions within the sensible world, and they have the right to prevent him from doing this. If he nevertheless does this – if, e. g., he does not obey the laws of the state – then he is rightfully punished, no matter what he may inwardly think about the laws in question. Moreover, he has to reproach himself in his conscience [for acting in this manner], for his action is immoral. (GA I/5: 226; SL 4: 252)

Politics is certainly for Fichte a question which has to be treated by scholars, but only by a small part of them, the governants, who do in fact have specific duties (cf. GA I/5: 310 ff.; SL 4: 356 ff.).

---

[42] "The correct relationship between the higher and lower classes, the appropriate mutual interaction between the two, is, as such, the true underlying support upon which the improvement of the human species rests. The higher classes constitute the mind of the single large whole of humanity; the lower classes constitute its limbs; the former are the thinking and designing [*Entwerfende*] part, the latter the executive part" (GA I/5: 316; SL 4: 364).

The conclusion of Fichte's general discussion of a theory of ethical life does mark in the most radical way his distance from Hegel. Fichte does not only stress the priority of society over the state and the perspective of the *ought*, a normativity of the *Sollen*, but he outlines even a utopian plan of the extinction of all the institutions which he has just presented to the readers. In the long run, every distinction, every difference and every institution should disappear, because the very idea of an institutional texture will become useless if the goal of the absolute agreement of all with all becomes a reality:

> Under the presupposition of such agreement the distinction between a learned and an unlearned public falls away, as do the church and the state. Everyone has the same convictions, and the conviction of any single person is the conviction of every person. The state falls away as a legislative and coercive power. The will of any single person is actually universal law, for all other persons will the same thing; and there is no need for constraint, because everyone already wills on his own what he is supposed to will. This ought to be the goal of all our thinking and acting, and even of our individual cultivation. (GA I/5: 226–27; SL 4: 253)

9.6 Concluding Remarks: Ethical Life and Doctrine of Duties

Moving from Hegel's first explicit distinction between *Moralität* and *Sittlichkeit*, we have proposed to read the theory of society of Fichte's *System of Ethics* as a theory of ethical life, that is as implying a similar, although less explicit and different, distinction. *Moralität* does designate the space and the point of view of an individual morality, just for this trait seen as only formal, and *Sittlichkeit* a collective, social and institutional morality, where that form can find a content or a material and where the individual can find his own proper ethical realization as a means of reason. Nevertheless, similar points and may be a relatively common framework of Fichte's and Hegel's views do not imply any kind of identity of their conceptions. It suffices to think of Fichte's normative attitude of a *Sollen* or his priority of society over the state.

One last remark. The questions of duties and of a doctrine of duties arise for both Fichte and Hegel, from the systematic point of view, *after* or at least in the framework of a theory of ethical life. In this regard too, there are both interesting similarities and remarkable differences. The very fact that the doctrine of duties belongs to a theory of ethical life illustrates the distance between the traditional doctrine of duties, including Kant and Fichte's and Hegel's views. The doctrine of duties of the seventeenth- and eighteenth-century moves from an agent and describes his duties towards himself, towards the others and towards God. Kant accepts the core of this doctrine, although he mentions the duties towards God, limiting at the same time the domain of morality to the duties towards human beings (ourselves and the others).

The scene is completely different with Fichte and Hegel. Both proceed to a kind of *objectivation* of the doctrine of duties.[43] The doctrine of duties is a further determination of the theory of ethical life which is the theory of a social and institutional whole: Moving from this whole, it is possible to determine the duties of the individuals also considering their social role. Both Fichte and Hegel propose therefore a kind of *objective* doctrine of duties. Nevertheless, there are important differences between the two thinkers also in this regard.

Hegel will abandon clearly and radically the model of the traditional doctrine of duties, somehow announcing this turn:

> The ethical *doctrine of duties*[44] (I mean the *objective* doctrine, not that which is supposed to be contained in the empty principle of moral subjectivity, because that principle determines nothing – see § 134) is therefore comprised in the systematic development of the circle of ethical necessity which follows in this *Third Part*. The difference between this exposition and the form of a *doctrine of duties* lies solely in the fact that, in what follows, the specific determinations of ethical life emerge as necessary relationships, but that there the exposition ends, without being supplemented in each case by the addition: *this determination is therefore a duty for the human being*. (§148 R)

One can wonder if there is a proper Hegelian doctrine of duties,[45] but, if any, this doctrine is different from that of Fichte. Duties are social and institutional determinations of the members of the ethical life. His philosophical horizon is a completely new one: It is the horizon of the nineteenth century, of a "second nature" of man shaped through society and history.

Fichte, on the contrary, is still a philosopher of the eighteenth century, closely connected with Kant and with the tradition of the doctrine of duties of modern practical philosophy. His view is different from that of the tradition and he tries to use an old form for a new content. His taxonomy of duties takes place in the context of a new framework, the ethical life, but

---

[43] Cf. Fonnesu (2004).
[44] It is noteworthy that exactly here we find a handwritten note: "*Ethisch* – statt moralisch – sittlich" (cf. Hegel 1970b/2008, 297).
[45] Cf. Peperzak (1982).

the structure itself of a doctrine of duties, although modified, is still present, and the duties of individuals are determined not only by their social function or *status*,[46] although the relationship with the ethical life does play a role. In this respect too, Fichte proves to be a philosopher of the transition between different worlds, or at least between different ways to understand human morality.[47]

[46] Cf. Chapter 10 by Stefano Bacin in this volume.
[47] This research arises in the framework of the project "Conceptual history and criticism of modernity" (FFI2017-82195-P), directed by Faustino Oncina Coves (University of Valencia, Spain).

CHAPTER 10

My Duties and the Morality of Others
Lying, Truth, and the Good Example in Fichte's Normative Perfectionism

Stefano Bacin

10.1 Introduction

The final part of Fichte's *System of Ethics* shares with most eighteenth-century treatments of normative ethics a general misfortune in later philosophical discussion and scholarship. Even Kant's ethics in the "Doctrine of Virtue" has long been neglected until rather recently, after all. According to a widespread, mostly implicit, assumption, those discussions are not as significant as the corresponding foundational accounts. Now, this underlying thought makes it impossible to fully appreciate the overall project of a work like Fichte's *System of Ethics*. One of the remarkable traits of Fichte's *System of Ethics* is that it encompasses not only a detailed investigation of the foundations of morality and the reality of its demands but also an extended survey of the main substantive contents of those demands. The *System of Ethics* has the ambitious aim of delivering both an explanation of moral normativity in general and the justification of specific demands. This is not in contrast with the general systematic task. Quite the opposite, in fact. The title of the work has to be taken literally: As a system, it must include both theoretical and practical issues, that is general and applied aspects of ethics. The project of a systematic treatment of moral theory, that is a genuine *Sittenlehre*, in fact, had to include an examination of the main ethical obligations – a doctrine of duties. The normative development is a confirmation, a last step of the complex justification of the principle.[1] The *System* is, as the title says, not just a groundlaying, but a full development of a theory encompassing the investigation of a principle, a deduction of its reality, and the final confirmation in an account of specific obligations, which provides answers to the main normative questions. In this spirit, then, the final part of the work, beginning in § 19, is

---

[1] See also Chapter 8 by Angelica Nuzzo in this volume.

presented as "the proper doctrine of duties," which is "proper," or genuine, both because it discusses some of the main substantive issues of morality in their specific terms, after the general obligations to the body, and the intellectual faculties elucidated in § 18, but also because it is supported by a scientific justification, unlike the previous, unsatisfying attempts. Fichte's foundational claims are thus to be appreciated by taking the *System of Ethics* seriously also as a work of normative ethics, by giving careful consideration to the last part and its task.

A possible obstacle to a careful consideration is that Fichte's treatment of ethical obligations might appear less original than what the previous section had suggested. After § 18 has stressed the collective dimension of ethical demands, with notable resemblances to Hegel's later views,[2] Fichte's doctrine of duties devotes much more space to the discussion of moral demands that do *not* depend on the role of a rational agent in his community. Unlike Hegel, then, Fichte does *not* hold that the only proper content for the doctrine of duties can be provided by the normative indications of social roles. In Fichte's view, the proper doctrine of duties is not merely "the development of the relationships which … are … actual in their entirety, to wit in the state."[3] For this reason Fichte distinguishes between universal and particular duties (GA I/5: 232 f.; SL 4: 259): The former are obligations that regard the relationships of rational agents without further qualification, whereas the latter are determined by the agent's social role.[4]

Besides an insufficient attention to the overall project of the *System of Ethics* and the original traits of its doctrine of duties, however, a further obstacle to the understanding of Fichte's discussion of ethical obligations lies in that its proper aim is not unambiguous. Fichte maintains in § 17 that conscience "would suffice for actual acting …. This, however, is not sufficient for the purposes of science" (GA I/5: 190; SL 4: 208).[5] Such a statement could suggest that what Fichte presents is a theory of morality for

---

[2] Similarities and differences between Fichte's and Hegel's views of morality are discussed in Chapter 8 by Angelica Nuzzo and Chapter 9 by Luca Fonnesu in this volume.

[3] Hegel (1821/1970, § 148A).

[4] This general taxonomy is original to Fichte in several respects and provides the frame in which he revises and, ultimately, discards traditional classification of duties, as we shall see in Section 10.4. When commentators address the question of possible sources of this classification at all, they often mention Baumgarten (see Wood 2016a, 236f., and Chapter 1 by Wood in this volume). I do not see any true indication for assuming that Baumgarten's views may have been significant for Fichte, who never mentions them. If the recent Kant scholarship has acknowledged that they played a major role for Kant (see e.g. Bacin 2015a; Fugate & Myers 2018), this does not entail that the same holds true for Fichte as well.

[5] See Chapter 6 by Dean Moyar in this volume.

scientific purposes only, and for the sake of the system. Such a reading would entail that the genuine theoretical work is done by the first two parts of the work, whereas the last one would have the mere task to present the main normative implications of the foundational claims, like significant corollaries that exemplify the meaning and display the reach of the truths gained through the theorems from which they are derived. The resulting doctrine of duties would then have no profound practical significance, because the criteria already available to conscience are sufficient for moral guidance. Such a reading, however, would not explain how the *System of Ethics* aims at contributing to morality. A careful consideration of Fichte's doctrine of duties, I believe, suggests a different understanding of the general purpose of the work, as I shall show.

In the following, I shall thus examine some of the most distinctive elements in the doctrine of duties of the *System of Ethics*, which both gives prominence to incisive aspects of Fichte's analysis and sheds light on his general approach to matters of normative ethics. In his original account of key moral demands, namely the demand of veracity and the duty of setting a good example, the almost paradoxical connection between one's obligation and the morality of other people emerges as the central point of Fichte's theory. Consequently, I shall propose a general characterisation of his normative ethics and suggest that Fichte's view of morality amounts to a special version of normative perfectionism. In turn, Fichte's perfectionism is qualified by the underlying claim of the agent-neutral character of morality, which entails a rejection of any self-other asymmetry.[6] In this light, Fichte's view combines elements that would take centre stage in the debate on moral philosophy in the following century.

10.2 Obligations of Accuracy: Lying and Communication

A first distinctive feature of Fichte's conception of morality emerges in his treatment of the obligations concerning the communication with others. Fichte's classification of the duties to others distinguishes between (a) the duties concerning the formal freedom of the others, (b) those that have to do with the (apparent) contrast of freedom in rational agents, and (c) those that demand to promote morality. Fichte puts the duties regarding communication into the first class, because he construes them as obligations

---

[6] I do agree with Wood (2016a) and Ware (2018) that Fichte's view resists easy classification, as is often the case with original and complex historical views. Nevertheless, suggesting a classification allows to emphasise its distinctive features, which in turn helps to re-consider its place in the history of ethics in broader terms.

that aim to secure and augment the exercise of formal freedom in other agents. In Part I of the *System of Ethics*, Fichte has argued that "a free being … acts in accordance with a concept of an effect" (GA I/5: 75; SL 4: 66; cf. e.g. GA I/5: 166; SL 4: 179). More specifically, formal freedom is causality of rational agents that is determined in light of cognition.[7] The correctness of that cognition, thus, is integral to the full development of the freedom of the others and "must therefore be my goal [*Zweck*] as well, just as much as and for the same reason that the correctness of my own practical cognition is my end [*Zweck*]" (GA I/5: 252; SL 4: 283). This gives to the obligations regarding other agents' knowledge a distinctive prominence in Fichte's theory.[8]

Fichte's originality in considering the obligations concerning communication is twofold. First, his justification of those obligations takes a quite different path than most previous discussions of the morality of lying. Second, and relatedly, along with the traditionally recognised prohibition of lying, Fichte also isolates a corresponding positive obligation, which he presents as "the command to promote correct insight on the part of others and actually to communicate to them any truth we ourselves might know" (GA I/5: 258; SL 4: 290). I shall clarify these two points in turn.

The first original feature of Fichte's view is that his justification of the unconditional prohibition of lying centres on the effects of lying on the formal freedom of other rational agents or, more exactly, the role that the *content* of the communication should play in the determination of the formal freedom of others. Fichte mainly emphasises his opposition to conceptions that admit only conditional prohibitions of lying; although an unconditional condemnation that leaves no space for exceptions was in fact not entirely new, even leaving Kant's view aside.[9] The most distinctive feature of Fichte's view of lying, however, is the moral significance attributed to communication and its epistemic content. In his view, lying is immoral because it hinders freedom. While previous accounts had already pointed out that lying is an interference with the freedom of others as long as it is harmful, Fichte maintains that, independently from any harm, its hindrance to the freedom of others is construed in terms of *cognition*. If I give another person "an incorrect cognition," that is if I lie to him, "he has been made into a means for my end" (GA I/5: 253; SL 4: 283). Even if lying

---

[7] On Fichte's conception of formal freedom, see Chapter 5 by Daniel Breazeale in this volume.
[8] See also Kosch (2018, 73).
[9] See Annen (1997). Oddly enough, Annen's otherwise helpful survey of the discussion on lying in eighteenth-century German philosophy does not even mention Fichte's *System of Ethics*, although he considers also later works of less prominent writers.

leads another person to act in conformity with moral demands, that is to act legally, it nevertheless prevents his morality, as "[t]he other person is not supposed to do what is right on the basis of some error, but ought to do it out of love for the good" (GA I/5: 253; SL 4: 284).

Fichte's content-centred construal of lying is original with respect to the previous debate and takes a path that has rarely been suggested in the discussions on the morality of lying overall. He characterises the content of the declarations, insofar as it can be matter of lying, as "practical cognition" (GA I/5: 252 f.; SL 4: 283ff.), as opposed to a purely speculative cognition.[10] This would appear to leave open the possibility that a purely speculative cognition, that is one that cannot possibly have implications for the deliberations of a rational agent, could not be content of a morally relevant declaration. Fichte holds, however, that there is no purely speculative cognition, that there cannot be such a thing. In a remarkable passage he explains:

> We therefore would have to distinguish between immediately practical items of knowledge [*Kenntnisse*] and purely theoretical ones. But according to a thoroughgoing transcendental philosophy, all theory is related to practice, and no theory is possible without such a relationship to practice. The distinction in question is therefore a merely relative one. The very same thing that is purely theoretical for one individual or for one era can be practical for another individual or era. (GA I/5: 259; SL 4: 291)

"Practical cognition," thus, is any piece of knowledge, insofar as it is, or can be, regarded as a potential basis for rational action. Because of this emphasis on the pragmatic function of belief, Fichte's view also strongly differs from those that appeal to a purported intrinsic value of truth as such.

The contrast with Kant's account of the ethical duty not to lie might be phrased by opposing two moral ideals. While Kant regards lying primarily as a violation of sincerity, Fichte suggests that what is blameworthy in lying is primarily an intentional failure of *accuracy*.[11] Fichte does write that "absolute sincerity and truthfulness is something I simply owe everyone" (GA I/5: 252; SL 4: 283), in the terms in which the issue was traditionally framed. However, Fichte equates owing sincerity with: "I am not permitted to say *anything that contradicts the truth*" (GA I/5: 252; SL 4: 283). In other terms, in Fichte's view, the traditional distinction between truth

---

[10] Note that Fichte thereby vacates one of the two distinctive features of practical cognition in Kant's understanding. Kant had defined practical cognition through a twofold distinction, according to which "practical" can be opposed either to "theoretical" or to "speculative." Speculative is, on Kant's account, a cognition that cannot possibly have implications for our actions. See Bacin 2015b.

[11] On the contrast between sincerity versus accuracy, see Williams (2002, 149, and *passim*). On Kant's account of the ethical duty not to lie, see Bacin (2013).

(*Wahrheit*) and veracity (*Wahrhaftigkeit*) fades away.[12] Fichte thus takes a different path than Kant's by departing from the definitions taken from the natural law vocabulary that Kant had drawn on (see VI 428). While truthfulness is a quality of the mind that lies in the consciously determined correspondence of declarations with the subject's beliefs, Fichte's construal of veracity is about the truth of the communication, not the truthfulness of the subject. In Fichte's account, a liar deserves blame not because he intentionally hides his beliefs but because he intentionally hides what is the *truth*, as far as he knows, thereby depriving the others of a possibly significant ("practical") piece of knowledge and thus impairing their formal freedom. What matters is primarily the epistemic value of the declaration, that is its providing *true* belief. In this light, lying is unconditionally wrong because it contrasts with the fundamental presupposition, demanded by the moral law, to assume that the others can morally improve themselves in free action.[13]

The importance of true knowledge for the determination of freedom makes the prohibition of lying unconditional. Fichte stresses accordingly his rejection of the permissibility of any supposedly necessary lie (*Notlüge*: GA I/5: 254ff.; SL 4: 286ff.),[14] also by discussing the same "customary school example" (GA I/5: 256, SL 4: 288; translation modified) of the would-be murderer at the door that is famously considered in Kant's essay on the *Supposed Right to Lie*.[15] Unaware of Kant's different take on the same case, Fichte's more elaborate discussion is an exercise in considering all possible alternatives to lying. As the duty not to lie demands, one should tell the truth to the assailant in the first place, on the necessary assumption of the possibility of his improvement (GA I/5: 253, SL 4: 284).[16] Alternately, the same presupposition would suggest to protect the would-be victim by talking the assailant out of his murderous intentions. In any

[12] Fichte already vacated the distinction in his 1791 sermon "On the Love of Truth" by using "truth" as corresponding to veracity (GA II,1: 147). Thereby, Fichte regards as lies also what previous writers called "logical untruths," that is, accidentally false statements.

[13] On the requirement of assuming the perfectibility of others, see GA I/5: 217, SL 4: 240; GA I/5: 248f., SL 4: 278f.; GA I/5: 253, SL 4: 284; cf. GA I/5: 280ff., SL 4: 318. See also De Pascale (2015, 186).

[14] While the English translation of the *System of Ethics* by Breazeale and Zöller renders *Notlüge* with "white lie," it would probably be more appropriate to use the directly corresponding term "necessary lie," because the distinctive feature of a *Notlüge* is not its being trivial, as the phrase "white lie" might suggest, but exactly that it is born out of necessity. See Dietz (2018, 289f.), and also Wood (2016a, 243).

[15] Everything suggests that Fichte's observations are independent from Kant's essay, which was published only a few months before the *System of Ethics*, in September 1797. I cannot examine thoroughly the contrast between Kant's and Fichte's views on lying here. For a brief comparison between their ways to discuss the murderer at the door case, see Timmermann (forthcoming, § 18).

[16] This eases the supposed tension pointed at by Wood (2016a, 243).

case, not even the risk for one's own life gives a reason to lie, directly contributing to the immorality of the other. Giving false information to the assailant, Fichte argues, is to be avoided at all costs.

This way of framing the issue follows from the account of agency given in the first part of the work. As to its normative implications, however, it does not account for the case of a declaration that, meant as a lie, in fact unwillingly delivers an *exact* cognition, on the basis of which another rational agent can act both from a good disposition and according to a perfectly suitable representation of the object of the action. In Fichte's account, such an unwillingly correct lie could not be regarded as immediately blameworthy. It could be blamed only if a further consideration is brought in – although the cognition is correct, the *interaction* between the subjects would still be distorted. However, this further condition makes an unwillingly correct lie a violation of a *different* demand than the prohibition of lying. This is in fact the point of another, positive duty regarding the same matter, which I shall now consider.

The second original aspect of Fichte's view on the morality of communication lies in that his content-centred construal of lying and veracity leads him to go beyond traditional accounts and envisage a corresponding positive obligation to "promote correct insight on the part of others." As lying is prohibited insofar as it limits the formal freedom of others through false information, the same care for the epistemic basis of the practice of that freedom demands from every moral agent "to communicate ... any truth" he might know (GA I/5: 258; SL 4: 290). Because every rational agent ought to promote what Fichte calls the efficacy of others as rational agents, that is a causal realisation of their formal freedom as adequate as possible, sharing with them the knowledge we can count on is a specific duty. As Fichte writes:

> [E]ven without being summoned by him [sc.: the other] to do this, I owe it to him to communicate correct cognition to him. This is a necessary end to me already through myself [*es ist mir schon durch mich selbst nothwendiger Zweck*]. (GA I/5: 258; SL 4: 290; translation modified)

Unlike the prohibition of lying, the specific duty to communicate the truth is an original addition of Fichte's examination of moral obligations, which thereby displays a not merely reconstructive character with regard to the traditional, pre-philosophical view of morality. Compared to the discussion of lying, which could draw on a long history of previous accounts, however, the positive duty of sharing our knowledge is ultimately less clear as to its applications. One issue with the application follows from the extension to any possibly relevant piece of knowledge, because the only relevant criterion is which information can be helpful to a more secure, informed, and efficacious action of the other (i.e. "which truth is practical to this individual": GA I/5: 258; SL 4: 290). On the other hand, although Fichte declares that particular obligations enjoy priority, that is *deliberative* priority, over universal duties (cf. GA I/5: 269; SL 4: 304), the specific obligations of the scholar that he presents later on (§ 29) can be reduced to, or follow from, the general duties regarding sharing of true knowledge.

10.3 Behaving Morally and the Morality of Others: The Duty to Set a Good Example

If Fichte's view of the duties regarding communication points out how correct cognition is a necessary condition for the successful exercise of formal freedom, another aspect of his doctrine of duties stresses the direct contribution that every rational agent should give to the morality of others. The duty to set a good example plays, accordingly, an important role in Fichte's account.[17] Whereas the duties regarding communication address the epistemic basis of the deliberations of other people, the duty to set a good example should address the moral disposition of the others, that is specifically their morality. This demand is, according to Fichte, entailed in the general rule: "show your fellow human beings things worthy of respect" (GA I/5: 279; SL 4: 317). If this rule is applied to one's own actions, it yields the duty of setting a good example:

> And we can hardly show them anything better suited to this purpose than our own moral way of thinking and our own moral conduct. (GA I/5: 279; SL 4: 317)

A praiseworthy conduct would not only be morally good per se, but it would also contribute to the morality of others through a stimulation of the feeling of respect. The point of the duty of setting the good example, as Fichte presents it, follows from the thought expressed in Kant's remark that "respect is a tribute that we cannot refuse to pay to merit" (5: 77). Fichte gives almost a paraphrase of that passage: "as soon as this affect finds its object it expresses itself unavoidably; everything worthy of respect is most certainly respected" (GA I/5: 279; SL 4: 317). Examples of good behaviour would strengthen this feeling in the other, thereby contributing

---

[17] The significance of that duty in Fichte's conception had already been noticed very early by C. F. Stäudlin (1798, 453f.).

to the goal that his actions would not only be legal but also genuinely moral (see GA I/5: 279ff.; SL 4: 318ff.). Fichte accordingly sees the point of this duty in "moral cultivation [*moralische Bildung*]" (GA I/5: 279; SL 4: 317). The purpose of the demand is, again, to strengthen the causal interplay of rational agents, insofar as it builds on the proper motivation. The efficacy of actions matters as long as they can count as a causal expression of reason.

The combination of a general maxim of moral education with a qualification that entails an exhortation to the other agent through one's own conduct has intuitive appeal. Fichte's suggestion to consider a specific obligation to set a good example grasps the plausible thought that one's own conduct does not matter exclusively as a feature of the moral worth or character of the individual agent, but can have an impact on others as well, even if they are not the addressee of the actions at issue. However, from the standpoint of a normative theory, Fichte's thought is peculiar in two regards at least.

First, the content of such an obligation sounds puzzling. As Fichte puts it in § 18, because "[w]hat I will is morality as such" and "it does not matter in the least whether this is *in* me or is *outside* me," "my end is achieved if the other person acts *morally*" (GA I/5: 210; SL 4: 232). This claim not only expresses the fundamental interdependence of moral agents, but it also generates here a definite obligation. The duty of setting a good example is thus put forward as a crucial part of one's striving towards that end. That construal of the obligation, however, has a significantly paradoxical overtone. Is it even possible to promote the moral perfection of others? In the *Metaphysics of Morals*, Kant has famously denied it, arguing that

> it is a contradiction for me to make another's *perfection* my end and consider myself under obligation to promote this. For the *perfection* of another human being, as a person, consists just in this: that *he himself* is able to set his end in accordance with his own concepts of duty; and it is self-contradictory to require that I do (make it my duty to do) something that only the other himself can do. (6: 386)[18]

Unaware of Kant's position on the matter, Fichte stresses that the duty requires *contributing* to the perfection of others, while leaving the actual deliberation to the other. Most part of Fichte's examination of the demand of giving a good example, in fact, is devoted to clarify the boundaries of that contribution. Still, this specific duty demands something that, if not

---

[18] For a critical discussion of Kant's view, see Denis (1999).

impossible to achieve, is impossible to assess, even from the individual agent's standpoint.[19] The genuine difference between Kant's and Fichte's views, however, concerns not the possibility to contribute to the agency of another subject, but the end at issue. For Fichte this obligation is not about the moral improvement of others, but one's contribution to the realisation of morality, both in oneself and in others.

Second, the distinctiveness of this duty is unclear. Can setting a good example be the content of a *specific* duty? Or is it just a pervasive aspect of the moral significance of complying with the demands of morality in general?[20] Now, Fichte can clarify this doubt and make sense of a requirement of that sort in two ways. He can argue that it is a specific duty insofar as it determines the task of a social role. Also, he can construe it as a sort of second-order duty, which is complied with by complying with other demands. Characteristically, Fichte's view ultimately includes *both* solutions.

In the more straightforward solution, corresponding to the latter option, the universal duty of setting a good example develops in the *particular* duty of the "moral teacher":

> The proper and characteristic duty of the teacher of the people is to set a good example. He does not provide such an example simply for his own sake, but for the sake of the entire community that he represents. (GA I/5: 307; SL 4: 352; cf. GA I/5: 307; SL 4: 204 f.)

The universal obligation to set a good example evolves in a specific duty regarding the promotion of the morality of others, through his restriction to a particular social role.[21] Fichte cannot be content with this solution, mainly because it would make the contribution to the morality of others not a universal task for every subject, but only for a restricted class of subjects. The underlying claim that "my end is achieved if the other person acts *morally*" (GA I/5: 210; SL 4: 232) does not concern only a social role, but each and every rational agent. More interestingly, then, the duty of setting a good example, as a *universal* duty, cannot be restricted to a specific conduct. Rather, it describes a general task in the moral life of every individual who

---

[19] Probably to make sense of this peculiar character, Kosch calls the duty of the good example an "indirect duty" (Kosch [2018], 71). The label does not fully correspond to Fichte's thought, though, and might lead to misunderstandings. The bindingness of the duty of the good example does not depend on prior ('direct') obligations. (Kant uses the phrase 'indirect duty' in this sense with regard to securing one's own happiness in order to remove obstacles to the practice of morality: see G, 4: 399.) The content of the duty of the good example cannot be reduced to a specific conduct, as I shall clarify soon, but this does not entail that its obligatoriness is to be construed differently than that of other duties.

[20] This issue has already been hinted at by Schleiermacher (1803, 304).

[21] Compare the "exemplary conduct [*exemplarische Führung*]" (6: 479) of the teacher in Kant's "Doctrine of Virtue."

has to be aware of the normative meaning of his conduct. The only specific aspect of the requirement is that of "publicity," as Fichte puts it (see GA I/5: 284; SL 4: 323 f.). Transparency allows one's actions, in principle, to have a larger impact on other subjects. The duty of setting a good example, thus, demands that the agent be open as to the grounds of his resolutions. In Fichte's view, thus, the specificity of this obligation is determined not by its object, but by a further constraint on actions, even if this concerns the entire scope of the conduct of an agent.[22] Unlike imperfect duties, the duty of setting a good example does not really leave open how the obligation is most appropriately complied with, in the given circumstances, because the duty applies to each and every aspect of the actions of a subject.

The duty of setting a good example thus gives an argument against a simple consequentialist reading of Fichte's view. The goal is here contributing to the *morality* of others, not to the mere instrumental adequacy or the conformity to law of their actions. Moreover, the duty of setting a good example is about contributing to morality in a way that cannot be assessed in terms of outcomes, if only because they must be left to the free determination of others. Here again, the obligation is about contributing to the full development of rational nature, even in others. Fichte talks therefore of "education [*Bildung*] to morality."

The most important part of the significance of the duty to set a good example, thus, lies in the demand to go, in one's own conduct, beyond the efficacy of the acts of an individual. The demand to contribute to the morality of others, as far as it is in one's power, pushes the individual agency beyond its limits. What matters here is not the full development of the capacities of others but a more efficacious and pervasive advancement towards self-sufficiency. Education to morality, thus, is about strengthening *all* rational agents and their moral disposition through a robust, clear, transparent embodiment of morality. In this sense, the duty of setting a good example is about a conscious striving towards an embodiment of the moral law that goes beyond one's own individual self.

10.4 Impersonal Morality

The specific obligations that I have considered show that Fichte's view of morality in the doctrine of duties focuses on the efficacy and the grounds of the causal interplay of rational agents towards their common overarching

---

[22] Thus, also this consideration confirms that Fichte's normative ethics does not leave conceptual space to the distinction between perfect and imperfect duties (see Section 10.4).

end of self-sufficiency. Fichte's treatment of duties regarding communication points out that the correctness of practical cognition of others "must … be my end … just as much as and for the same reason that the correctness of my own practical cognition is my end" (GA I/5: 252; SL 4: 283). Analogously, "my end is achieved if the other person acts *morally*" (GA I/5: 210; SL 4: 232), because it is utterly irrelevant whether morality is realised by the one or the other subject. This double focus is in fact only a part of a comprehensive conception, which revolves around the thought that an agent's duty is, in its most substantial part, about the morality of others. Fichte's account of moral demands shows that the differences among individuals are of no importance from a normative point of view.

A reassessment of supposedly agent-centred aspects of morality is already apparent in Fichte's remarks concerning the purported duties to oneself. Fichte maintains that if such duties *regard* one's own individual person, they are in fact not *owed* to one's self as such. What is traditionally called a duty to oneself is

> not, properly speaking, a duty with respect to [*gegen*] myself and for the sake of myself, which is how one customarily puts it; for in this situation as well I am and remain a means for a final end outside of myself. (GA I/5: 231; SL 4: 257)

Such duties are in fact merely self-*regarding* obligations. The argument on the purported duties to the self parallels a similar reduction that earlier writers had suggested in arguing that the so-called duties to the self are in fact owed to God.[23] Fichte's point is now, analogously, that the moral significance of self-regarding actions does not lie in their self-regarding features, but exclusively in the way they make me able to contribute to the final end of reason. When he calls self-regarding duties "conditioned duties" (GA I/5: 232; SL 4: 257), he does not merely propose a new label but also emphasises this perspective change. Any qualitative difference from other regarding actions is thus irrelevant, in this respect. An important agent-centred aspect of common-sense morality thereby undergoes a significant revision.

A further step in the same direction is taken in § 24 of the *System of Ethics*, where Fichte discusses, under a rather opaque label, the "duties with respect to conflict between the formal freedom of rational beings" (GA I/5: 266; SL 4: 300). Some early readers of the *System of Ethics* referred to this section for Fichte's treatment of possible conflicts of duties.[24] More exactly, the section

---

[23] See for example Clarke (1706, 97).

[24] See Reinhard (1801, § 201) and Stäudlin (1798, 453f.). (These remarkable examples of the otherwise scarce early reception of the *System of Ethics* have never been considered, to the best of my knowledge. See Zöller [2015], who only mentions a few early reviews of the *System*.)

Lying, Truth, & Good Example in Fichte's Normative Perfectionism 213

argues for the impossibility of such conflicts, in light of the general claim that the formal freedom of different individual rational agents cannot possibly be in contrast. Should the conditions for the exercise of formal freedom by different individuals – that is their life, body, and property – conflict, Fichte argues that there is no general criterion to address the issue and solve the resulting perplexity. While previous writers had suggested that a criterion was provided by the necessary prioritisation of one's own person to others',[25] Fichte holds the opposite view. He goes so far as maintaining that on the matter

> [t]he law remains completely silent, and since my actions are supposed to be animated by nothing but the moral law, I ought not to do anything at all, but should calmly await the outcome. (GA I/5: 268; SL 4: 303)

When he considers the possibility of moral contrast between the destinies of different persons, his underlying view emerges most clearly: There is no qualitative, morally relevant difference between rational agents. There is no normative priority or asymmetry between the self and others, as "we are both tools of the moral law in *the same way*" (GA I/5: 268; SL 4: 303). Fichte maintains that the person of the other matters to me just as much as my own, by virtue of one same final end (see GA I/5: 250; SL 4: 280). At one point, he observes that obligations regarding relatives have priority insofar as they are "particular duties" (GA I/5: 269; SL 4: 304), that is non-transferrable duties that are determined according to the social role of the individual agent. Thus, only the specific order of a society can establish overriding relations between demands, while the general interpersonal morality of "universal duties" is not able to discern any standard of prioritisation.[26] Provided that no particular duties apply, no asymmetry between persons has any normative bearing.

As is the case with self-regarding duties, also the duties to others are not properly owed to the individual persons of the others, in Fichte's view. Both traditional classes of obligations are in fact "duties to the whole [*gegen das Ganze*]" (GA I/5: 232; SL 4: 258; translation modified). In Fichte's distinction between conditioned and universal duties (see GA I/5: 232; SL 4: 257), the very difference between duties to oneself and to others is thus not merely re-phrased, but profoundly revised, and ultimately taken back. Obligations are not due to anyone in particular, but they merely demand actions regarding someone, be it one's own self or others. This marks an

---

[25] See for example Wolff (1750, § 64).
[26] Fichte already vacated the distinction in his 1791 sermon "On the Love of Truth," by using "truth" as corresponding to veracity (GA II/1: 147). Thereby Fichte regards as lies also what previous writers called "logical untruths," that is, accidentally false statements.

important difference to previous views, Kant's included, which follows from the normative irrelevance of individual distinctions.

Fichte's dismissal of agent-centred differences, in fact, is introduced in general terms at the outset of the doctrine of duties through a re-formulation of Kant's Formula of the End in Itself.[27] Fichte puts forward as the principle that underlies all moral demands the claim that "I am *for myself* – i.e., before my own consciousness – only an instrument, a mere tool of the moral law, and by no means the end of the same" (GA I/5: 230; SL 4: 255). To the individual rational agent, who faces practical issues, the moral law is thus primarily a general demand of contributing to the efficacy of rational action. In this perspective, the other moral subjects are seen as ends: "Before my own consciousness, these others are not means but the final end" (GA I/5: 230; SL 4: 255). These remarks already imply a notable difference from Kant's emphasis on humanity both in one's person and the others'. Yet, as so often in the *System of Ethics*, Fichte maintains the convergence of their views:

> This Kantian proposition is compatible with mine, when the latter has been further elaborated. For every rational being outside me, to whom the moral law certainly addresses itself in the same way that it addresses itself to me, namely, as the tool of the moral law, I am a member of the community of rational beings; hence I am, from his viewpoint, an end *for him*, just as *he* is, from my viewpoint, an end *for me*. (GA I/5: 230; SL 4: 255 f.)

However, this reassurance is soon followed by a further important clarification:

> Everyone is an end, in the sense that everyone is a *means* for realizing reason. This is the ultimate and final end of each person's existence; this alone is why one is here, and if this were not the case, if this were not what ought to happen, then one would not need to exist at all. (GA I/5: 230; SL 4: 256)

The consideration of all agents as ends is, in the deliberative perspective, a first glimpse of the teleological structure of morality. The notion of end, in fact, does not properly apply to persons per se, but to the realisation of reason, which is only possible through rational agents. The difference from Kant's view lies already in the meaning of "end," which changes from denoting an object of volition to denoting (part of) a goal to be achieved. Whereas Kant had observed in the *Groundwork for the Metaphysics of Morals* that every rational agent should be regarded "not as an end to be effected but as an independently existing end" (4: 437), Fichte argues that other persons are to be regarded as ends not as a limiting condition to

---

[27] On this, see also Guyer (2019, 273–275).

Lying, Truth, & Good Example in Fichte's Normative Perfectionism 215

subjective ends, but as a part of the general end to be pursued.[28] Correspondingly, all ethical demands presuppose the perfectibility of all rational agents as such.[29]

While Kant's terms were functional to an anti-teleological view of morality, Fichte deploys them to stress the teleological outlook of his own conception from the outset. Also, while Kant's view acknowledges agent-centred distinctions and gives them a central position in his normative ethics, Fichte's account reaches a very different conclusion. His construal of the terms of the Formula of the End in Itself amounts to a dismissal of any self-other asymmetry. As Fichte puts it, "every virtuous person ... ought to forget himself in his end" (GA I,5: 303; SL 4: 347; cf. e.g. GA I/5: 230; SL 4: 255 f.).[30] The end of morality is not related to the perspective of the first or the second person, but is just the same for every rational agent. In *this* sense, his view is to be characterised as agent-neutral, namely as a theory that determines for every moral agent exactly the same ultimate aim.[31] As he reportedly puts it in his lectures, "the object of the moral law was reason in general, the entire community of rational beings ... is reason, as we have seen. Reason itself, as end, is posited outside of me, although it can only be realised through myself as individual" (GA IV/1: 123, VM; my translation; cf. GA I/5: 229, SL 4: 254 f.).

Fichte's view thus counters assumptions that are deeply rooted both in moral philosophy and in ordinary moral thinking. Some decades later, Sidgwick observed that

> [i]t would be contrary to Common Sense to deny that the distinction between anyone individual and any other is real and fundamental, and that consequently "I" am concerned with the quality of my existence as an individual in a sense, fundamentally important, in which I am not concerned with the quality of the existence of other individuals: and this being so, I do not see how it can be proved that this distinction is not to be taken as fundamental in determining the ultimate end of rational action for an individual. (Sidgwick 1874, 498)

That the ultimate end is not determined in relation to the distinction between different individuals is exactly what Fichte maintains as the first and foremost normative claim of his examination of ethical duties. The

---

[28] Notably, the corresponding passage in Fichte's lectures on morals (GA IV/1: 124) clarifies that he referred not to the *Groundwork*, but to the second *Critique* (5: 87), where the notion of "independently existing end" is not present.

[29] GA I/5: 217, SL 4: 240; GA I/5: 248f., SL 4: 278f.; GA I/5: 253, SL 4: 284; cf. GA I/5: 280ff., SL 4: 318f.

[30] Regarding Fichte's conception as an *Ethik der Person* (Maesschalk 2015), thus, is misleading as it precludes to appreciate this distinctive trait.

[31] See for example Dreier (1993, 22).

idea of the agent-neutrality of moral demands is thus a fundamental trait of his normative ethics. Fichte makes precisely this point by arguing that "all free beings necessarily share the same end," clarifying it as follows:

> [T]he purposive [*zweckmäßige*] conduct of one person would at the same time be purposive for all others and … the liberation of one would at the same time be the liberation of all the others. Is this the case? …. [E]verything and everything for us in particular, i.e., the *distinctive character of our presentation of ethics* – depends upon the answer to this question. (GA I/5: 209; SL 4: 230 f.; my emphasis)

The doctrine of duties makes it clear that Fichte answers his question in the affirmative: The "purposive conduct of one person" is indeed, crucially, "at the same time … purposive for all others." This important claim in fact determines the distinctive character of his view. As Fichte observes in the *Wissenschaftlehre nova methodo*, "[e]thics does not deal with any particular individual; instead, it deals with reason as such or in general" (GA IV/3: 521; WLnm, 242). Now, if ethics is "the theory of our consciousness of our moral nature in general and of our specific duties in particular" (GA I/5: 35; SL 4: 15), then the primary contribution of Part Three to the general project is to clarify that the demands yielded by that moral nature are not cast in individual, but in impersonal terms.

10.5 Normative Perfectionism beyond Asymmetry

Once we appreciate the agent-neutral character of Fichte's view of morality, we might suggest to interpret it as consequentialist. Michelle Kosch has argued that "the rejection of agent-centred restrictions" is one of the main reasons for thinking that Fichte's view is "consequentialist in structure."[32] Now, an important weakness of a consequentialist reading of his normative ethics is that it leads to overlook Fichte's insistence on the requirement for morality even in what he presents as a "doctrine of legality."[33] Fichte stresses that even the *content* of main specific ethical obligations requires not mere conformity to the letter of moral demands, but proper causality from concepts. Fichte

---

[32] Kosch (2018, 89). Kosch assumes that the agent-neutrality claim necessarily distinguishes between consequentialist and deontological theories, which is disputable (see e.g. Dreier [1993, 22f.]). Furthermore, departing from Wood (2014, 2016a), Kosch (2018), and Ware (2018), I avoid the ultimately unclear term "deontology" and prefer to use "non-consequentialism" instead. For a detailed consideration of the limits of "deontology," and the suggestion to drop the term altogether, see Timmermann (2015).

[33] On Fichte's slightly misleading understanding of "legality" in the *System of Ethics*, see Chapter 9 by Luca Fonnesu in this volume.

Lying, Truth, & Good Example in Fichte's Normative Perfectionism 217

emphasises this requirement no less than three times.[34] As he puts it, "[o]ne cannot will legality at all, except for the sake of morality" (GA I/5: 261; SL 4: 294). Thus, the mere (either actual or intended) consequences determine neither the moral worth of actions nor the deliberative standard. Unlike standard forms of consequentialism, Fichte's view does not regard any state of affairs as the aim with regard to which the worth of actions is determined.[35] On the other hand, however, morality consists in a fuller form of causal determination of reason than mere legality. As Fichte's analysis of specific duties displays, all their requirements aim at the development of the efficacy of reason towards full self-sufficiency. In his account, the teleological structure of morality is also embedded in the perspective of the individual agent, who regards other agents as ends. Morality is thus construed in terms of relations to ends, with the crucial clause that these are not ends external to free agency.

To accommodate its non-consequentialist yet teleological character, Fichte's conception of morality should be regarded as a version of perfectionism.[36] More specifically, Fichte develops a form of normative perfectionism, as opposed to a biological perfectionism. While the latter is based on the features of agents as a biological species, normative perfectionists like Fichte put forward a theory of morality that justifies moral obligations on the basis of the general end of the development of the rational nature of agents.[37] As we have seen in previous sections, Fichte's doctrine of duties accordingly justifies specific moral obligations insofar as they converge towards a larger development of rational nature. In contrast to most other forms of normative perfectionism, however, Fichte's perfectionism is significantly qualified by the central idea of agent-neutrality.[38] The ultimate end towards which morality strives is not, as we have seen, the full development of any individual self, but the full realisation of reason.

A striking but indicative consequence of the agent-neutral qualification of perfectionism is that "virtue" as a specific notion plays virtually no role in Fichte's normative theory. The *System of Ethics* is arguably unique, among eighteenth-century works on moral philosophy, in the extremely limited importance of the notion of virtue.[39] The word is here used only in non-specific terms, synonymously for the moral worth of an

---

[34] See GA I/5: 254, 261; SL 4: 284, 285, 294.   [35] See also Wood (2014, 151f.).

[36] I thus find myself in agreement with Ware (2018) and Moggach (2018) on regarding Fichte as a perfectionist.

[37] See Brink (2019), who mentions Aristotle, Mill, and Green as examples of normative perfectionism.

[38] On the general profile of an agent-neutral perfectionism, see Hurka (1993, 63f.).

[39] David James' emphasis given to virtue in his reconstruction of Fichte's social philosophy (James 2011) goes admittedly beyond Fichte's own vocabulary in the Jena practical philosophy, referring forward to the larger role of the notion of virtue in the *Addresses to the German Nation* (see James

agent. More importantly, in the *System of Ethics* there is no space for virtue as an agent's character.[40] When Fichte comes closest to a precise statement of his notion of virtue, he characteristically maintains: "True virtue consists in acting, in acting for the community, by means of which one may forget oneself completely" (GA I/5: 231; SL 4: 256), which amounts to rejecting a traditional, agent-centred notion of virtue. Virtue has thus no bearing for normative ethics, in Fichte's view, because the normative issues are not about the development of the individual agent.

More importantly, Fichte's agent-neutral conception of morality distinguishes his form of normative perfectionism from most others by dismissing any genuine self-other asymmetry. As his analysis of specific duties shows, it has no normative bearing to the realisation of morality whether an action affects one's own self or other persons. Every subject has the duty to further morality in others "as much as" in oneself "and for the same reason" (cf. GA I/5: 252; SL 4: 283). Ethical obligations do not address the individual person's perspective, but demand to go beyond it: "The sole duty of everyone is to further the end of reason; the latter comprehends within itself all other ends" (GA I/5: 285, SL 4: 325). The distinctive "good" of individual rational agents that other normative perfectionists, such as Green, acknowledge fades away as such. In a radical construal of the impartiality of moral demands, Fichte holds that all individual agents equally matter as means to the development of reason in general.

In spite of some counterintuitive elements, that is chiefly its agent-neutral character, Fichte's normative perfectionism presents rational agents with a moral theory that intends to provide the necessary normative orientation fitting the boundaries of the deliberative boundaries of finite reason. In a remarkable passage, where Fichte considers how one should decide when confronted with the necessity of sacrificing either the life of an older person or that of a younger person, he argues as follows:

> [I]t is simply impossible to judge from whose preservation more or less good will follow, for the finite understanding has no voice when it comes to determining what will and what will not prove to be more advantageous in a certain situation, and every argument of this sort is impertinent and presumptuous. This is a decision that must be left to the rational governance of the world – which is something that one believes in from this [moral] point

---

[2011, 17ff., 139]). While talking of virtue is helpful to clarify the relationship between right and morality in Fichte's conception, it does not waive the marginality of that notion in ethics and the contrast to previous ways of deploying it.

[40] Similarities and differences between Fichte's and Hegel's views of morality are discussed in this volume in Chapter 8 by Angelica Nuzzo and Chapter 9 by Luca Fonnesu.

Lying, Truth, & Good Example in Fichte's Normative Perfectionism 219

of view. *Finite understanding knows only that at each moment of one's life one ought to do what duty calls upon one to do at that moment*, without worrying about how much good will follow from doing this and how this might happen. (GA I/5: 268; SL 4: 303; my emphasis)[41]

The philosophical investigation uncovers the teleological structure of morality, showing that it is oriented to the promotion of a final, all-encompassing end. On a larger scale, morality is organised towards the ultimate end of the full realisation of reason's power, to which all moral actions contribute. As Fichte writes, "[r]eason is thoroughly determined; therefore, everything that lies within the sphere of reason … must also be determined" (GA I/5: 191; SL 4: 208). This cannot be the standard of judgment in the given circumstances, but it is this structure that ultimately justifies specific ethical demands.

10.6 Practical Cognition: The Purpose of Fichte's Moral Theory

Its general characterisation notwithstanding, the overall purpose of Fichte's normative view still remains unclear. As I mentioned at the outset, Fichte's claim that the underlying purpose of the *System of Ethics* is "scientific" could easily be understood to the effect that the work merely provides a philosophical explanation of morality as part of the system of the *Wissenschaftslehre*. But how would the extensive doctrine of duties of the last part of the work sit in such a project, then? If a directly prescriptive theory would obviously not be compatible with the most fundamental tenets of Fichte's thought and his view of freedom in particular, the aim of the normative theory cannot be a mere reconstruction of ordinary moral thinking either. In dismissing the relevance of any self-other asymmetry, the scientific investigation of morality leads to a revision of moral common sense.

In contrast to a mere descriptive or reconstructive endeavour, the task of the doctrine of duties in the *System of Ethics* is rather to provide the epistemic grounds for a full development of the moral nature of rational agents. In the lectures on moral philosophy that prepared the *System of Ethics*, Fichte reportedly observed that "the human being with a moral disposition [*moralisch gesinnt*]" will "have to design a certain plan for himself, because the entire whole of reason [*das ganze All der Vernunft*] cannot be presented." Thus "he will have to speculate, for the sake of moral action. If he meets doubt in his acts, he will have to speculate further." Now, the distinctive task of the "scholar" is exactly to entertain this

---

[41] See also Ware (2018, 575).

theoretical activity for the sake of morality in general: "The scholar, who occupies himself with speculation, acts too, for exactly his speculation is his end and his action" (GA IV/1: 132, VM; my translation). While this remark is phrased in terms that do not find direct correspondence in the *System of Ethics*, the thought aptly conveys the task of the theory presented in the published work, too. A normative theory as outlined in its final part follows the purpose to contribute to the morality of others by clarifying the coherent plan of the "whole of reason."

Fichte thus understands the task of moral philosophy in strongly moral terms. What Fichte attributes to the "duty of a scholar," namely "to seek and to disseminate truth that is purely theoretical" but "ought to become practical" (GA I/5: 259; SL 4: 291), serves here also as a metaphilosophical maxim that requires to present the results of the philosophical investigation as practical cognition. In violation of that duty, the bad moral philosopher has a share in the responsibility for the viciousness of his community. For this reason, the defence of necessary lies is so seriously blameworthy.[42] In contrast, an accurate, scientific, "proper" doctrine of duties should be regarded not only as integral to the overall project, but in fact as its main purpose. The scientific account developed in the first two parts of the work requires to be brought to completion in the third part, through which it can contribute to the advancement of morality.

Although it departs from deeply rooted assumptions in ordinary moral thinking, the philosophical reconstruction of the series of actions leading to self-sufficiency thus provides better epistemic grounds for rational deliberation. This gives to Fichte's theory a practical significance without imposing on it a prescriptive character. In Fichte's terms, the *System of Ethics*, especially its "proper doctrine of duties," should be understood as providing an articulate body of practical cognition. If conscience "would suffice for actual acting" (GA I/5: 190; SL 4: 208), conscience supported by science, that is a systematic overview of the contents of morality, draws on true practical cognition. Moral philosophy thus represents an all-important contribution to the advancement of morality. The final observation that "the common man will become ever more capable of advancing with the culture of the age" (GA I/5: 317; SL 4: 365) is a fitting conclusion for the *System of Ethics*, as Fichte remarks, not merely because it underscores the thought of the cooperation between the different components of society, but also because it articulates the proper task of his own normative theory in promoting morality.

---

[42] See GA I/5: 256; SL 4: 288: "Defense of necessary lies is also the most perverted thing possible among human beings."

Bibliography

Ameriks, Karl. 2000. *Kant and the Fate of Autonomy*. Cambridge: Cambridge University Press.

Ameriks, Karl. 2003. "On Being Neither Post- Nor Anti-Kantian: A Reply to Breazeale and Larmore Concerning The Fate of Autonomy." *Inquiry* 46: 272–292.

Annen, Martin. 1997. *Das Problem der Wahrhaftigkeit in der Philosophie der deutschen Aufklärung: Ein Beitrag zur Ethik und zum Naturrecht des 18. Jahrhunderts*. Würzburg: Königshausen & Neumann.

Bacin, Stefano. 2013. "'The Perfect Duty to Oneself Merely as a Moral Being' (TL 6: 428–437)." In *Kant's "Tugendlehre." A Comprehensive Commentary*, edited by Andreas Trampota, Oliver Sensen, and Jens Timmermann, 245–268. Berlin: De Gruyter.

Bacin, Stefano. 2015a. "Kant's Lectures on Ethics and Baumgarten's Moral Philosophy." In *Kant's Lectures on Ethics: A Critical Guide*, edited by Lara Denis and Oliver Sensen, 15–33. Cambridge: Cambridge University Press.

Bacin, Stefano. 2015b. "Erkenntnis, praktische." In *Kant-Lexikon*, edited by Marcus Willaschek, Georg Mohr, Jürgen Stolzenberg, and Stefano Bacin, 549–551. Berlin and Boston: De Gruyter.

Bacin, Stefano. 2017. "'Ein Bewußtsein, das selbst Pflicht ist': Fichtes unkantische Auffassung des Gewissens und ihr philosophischer Kontext." In *Fichte und seine Zeit*, vol. 2: *Streitfragen*, edited by Matteo d'Alfonso, Carla De Pascale, Erich Fuchs, and Marco Ivaldo, 306–325. Leiden and Boston: Brill.

Baur, Michael, trans. 2000. *Foundations of Natural Right according to the Principles of the Wissenschaftslehre*. Cambridge: Cambridge University Press.

Beiser, Frederick C. 2002. *German Idealism: The Struggle against Subjectivism, 1781–1801*. Cambridge, MA: Harvard University Press.

Bowman, Curtis and Estes, Yolanda, trans. 2010. *J. G. Fichte and the Atheism Dispute (1798–1800)*. London: Routledge.

Breazeale, Daniel, trans. 1988. *Fichte: Early Philosophical Writings*. Ithaca, NY: Cornell University Press.

Breazeale, Daniel, trans. 1992. *Foundations of Transcendental Philosophy (Wissenschaftslehre) nova methodo*. Ithaca, NY: Cornell University Press.

Breazeale, Daniel, trans. 1994. *Introductions to the Wissenschaftslehre and Other Writings*. Indianapolis: Hackett.

Bibliography

Breazeale, Daniel, trans. 2001a. "J. G. Fichte: Review of Friedrich Heinrich Gebhard, On Ethical Goodness as Disinterested Benevolence (Gotha: Ettinger, 1792)." *Philosophical Forum* 32 (4): 297–310.

Breazeale, Daniel, trans. 2001b. "J. G. Fichte: Review of Leonhard Creuzer, Skeptical Reflections on the Freedom of the Will (Giessen: Heyer: 1793)." *Philosophical Forum* 32 (4): 289–296.

Breazeale, Daniel. 2003. "Two Cheers for Post-Kantianism: A Response to Karl Ameriks." *Inquiry* 46: 239–259.

Breazeale, Daniel and Zöller, Günter. 2005. "Introduction." In *The System of Ethics: According to the Principles of the Wissenschaftslehre*, edited by J. G. Fichte, vii–xxxiii. Cambridge: Cambridge University Press.

Breazeale, Daniel and Zöller, Günter, trans. 2005. *The System of Ethics: According to the Principles of the Wissenschaftslehre*. Cambridge: Cambridge University Press.

Breazeale, Daniel. 2012. "In Defense of Fichte's Account of Ethical Deliberation." *Archiv für Geschichte der Philosophie* 94 (2): 178–207.

Breazeale, Daniel. 2015. "Der systematische Ort der Sittenlehre Fichtes." In *Fichtes System der Sittenlehre: Ein kooperativer Kommentar*, edited by Jean-Christophe Merle and A. Schmidt, 267–293. Frankfurt: Klostermann.

Breazeale, Daniel. 2018. "In Defense of Conscience: Fichte vs. Hegel." *Fichte-Studien* 45: 113–132.

Brink, David O. 2019. "Normative Perfectionism and the Kantian Tradition." *Philosophers' Imprint* 19 (45): 1–28.

Burman, Erik Olof. 1891. *Die Transcendentalphilosophie Fichte's und Schelling's dargestellt und erklärt*. Uppsala: Almqvist.

Cesa, Claudio. 1986. "Notstaat: Considerazioni su un termine della filosofia politica di Hegel." In *Scritti per Mario Delle Piane*, 135–151. Napoli: ESI.

Cesa, Claudio. 1992. "In tema di intersoggettività." In *J.G. Fichte e l'idealismo trascendentale*, 189–233. Bologna: Il Mulino.

Cesa, Claudio. 2013. *Verso l'eticità: Saggi di storia della filosofia*. Pisa: Edizioni della Normale.

Clarke, Samuel. 1706. *A Discourse Concerning the Unchangeable Obligations of Natural Religion, and the Truth and Certainty of the Christian Revelation*. London.

Dancy, Jonathan. 1993. *Moral Reasons*. Oxford: Blackwell.

Dancy, Jonathan. 2004. *Ethics without Principles*. Oxford: Oxford University Press.

De Pascale, Carla. 1995. *Etica e diritto: La filosofia pratica di Fichte e le sue ascendenze kantiane*. Bologna: il Mulino.

De Pascale, Carla. 2003. *"Die Vernunft ist praktisch". Fichtes Ethik und Rechtslehre im System*. Berlin: Duncker & Humblot.

De Pascale, Carla. 2015. "Die allgemeinen Pflichten (§§ 22–25)." In *Fichtes System der Sittenlehre: Ein kooperativer Kommentar*, edited by Jean-Christophe Merle and Andreas Schmidt, 183–202. Frankfurt: Klostermann.

Denis, Lara. 1999. "Kant on the Perfection of Others." *The Southern Journal of Philosophy* 37: 21–41.

Bibliography

Dietz, Simone. 2018. "White and Prosocial Lies." In *The Oxford Handbook of Lying*, edited by Jörg Meibauer, 289–300. Oxford: Oxford University Press.

Düsing, Edith. 1986. *Intersubjektivität und Selbstbewusstsein: Behaviouristische, phänomenologische und idealistische Begründungstheorien bei Mead, Schütz, Fichte und Hegel*. Köln: Dinter.

Dreier, James. 1993. "Structures of Normative Theories." *The Monist* 76: 22–40.

Eberhard, Johann August. 1799. *Ueber den Gott des Herrn Professor Fichtes und den Götzen seiner Gegner: Eine ruhige Prüfung seiner Appellation an das Publikum in einigen Briefe*. Halle: Hemmerdge and Schwetschke.

Fischer, Kuno. 1869. *Geschichte der neuern Philosophie: Fichte und seine Zeit*. Heidelberg: Wassermann.

Fonnesu, Luca. 1993. *Antropologia e idealismo: La destinazione dell'uomo nell'etica di Fichte*. Roma: Laterza.

Fonnesu, Luca. 1996. "Die Aufhebung des Staates bei Fichte." *Fichte-Studien* 11: 85–97.

Fonnesu, Luca. 1999. "Metamorphosen der Freiheit in Fichtes Sittenlehre." In *Zur Einheit der Lehre Fichtes*, edited by Marco Ivaldo and Jose Villacañas, 255–271. Amsterdam: Rodopi.

Fonnesu, Luca. 2004. "Pflicht und Pflichtenlehre: Fichtes Auseinandersetzung mit der Aufklärung und mit Kant." In *Fichte und die Aufklärung*, edited by Carla De Pascale, Erich Fuchs, Marco Ivaldo, and Gunter Zöller, 133–146. Hildesheim and New York: Olms.

Fonnesu, Luca. 2010. *Per una moralità concreta: Studi sulla filosofia classica tedesca*. Bologna: Il Mulino.

Fonnesu, Luca. 2019. "Kant on Communication." *Studi kantiani* 32: 11–23.

Fugate, Courtney D. and Hymers, John, eds. 2018. *Baumgarten and Kant on Metaphysics*. Oxford: Oxford University Press.

Gibbard, Allan. 1999. "Morality as Consistency in Living: Korsgaard's Kantian Lectures." *Ethics* 110: 140–164.

Goh, Kien-How. 2012. "Between Determinism and Indeterminism: The Freedom of Choice in Fichte's *System der Sittenlehre*." *European Journal of Philosophy* 23 (3): 439–455.

Grimm, Jacob Wilhelm Grimm. 1905. *Deutsches Wörterbuch von Jacob und Wilhelm Grimm*, Bd.X.1. Leipzig: Hirzel.

Green, Garrett, trans. 2010. *Attempt at a Critique of All Revelation*. Cambridge: Cambridge University Press.

Gregor, Mary J. trans. 1996. *Kant: Practical Philosophy*, edited by Mary J. Gregor. Cambridge: Cambridge University Press.

Guyer, Paul. 2019. "Freedom as an End in Itself: Fichte on Ethical Duties." In *The Palgrave Fichte Handbook*, edited by Steven Hoeltzel, 257–283. London: Palgrave.

Habermas, Jürgen. 1988. "Moralität und Sittlichkeit: Treffen Hegels Einwände gegen Kant auch auf die Diskursethik zu?" *Revue internationale de philosophie* 42: 320–340.

Harris, Henry Silton. 1972. *Hegel's Development: Toward the Sunlight, 1770–1801*. Oxford: Clarendon Press.

Bibliography

Heath, Peter and Lachs, Joseph, trans. 1982. *The Science of Knowledge*. Cambridge: Cambridge University Press.

Hegel, Georg Wilhelm Friedrich. 1970. *Werke in 20 Bänden*, edited by Eva Moldenhauer and Karl Markus Michel. Frankfurt: Suhrkamp.

Hegel, Georg Wilhelm Friedrich. 1801/1977. *The Difference between Fichte's and Schelling's System of Philosophy*, translated by Walter Cerf and H.S. Harris. Albany: SUNY Press.

Hegel, Georg Wilhelm Friedrich. 1802/1970. *Über die wissenschaftlichen Behandlungsarten des Naturrechts, seine Stelle in der praktischen Philosophie und sein Verhältnis zu den positiven Rechtswissenschaften* (*Werke*, Frankfurt: Suhrkamp 1970, vol. II). Translated by T.M. Knox, introduction by H.B. Acton, foreword by J.R. Silber, Philadelphia. University of Pennsylvania Press.

Hegel, Georg Wilhelm Friedrich. 1821/1970. *Grundlinien der Philosophie des Rechts* (*Werke*, Frankfurt: Suhrkamp 1970, vol. VII). Translated by T.M. Knox, revised, edited and introduced by Stephen Houlgate. New York: Oxford University Press. 2008.

Henrich, Dieter. 1992. *Der Grund im Bewußtsein: Untersuchungen zu Hölderlins Denken (1794–1795)*. Stuttgart: Klett-Cotta.

Henrich, Dieter. 2003. *Between Kant and Hegel: Lectures on German Idealism*, edited by David S. Pacini. Cambridge, MA: Harvard University Press.

Henrich, Dieter. 2004. *Grundlegung aus dem Ich: Untersuchungen zur Vorgeschichte des Idealismus, Tübingen-Jena (1790–1794)*. Frankfurt: Suhrkamp.

Höffe, Otfried. 2013. "Kantian Ethics." In *The Oxford Handbook of the History of Ethics*, edited by Roger Crisp, 465–482. Oxford: Oxford University Press.

Honneth, Axel. 2011. *Das Recht der Freiheit: Grundriss einer demokratischen Sittlichkeit*. Frankfurt: Suhrkamp.

Hornig, Gottfried. 1980. "Perfektibilität: Eine Untersuchung zur Geschichte und Bedeutung dieses Begriffs in der deutschsprachigen Literatur." *Archiv für Begriffsgeschichte* 24: 221–257.

Hume, David. 1739–40/1888. *A Treatise of Human Nature*. Oxford: Oxford University Press.

Hurka, Thomas. 1993. *Perfectionism*. Oxford, New York: Oxford University Press.

Irwin, Terence. 2004. "Kantian Autonomy." In *Agency and Action*, edited by John Hyman and Helen Steward, 137–164. Cambridge: Cambridge University Press.

Irwin, Terence. 2009. *The Development of Ethics, Volume 3: From Kant to Rawls*. Oxford University Press.

Ivaldo, Marco. 1992. *Libertà e ragione: L'etica di Fichte*. Milano: Mursia.

Jacobi, Friedrich Heinrich. 1798/1994. "Von Religion, Lehrmeinungen, Gebrauchen." In *Johann Gottfried von Herder, Werke in zehn Bänden 9/1: Theologische Schriften*, edited by Christoph Bultmann and Thomas Zippert, 725–857. Frankfurt: Deutscher Klassiker Verlag.

Jacobs, Wilhelm G. 2017. "Review of Merle and Schmidt 2015." *Archiv für Geschichte der Philosophie* 99: 233–236.

Bibliography

James, David. 2011. *Fichte's Social and Political Philosophy: Property and Virtue.* Cambridge: Cambridge University Press.

James, David. 2016. "The Political Theology of Fichte's Staatslehre: Immanence and Transcendence." *British Journal for the History of Philosophy* 24 (6): 1157–1175.

Katsafanas, Paul. 2015. "Ethics." In *Oxford Handbook of Nineteenth-Century German Philosophy*, edited by Michael Forster and Kristin Gjesdal, 474–493. Oxford: Oxford University Press.

Kierkegaard, Søren. 1980. *The Concept of Anxiety*, edited and translated by Albert B. Anderson and Reidar Thomte. Princeton, NJ: Princeton University Press.

Korsgaard, Christine. 1996. *Sources of Normativity*. Cambridge: Cambridge University Press.

Kosch, Michelle. 2011. "Formal Freedom in Fichte's System of Ethics." *Internationales Jahrbuch des Deutschen Idealismus/international Yearbook of German Idealism* 8: 150–168.

Kosch, Michelle. 2014. "Practical Deliberation and the Voice of Conscience in Fichte's 1798 System of Ethics." *Philosophers' Imprint* 14: 1–16.

Kosch, Michelle. 2015. "Agency and Self-Sufficiency in Fichte's Ethics." *Philosophy and Phenomenological Research* 91 (2): 348–380.

Kosch, Michelle. 2018. *Fichte's Ethics*. Oxford, New York: Oxford University Press.

Lauth, Reinhard. 1962. "Le problème de l'interpersonnalité chez Fichte." *Archives de philosophie* 25: 325–344.

Larmore, Charles. 2003. "Back to Kant? No Way." *Inquiry* 46: 260–271.

Lessing, Gotthold Ephraim. 2005. *Philosophical and Theological Writings*, edited and translated by H. B. Nisbet. Cambridge: Cambridge University Press.

Loewe, Johann Heinrich. 1862. *Die Philosophie Fichte's nach dem Gesammtergebnisse ihrer Entwickelung und in ihrem Verhältnisse zu Kant und Spinoza: Mit einem Anhange ueber den Gottesbegriff Spinoza's und dessen Schicksale.* Stuttgart: Nitzschke.

Macor, Laura Anna. 2013. *Die Bestimmung des Menschen: Eine Begriffsgeschichte (1748–1800).* Stuttgart-Bad Cannstatt: Frommann-Holzboog.

Maesschalck, Marc. 2015. "Die Lehre von den bedingten Pflichten (§§ 19–21)." In *Fichtes System der Sittenlehre: Ein kooperativer Kommentar*, edited by Jean-Christophe Merle and Andreas Schmidt, 157–182. Frankfurt: Klostermann.

Martin, Wayne. 1997. *Idealism and Objectivity: Understanding Fichte's Jena Project*, 36–52. Stanford: Stanford University Press.

Martin, Wayne. 2018. "Fichte's Creuzer Review and the Transformation of the Free Will Problem." *European Journal of Philosophy* 26: 717–729.

Merle, Jean-Christophe and Schmidt, Andreas, eds. 2015. *Fichtes System der Sittenlehre: Ein kooperativer Kommentar.* Frankfurt: Klostermann.

Moggach, Douglas. 2018. "Contextualising Fichte: Leibniz, Kant, and Perfectionist Ethics." *Fichte-Studien* 45: 133–153.

Moyar, Dean. 2008. "Unstable Autonomy: Conscience and Judgment in Kant's Moral Philosophy." *Journal of Moral Philosophy* 5 (3): 327–360.

Bibliography

Nagel, Thomas. 1970. *The Possibility of Altruism*. Princeton, NJ: Princeton University Press.

Naulin, Paul. 1969. "Philosophie et communication chez Fichte." *Revue internationale de philosophie* 23: 410–441.

Neuhouser, Frederick. 1990. *Fichte's Theory of Subjectivity*. Cambridge: Cambridge University Press.

Nuzzo, Angelica. 2011. "Théorie de l'éthique et éthique appliquée chez Fichte: *Sittenlehre* ou *Metaphysik der Sitten?*" *Revue de Métaphysique et de Morale* 3: 319–333.

Nuzzo, Angelica. 2012. *Memory, History, Justice in Hegel*. London/New York: Palgrave Macmillan.

Nuzzo, Angelica. 2013. "Contradiction in the Ethical World. Hegel's Challenge for Times of Crisis." In *Freiheit: Akten der Stuttgarter Hegel Kongress 2011*, edited by Gunnar Hindrichs and Axel Honneth, 627–648. Frankfurt: Klostermann.

Nuzzo, Angelica. 2015. "Kant's Pure Ethics and the Problem of Application." In *Politics and Teleology in Kant*, edited by Paul Formosa, Avery Goldman, and Tatiana Patrone, 245–261. Cardiff: University of Wales Press.

Nuzzo, Angelica. 2016. "Moral Motivation in Post-Kantian Philosophy: Fichte and Hegel." In *Moral Motivation*, edited by Iakovos Vasiliou, 227–252. Oxford: Oxford University Press.

Peperzak, Adriaan. 1982. "Hegels Pflichten- und Tugendlehre." *Hegel-Studien* 17: 97–117.

Peperzak, Adriaan. 2001. *Modern Freedom. Hegel's Legal, Moral, and Political Philosophy*. Dordrecht/Boston/London: Kluwer.

Piché, Claude. 2000. "Le mal radical chez Fichte." In *Fichte: Le moi et la liberté*, edited by Jean-Christophe Goddard. 209–231. Paris: Presses Universitaires de France.

Pinkard, Terry. 2002. *German Philosophy 1760–1860*. Cambridge: Cambridge University Press.

Pippin, Robert. 2008. *Hegel's Practical Philosophy*. Cambridge: Cambridge University Press.

Pippin, Robert. 2016. "Über Selbstgesetzgebung." In *Die Aktualität des Deutschen Idealismus*, edited by Robert Pippin, 52–84. Frankfurt: Suhrkamp.

Platner, Ernst. 1782/86. *Philosophische Aphorismen: Nebst einigen Anleitungen zur philosophischen Geschichte*. Leipzig: Schwickert Verlag.

Preul, Reiner. 1969. *Reflexion und Gefühl: Die Theologie Fichtes in seiner vorkantischen Zeit*. Berlin: De Gruyter.

Preuss, Peter, trans. 1987. *The Vocation of Man*. Indianapolis: Hackett.

Rauscher, Frederick. 2002. "Kant's Moral Anti-Realism." *Journal of the History of Philosophy* 40 (3): 477–499.

Regan, Donald H. 2002. "The Value of Rational Nature." *Ethics* 112: 267–291.

Reinhard, Franz Volkmar. 1801. *System der christlichen Moral*. Vol II. 3rd ed. Reutlingen: Grözinger.

Rohs, Peter. 1992. "Der materiale Gehalt des Sittengesetzes." *Fichte-Studien* 3: 170–183.

Bibliography

Rödl, Sebastian. 2007. *Self-Consciousness*. Cambridge, MA: Harvard University Press.

Schelling, Friedrich Wilhelm Josef. 1856ff. *Schellings sämmtliche Werke*. Stuttgart: Cotta.

Schelling, Friedrich Wilhelm Josef. 1976ff. *Historisch-Kritische Ausgabe*. Stuttgart: Frommann-Holzboog.

Schick, Friedrike. 2015. "Vermittlungen zwischen Natur und Freiheit–der Naturtrieb in §8 des *Systems der Sittenlehre*." In *Fichtes System der Sittenlehre: Ein kooperativer Kommentar*, edited by Jean-Christophe Merle and Andreas Schmidt, 75–92. Frankfurt: Klostermann.

Schleiermacher, Friedrich. 1803/2002. "*Grundlinien einer Kritik der bisherigen Sittenlehre.*" In *Kritische Gesamtausgabe*, I.4, edited by Eilert Herms, Günter Meckenstock, and Michael Pietsch. 27–357. Berlin: De Gruyter.

Schlösser, Ulrich. 2001. *Das Erfassen des Einleuchtens: Fichtes Wissenschaftslehre 1804*. Berlin: Philo Verlag.

Schmidt, Andreas. 2015. "Die Deduktion des Prinzips der Sittlichkeit (§§1–3)." In *Fichtes System der Sittenlehre: Ein kooperativer Kommentar*, edited by Jean Merle and Andreas Schmidt, 39–56. Frankfurt: Klostermann.

Sidgwick, Henry. 1874/1981. *The Methods of Ethics*. Indianapolis: Hackett.

Siep, Ludwig. 1992. *Praktische Philosophie im Deutschen Idealismus*. Frankfurt: Suhrkamp Verlag.

Siep, Ludwig. 2009. "Staat und Kirche bei Fichte und Hegel." In *Symposion Johann Gottlieb Fichte. Herkunft und Ausstrahlung seines Denkens. München 5. und 6. März 2009*, edited by Werner Beierwaltes and Erich Fuchs, 47–63. München: Verlag der Bayerischen Akademie der Wissenschaften.

Siep, Ludwig. 2010. *Aktualität und Grenzen der praktischen Philosophie Hegels: Aufsätze 1997–2009*. München: Fink.

Städlin, Carl Friedrich. 1798. *Grundrisse der Tugend- und Religionslehre zu akademischen Vorlesungen für zukünftige Lehrer in der christlichen Kirche: Erster Theil, welcher die Tugendlehre enthält*. Göttingen: Vandenhoeck & Ruprecht.

Stern, Robert. 2012. *Understanding Moral Obligation: Kant, Hegel, Kierkegaard*. Cambridge: Cambridge University Press.

Süskind, Friedrich Gottlieb. 1794. *D. Gottlob Christian Storr's Bemerkungen über Kant's philosophische Religionslehre, aus dem Lateinischen: Nebst einigen Bemerkungen des Uebersetzers über den aus Principien der praktischen Vernunft hergeleiteten Ueberzeugungsgrund von der Möglichkeit und Wirklichkeit einer Offenbarung in Beziehung auf Fichtes Versuch einer Critik aller Offenbarung*. Tübingen: J. G. Cotta.

Timmermann, Jens. 2015. "What's Wrong with 'Deontology'?" *Proceedings of the Aristotelian Society* 115: 75–92.

Timmermann, Jens. forthcoming. *Kant on the Supposed Right to Lie*. Cambridge: Cambridge University Press.

Verweyen, Hansjürgen. 1975. *Recht und Sittlichkeit in J. G. Fichtes Gesellschaftslehre*. Freiburg; Munchen: Alber.

Verweyen, Hansjürgen. 1995. "Fichtes Religionsphilosophie: Versuch eines Gesamtüberblick." *Fichte-Studien* 8: 193–224.

Bibliography

Walch, Johann Georg. 1726. *Philosophisches Lexicon*. Halle: Gleditsch.

Wallace, R. Jay. 2006. *Normativity and the Will: Selected Essays on Moral Psychology and Practical Reason*. Oxford: Clarendon Press.

Ware, Owen. 2015. "Agency and Evil in Fichte's Ethics." *Philosophers' Imprint* 15 (11): 1–21.

Ware, Owen. 2017. "Fichte on Conscience." *Philosophy and Phenomenological Research* 95 (2): 376–394.

Ware, Owen. 2018. "Fichte's Normative Ethics: Deontological or Teleological?" *Mind* 127 (506): 565–584.

Ware, Owen. 2019. "Fichte's Method of Moral Justification." *British Journal for the History of Philosophy* 27 (6): 1173–1193.

Ware, Owen. 2020. *Fichte's Moral Philosophy*. New York: Oxford University Press.

Ware, Owen. 2021. *Kant's Justification of Morality*. Oxford: Oxford University Press.

Williams, Bernard. 2002. *Truth and Truthfulness: An Essay in Genealogy*. Princeton, NJ: Princeton University Press.

Wolff, Christian. 1750. *Institutiones Juris Naturae et Gentium*. Halle: Renger.

Wood, Allen W. 2000. "The 'I' as Principle of Practical Philosophy." In *The Reception of Kant's Critical Philosophy*, edited by Sally Sedgwick, 93–108. Cambridge: Cambridge University Press.

Wood, Allen W. 2014. "Leaving Consequentialism Behind." In *The Free Development of Each: Studies on Freedom, Right, and Ethics in Classical German Philosophy*, 144–163. Oxford: Oxford University Press.

Wood, Allen W. 2016a. *Fichte's Ethical Thought*. Oxford/New York: Oxford University Press.

Wood, Allen. 2016b. "Fichte's Philosophy of Right and Ethics." In *The Cambridge Companion to Fichte*, edited by David James and Günter Zöller, 168–198. Cambridge: Cambridge University Press.

Wood, Allen W. 2017a. "Fichte." In *The Cambridge History of Moral Philosophy*, edited by Sacha Golob and Jens Timmermann, 410–420. Cambridge: Cambridge University Press.

Wood, Allen. 2017b. *Formulas of the Moral Law*. Cambridge: Cambridge University Press.

Zedler, Johann Heinrich. 1731–1754. *Zedlers Universallexikon*. Halle, Leipzig: Zedler.

Zöller, Günter. 1998. *Fichte's Transcendental Philosophy: The Original Duplicity of Intelligence and Will*. Cambridge: Cambridge University Press.

Zöller, Gunter. 2003. "Das Absolute und seine Erscheinung: Die Schelling-Rezeption des späten Fichte." *Internationales Jahrbuch des deutschen Idealismus* 1: 165–182.

Zöller, Günter. 2008. "Two Hundred Years of Solitude: The Failed Reception of Fichte's *System of Ethics*." *Philosophy Today* 52: 218–227.

Zoller, Gunter. 2015. "Die Rezeption und Wirkungsgeschichte von Fichtes *System der Sittenlehre*." In *Fichtes System der Sittenlehre: Ein kooperativer Kommentar*, edited by Jean-Christophe Merle and Andreas Schmidt, 247–266. Frankfurt: Klostermann.

Index

agent-neutral view of morality, 9, 117, 203, 215, 216, 217, 218
Ameriks, Karl, 28
Annen, Martin, 204
Anstoss, 91
application (of the principle of morality), 13, 14, 15, 16, 22, 23, 45, 54, 55, 56, 59, 67, 69, 124, 135, 151, 152, 153, 154, 155, 156, 157, 158, 159, 168, 171, 172, 176, 182, 207
Aristotle, 21, 217
Atheism Controversy, 44
Aufforderung, see summons (*Aufforderung*)
autonomy, 5, 7, 11, 14, 15, 47, 48, 49, 50, 58, 59, 61, 77, 78, 139, 140, 144, 148, 153, 155, 168, 169

Bacin, Stefano, 9, 109, 120, 125, 184, 200, 202, 205
Baumgarten, Alexander Gottlieb, 24, 202
Beiser, Frederick, 2
body, 8, 12, 16, 25, 57, 61, 92, 114, 123, 126, 153, 156, 160, 161, 163, 164, 165, 166, 168, 169, 170, 171, 172, 173, 174, 176, 185, 192, 202, 213, 220
Breazeale, Daniel, 6, 7, 28, 32, 81, 87, 101, 125, 127, 128, 130, 150, 183, 204, 206
Brink, David O., 217
Burman, Erik Olof, 75

categorical imperative, 4, 12, 13, 14, 15, 23, 26, 27, 30, 44, 45, 47, 66, 81, 129, 175, 191
Cesa, Claudio, 179, 182, 185
choice (*Willkür*), 7, 11, 18, 21, 22, 23, 24, 39, 41, 42, 72, 76, 79, 85, 86, 87, 88, 89, 90, 92, 93, 95, 97, 98, 99, 100, 103, 107, 109, 127, 128, 133, 134, 136, 139, 141, 143, 147, 152, 156, 163, 187
church, 8, 174, 175, 188, 190, 194, 195, 196, 197, 198
Clarke, Samuel, 212
cognition, practical, 204, 205, 212, 220, 220
communication, 16, 26, 82, 110, 128, 129, 188, 190, 191, 192, 194, 195, 196, 197, 203, 204, 206, 207, 208, 212
compulsion (*Zunötigung*), 30, 31, 32, 33

conscience, 3, 4, 7, 8, 18, 20, 21, 22, 23, 45, 66, 72, 76, 79, 82, 83, 109, 110, 111, 112, 113, 114, 115, 116, 117, 118, 119, 120, 121, 122, 123, 124, 125, 126, 127, 128, 129, 130, 135, 136, 140, 145, 147, 148, 150, 152, 158, 159, 175, 182, 183, 184, 188, 189, 190, 191, 193, 196, 197, 202, 220
consequentialism, 25, 27, 117, 119, 126, 211, 216
conviction, 19, 22, 23, 70, 105, 109, 111, 112, 116, 118, 119, 122, 129, 130, 135, 158, 182, 183, 184, 190, 191, 192, 194, 195, 196, 198
Crowe, Benjamin, 5
cultivation (*Bildung*), 7, 82, 131, 209

Dancy, Jonathan, 125
De Pascale, Carla, 3, 152, 189, 206
deduction of the principle of morality, 5, 6, 12, 85, 151
deliberation, 5, 40, 55, 72, 76, 79, 109, 110, 112, 113, 114, 116, 117, 118, 119, 121, 122, 124, 129, 130, 135, 220
Denis, Lara, 209
deontology, 125, 216
deontology (deontological ethics), 27, 126, 216
desire, 6, 17, 26, 42, 66, 69, 71, 72, 75, 76, 78, 79, 80, 83, 86, 97, 103, 139, 145
desire, faculty of (lower and higher), 81, 86, 152, 182
Dreier, James, 215, 216
drives, 3, 6, 8, 17, 23, 49, 57, 64, 66, 67, 69, 71, 72, 73, 74, 75, 76, 77, 78, 79, 80, 81, 82, 83, 86, 88, 94, 95, 96, 97, 98, 99, 101, 102, 104, 110, 112, 121, 122, 126, 128, 141, 153, 154, 160, 162, 163, 165, 170, 173, 174, 175
drive towards the entire self, 57
drive, ethical, 6, 17, 23, 72, 79, 80, 81, 82, 83, 84, 99, 110, 122, 127, 174
drive, formative (*Bildungstrieb*), 6, 49, 57, 69, 78, 80
drive, fundamental (*Urtrieb*), 72, 73, 82, 83, 162

229

Index

drives (cont.)
    drive, natural, 6, 8, 37, 38, 69, 72, 73, 75, 76, 77,
      78, 79, 80, 81, 82, 83, 86, 93, 95, 96, 99, 101,
      102, 103, 139, 156, 162, 164, 165, 168, 169, 172
    drive, pure, 17, 23, 31, 72, 73, 81, 82, 83, 92, 97,
      98, 99, 102, 103
    self-preservation, drive for, 78
Düsing, Edith, 185
duties
    (apparent) conflict of, 212
    conditioned, 212, 213
    doctrine of, 7, 8, 9, 18, 24, 67, 151, 158, 159, 181,
      184, 188, 189, 191, 198, 199, 201, 202, 203, 208,
      211, 214, 216, 217, 219, 220
    to oneself. *see* duties, conditioned
    universal vs particular, 213

Eberhard, Johann August, 44
education, moral, 41, 105, 106, 131, 188, 194, 197,
    209, 211
embodiment, 8, 58, 64, 153, 162, 163, 164, 166, 169,
    171, 174, 176, 211
end in itself, 4, 9, 13, 21, 24, 27, 32, 47, 165, 186
end, concept of an (*Zweckbegriff*), 36, 74, 76, 79,
    82, 83, 84, 112
ethical life (*Sittlichkeit*), 8, 9, 67, 83, 129, 151, 152,
    153, 158, 159, 161, 169, 174, 175, 176, 178, 179,
    180, 181, 182, 183, 184, 185, 186, 187, 188, 190,
    191, 196, 198, 199, 200, 227
evil, 7, 131, 132, 133, 134, 135, 136, 137, 140, 141, 142,
    143, 144, 145, 146, 147, 148, 188

feeling, 7, 16, 17, 23, 35, 42, 49, 66, 71, 74, 76, 80,
    82, 83, 88, 109, 110, 112, 114, 115, 116, 118, 121,
    123, 124, 127, 128, 129, 134, 135, 145, 187, 208
Fichte, Johann Gottlieb
    "First Introduction to the
      Wissenschaftslehre," 33
    "Second Introduction to the
      Wissenschaftslehre," 33, 34
    Attempt at a Critique of all Revelation, 85
    Foundations of Natural Right, 3, 10, 41, 67, 68,
      89, 91, 169, 181, 185, 189, 193, 221
    Review of F. H. Gebhard's *On Ethical
      Goodness as Disinterested Benevolence*, 87, 88
    Review of Leonhard Creuzer's *Skeptical
      Observations on Freedom of the Will*, 87, 88
    Wissenschaftslehre 1804, 59, 65
    Wissenschaftslehre nova methodo, 1, 5, 29, 35, 46,
      61, 92, 216
Fischer, Kuno, 75
Flatt, Johann Friedrich, 44
Fonnesu, Luca, 3, 8, 154, 159, 185, 190, 193, 199,
    202, 216, 218
Formula of the End in Itself, 215

formula philosophy, 6, 68
freedom, 10, 63, 87, 132, 169, 171
    formal freedom, 6, 7, 11, 86, 89, 90, 91, 92, 93,
      94, 95, 96, 97, 98, 99, 101, 102, 103, 106, 107,
      108, 175, 203, 204, 206, 207, 208, 212
    material freedom, 7, 11, 89, 90, 92, 93, 94, 95,
      96, 97, 98, 99, 100, 101, 102, 103, 104, 105,
      106, 107, 108

Gibbard, Allan, 38
God, 5, 11, 16, 24, 28, 30, 31, 32, 40, 41, 42, 43, 44,
    45, 46, 199, 212
Goh, Kien-How, 107
good example, 9, 203, 208, 209,
    210
Green, T.H., 217, 218
Guyer, Paul, 214

Habermas, Jürgen, 179
Harris, H.S., 44
Hegel, Georg Wilhelm Friedrich, 2, 3, 9, 44, 66,
    127, 128, 130, 150, 152, 153, 158, 159, 160, 161,
    162, 169, 174, 175, 176, 178, 179, 180, 181, 183,
    184, 185, 189, 191, 195, 198, 199, 202, 218
Henrich, Dieter, 35, 44
Hölderlin, Friedrich, 44
Honneth, Axel, 179
Hornig, Gottfried, 193
Hume, David, 50
Hurka, Thomas, 217

idealism (transcendental), 32, 33, 34, 43, 45
I-hood, 8, 24, 25, 33, 34, 43, 46, 73, 90, 93, 96, 98,
    101, 103, 108, 126, 150, 152, 161, 164, 165, 170,
    172, 174
individuality, 2, 7, 8, 23, 25, 26, 33, 41, 43, 60, 78,
    89, 92, 93, 94, 95, 98, 102, 103, 106, 109, 110,
    111, 113, 115, 117, 118, 125, 128, 131, 132, 133, 134,
    135, 136, 137, 139, 141, 142, 143, 144, 145, 146,
    147, 148, 149, 168, 169, 170, 172, 174, 175, 176,
    180, 181, 182, 183, 184, 186, 187, 188, 190, 191,
    196, 198, 205, 208, 209, 210, 211, 213, 215, 217,
    217, 218
inertia, 105, 135, 136, 138, 140, 141, 142, 144, 146,
    147, 148
instinct of reason, 5, 35
intelligence, 6, 33, 55, 57, 61, 62, 161,
    170, 172, 185
Irwin, Terence, 3, 39
Ivaldo, Marco, 3

Jacobi, Friedrich Heinrich, 42, 44, 59
Jacobs, Wilhelm G., 3
James, David, 7, 8, 146, 189,
    217

Index

231

Kant, Immanuel, 2, 3, 4, 5, 8, 9, 10, 11, 12, 13, 14, 15, 16, 17, 18, 19, 20, 21, 22, 23, 24, 26, 27, 28, 30, 36, 39, 40, 44, 45, 47, 48, 49, 50, 51, 61, 63, 64, 66, 67, 68, 69, 71, 81, 85, 86, 90, 111, 117, 120, 125, 129, 132, 133, 134, 136, 138, 141, 148, 150, 151, 152, 153, 154, 155, 156, 157, 158, 159, 160, 161, 163, 166, 168, 171, 175, 176, 179, 180, 181, 182, 184, 185, 186, 187, 188, 189, 190, 191, 192, 193, 198, 199, 201, 202, 204, 205, 206, 208, 209, 210, 214, 225
  "Doctrine of Virtue," 2, 4, 10, 13, 19, 21, 22, 23, 27, 210
  Critique of Judgment, 163, 171
  Critique of Practical Reason, 1, 2, 21, 64, 187, 215
  Critique of Pure Reason, 68, 157
  Formula of Humanity, 13, 24, 214
  Formula of the End in Itself. *see* Formula of Humanity
  Groundwork for the Metaphysics of Morals, 4, 10, 13, 18, 19, 20, 21, 30, 47, 61, 184, 214
  Religion within the Boundaries of Mere Reason, 132, 133, 134
Kierkegaard, Søren, 3, 8, 132, 137, 142, 143, 144, 145, 146, 147, 148, 149
Korsgaard, Christine, 29, 30, 31, 32, 37, 38, 39
Kosch, Michelle, 3, 25, 49, 90, 110, 115, 116, 117, 118, 119, 120, 126, 153, 204, 216

labour, 188, 189, 196
Larmore, Charles, 28
Lauth, Reinhard, 185
legality, 17, 183, 184, 187, 188, 190, 216
Lessing, Gotthold Ephraim, 41
Loewe, Johann Heinrich, 78
longing, 16, 66, 71, 72, 74, 75, 76, 80, 81, 93
lying, 9, 21, 136, 204, 205, 206, 207

Macor, Laura Anna, 185
Maesschalk, Marc, 215
Martin, Wayne, 33, 88
Marx, Karl, 3, 193
Merle, Jean-Christophe, 3
metaphysics of morals, 66, 152, 180, 182
method, synthetic vs analytical, 12
Mill, John Stuart, 217
Moggach, Douglas, 217
moral law, 8, 11, 12, 13, 15, 17, 24, 27, 29, 30, 34, 41, 42, 44, 45, 46, 48, 49, 64, 69, 70, 75, 79, 82, 87, 98, 99, 100, 105, 108, 111, 112, 122, 129, 132, 133, 134, 135, 136, 137, 138, 139, 140, 141, 142, 143, 144, 145, 148, 152, 153, 155, 168, 169, 171, 173, 174, 175, 176, 180, 186, 187, 189, 192, 193, 206, 211, 213, 214, 215
moral nature (of human beings), 2, 5, 29, 30, 31, 34, 35, 37, 142, 144, 145, 146, 193, 216, 219

moral teacher, 210
morality, 3, 4, 5, 7, 8, 9, 11, 12, 13, 14, 15, 17, 21, 23, 30, 31, 32, 48, 67, 70, 71, 75, 80, 83, 84, 85, 94, 96, 97, 104, 105, 106, 111, 117, 118, 122, 123, 125, 126, 135, 137, 138, 152, 153, 154, 156, 158, 159, 165, 166, 167, 169, 170, 173, 175, 176, 178, 179, 180, 181, 182, 183, 184, 187, 188, 189, 190, 193, 198, 199, 200, 201, 202, 203, 204, 205, 207, 208, 209, 210, 211, 212, 213, 215, 216, 218, 219, 219, 220
Moyar, Dean, 7, 120, 184, 202

Nagel, Thomas, 38
Naulin, Paul, 190
Neuhouser, Frederick, 35, 36, 37, 38, 90
normativity, 28, 29, 31, 32, 33, 35, 38, 39, 40, 42, 43, 45, 46, 198, 201
not-I, 25, 72, 135
Novalis (Friedrich von Hardenberg), 125
Nuzzo, Angelica, 8, 80, 152, 153, 154, 157, 162, 163, 185, 201, 218

Peperzak, Adriaan, 184, 199
perfectibility, 193, 206, 215
perfectionism, 9, 203, 217, 218
Piché, Claude, 138
Pinkard, Terry, 48
Pippin, Robert, 48
Platner, Ernst, 42
Preul, Reiner, 184

Rauscher, Frederick, 28
reflective judgment, 110, 112, 113, 114, 115, 117, 118, 119, 121, 122, 124, 127, 128, 129, 130
Regan, Donald H., 38
Reinhard, Franz Volkmar, 212
Reinhold, Karl Leonhard, 85, 86, 87, 88, 97
respect, 21, 24, 132, 133, 134, 136, 145, 174, 208
Rödl, Sebastian, 48
Rohs, Peter, 121, 124
Rousseau, Jean-Jacques, 19, 193

Schelling, Friedrich Wilhelm Joseph, 44, 56, 59, 181, 182
Schick, Friedrike, 75
Schiller, Friedrich, 180, 189
Schlösser, Ulrich, 5, 6, 59
Schmidt, Andreas, 3, 51, 62
scholar, 189, 193, 196, 197, 208, 219
self-determination, 35, 36, 37, 38, 40, 47, 48, 54, 55, 57, 60, 63, 64, 77, 87, 89, 90, 91, 94, 96, 100, 101, 102, 103, 127, 139, 162, 163, 168, 169, 187
self-other asymmetry, 203, 215, 218, 219

self-sufficiency, 3, 12, 13, 17, 24, 25, 26, 27, 40, 70, 71, 73, 81, 82, 84, 92, 97, 98, 99, 102, 104, 110, 113, 114, 117, 119, 122, 125, 128, 139, 139, 141, 144, 153, 154, 156, 159, 161, 164, 165, 166, 170, 172, 173, 174, 175, 176, 185, 186, 188, 211, 217, 220
Sidgwick, Henry, 215
Siep, Ludwig, 179, 181, 195
society, 2, 7, 8, 26, 27, 104, 105, 106, 131, 132, 137, 138, 140, 141, 174, 175, 176, 179, 186, 187, 188, 189, 190, 191, 192, 193, 194, 197, 198, 199, 213, 220
Spinoza, Baruch, 151, 153, 161, 165, 166, 167, 168, 173, 177
spontaneity, 6, 49, 52, 57, 60, 86, 87, 88, 89, 92, 93, 103, 104, 154, 156, 169, 171
state, 8, 188, 189, 190, 192, 193, 194, 195, 196, 197, 198
Stäudlin, Carl Friedrich, 208, 212
Stern, Robert, 28, 30
Storr, Gottlob Christian, 44, 45
striving (*Streben*), 5, 6, 16, 49, 54, 57, 58, 60, 64, 65, 70, 71, 72, 73, 74, 77, 78, 79, 80, 81, 82, 83, 92, 101, 106, 108, 195, 209, 211
summons (*Aufforderung*), 41, 170, 171, 172, 173
Süskind, Friedrich Gottlieb, 44, 45

Tathandlung (fact/act), 59, 91
teleological ethics, 16, 25, 26, 27, 121, 126, 186, 188, 214, 217, 219
Timmermann, Jens, 206, 216
tool of the moral law, 24, 100, 126, 166, 167, 173, 175, 213, 214, 214
truth, 114, 116, 118, 130, 135, 145, 180, 204, 205, 206, 207, 213, 220

Verweyen, Hansjürgen, 3, 41, 189
virtue, 217

Walch, Johann Georg, 180
Wallace, R. Jay, 39
Ware, Owen, 3, 6, 28, 64, 77, 81, 82, 83, 107, 110, 124, 140, 142, 182, 203, 216, 217, 219
Weisshuhn, Friedrich August, 1
will, 17, 18, 50, 51, 52, 56, 86, 87, 89, 163, 214
will, pure, 28, 40, 42
Wolff, Christian, 213
Wood, Allen, 3, 4, 15, 24, 25, 71, 81, 89, 107, 109, 119, 120, 125, 128, 131, 142, 153, 161, 173, 202, 203, 206, 216

Zedler, Johann Heinrich, 180
Zöller, Günter, 3, 33, 35, 183, 206, 212

CAMBRIDGE CRITICAL GUIDES

Titles published in this series (continued):

Kant's *Metaphysics of Morals*
EDITED BY LARA DENIS
Spinoza's *Theological-Political Treatise*
EDITED BY YITZHAK Y. MELAMED AND MICHAEL A. ROSENTHAL
Plato's *Laws*
EDITED BY CHRISTOPHER BOBONICH
Plato's *Republic*
EDITED BY MARK L. MCPHERRAN
Kierkegaard's *Concluding Unscientific Postscript*
EDITED BY RICK ANTHONY FURTAK
Wittgenstein's *Philosophical Investigations*
EDITED BY ARIF AHMED
Kant's *Critique of Practical Reason*
EDITED BY ANDREWS REATH AND JENS TIMMERMANN
Kant's *Groundwork of the Metaphysics of Morals*
EDITED BY JENS TIMMERMANN
Kant's *Idea for a Universal History with a Cosmopolitan Aim*
EDITED BY AMÉLIE OKSENBERG RORTY AND JAMES SCHMIDT
Mill's *On Liberty*
EDITED BY C. L. TEN
Hegel's *Phenomenology of Spirit*
EDITED BY DEAN MOYAR AND MICHAEL QUANTE

CPSIA information can be obtained
at www.ICGtesting.com
Printed in the USA
LVHW021222030821
694401LV00003B/217